C. JOHNSON

W9-AYS-953

C. JOHNSON

Exploring Art

ABOUT THE PROGRAM

Exploring Art takes a media approach to art, focusing on the elements and principles of art and how artists use various media and techniques, such as drawing, painting, printmaking, and sculpting. The concepts of aesthetics, art criticism, art history, and art production are applied and reinforced throughout the program.

ABOUT THE COVER ILLUSTRATION

The paints, chalk sticks, and printing block shown on the front and back covers are familiar examples of art media. The colorful swashes of color in the non-objective painting on the front cover show what students can create with a few basic art media.

Exploring Art

Gene Mittler, Ph.D.
Professor Emeritus
Texas Tech University

Rosalind Ragans, Ph.D.
Associate Professor Emerita
Georgia Southern University

**Glencoe
McGraw-Hill**

New York, New York   Columbus, Ohio   Woodland Hills, California   Peoria, Illinois

ABOUT THE AUTHORS

Gene Mittler

Gene Mittler is one of the authors of Glencoe's middle school/junior high art series, *Introducing Art, Exploring Art,* and *Understanding Art.* He is also author of *Art in Focus,* a chronological approach to art for Glencoe's senior high program, and *Creating and Understanding Drawings.* He has taught at both the elementary and secondary levels and at Indiana University. He received an M.F.A. in sculpture from Bowling Green State University and a Ph.D. in art education from the Ohio State University. He has authored grants and published numerous articles in professional journals and has lectured in the United States and abroad. Dr. Mittler is currently Professor Emeritus at Texas Tech University.

Rosalind Ragans

Rosalind Ragans is one of the authors of Glencoe's middle school/junior high art series, *Introducing Art, Exploring Art,* and *Understanding Art.* She served as senior author on the elementary program *Art Connections* for the SRA division of McGraw-Hill, and wrote the multi-level, comprehensive *ArtTalk* text for Glencoe's senior high program. She received a B.F.A. at Hunter College, CUNY, New York, and earned a M.Ed. in Elementary Education at Georgia Southern College and Ph.D. in Art Education at the University of Georgia. Dr. Ragans has taught art in grades K–12, and has earned several honors including National Art Educator of the Year for 1992. She is currently Associate Professor of Art Education Emerita at Georgia Southern University.

ABOUT ARTSOURCE®

The materials provided in the Performing Arts Handbook are excerpted from *Artsource®: The Music Center Study Guide to the Performing Arts,* a project of the Music Center Education Division. The Music Center of Los Angeles County, the largest performing arts center in the western United States, established the Music Center Education Division in 1979 to provide opportunities for lifelong learning in the arts, and especially to bring the performing and visual arts into the classroom. The Education Division believes the arts enhance the quality of life for all people, but are crucial to the development of every child.

Glencoe/McGraw-Hill

A Division of The **McGraw-Hill** Companies

Send all inquiries to:
Glencoe/McGraw-Hill
21600 Oxnard Street
Woodland Hills, CA 91367

ISBN 0-02-662356-0 (Student Text)
ISBN 0-02-662357-9 (Teacher's Wraparound Edition)

Printed in the United States of America.

2 3 4 5 6 7 8 9   004/043   03 02 01 00 99 98

EDITORIAL CONSULTANTS

Claire B. Clements, Ph.D.
Specialist, Special Needs
Associate Professor and Community Education
    Director at the Program on Human Development
    and Disability
The University of Georgia
Athens, Georgia

Robert D. Clements, Ph.D.
Specialist, Special Needs
Professor Emeritus of Art
The University of Georgia
Athens, Georgia

Cris Guenter, Ed.D.
Specialist, Portfolio and Assessment
Professor, Fine Arts/Curriculum and Instruction
California State University, Chico
Chico, California

Nancy C. Miller
Booker T. Washington High School for the
    Performing and Visual Arts
Dallas, Texas

Faye Scannell, M.A.
Specialist, Technology
Bellevue Public Schools
Bellevue, Washington

Dede Tisone-Bartels, M.A.
Specialist, Curriculum Connections
Crittenden Middle School
Mountain View, California

Jean Morman Unsworth
Art Consultant to Chicago
    Archdiocese Schools
Chicago, Illinois

CONTRIBUTORS/REVIEWERS

Lydia Bee
Art Specialist
Junction Middle School
Palo Cedro, California

Gale Gomez-Bjelland
Visual Arts Instructor
David A. Brown Middle School
Wildomar, California

Cheryl Hartman Brown, M.A.
Art Educator
Modesto, California

Carol M. Burris
Art Teacher
Columbus East High School
Columbus, Ohio

Ann E. Heintzelman
Art Teacher
Daleville Elementary School
Daleville, Indiana

Jane Rhoades-Hudak, Ph.D.
Teacher/Educator
Georgia Southern University
Statesboro, Georgia

Kenneth Sakatani, Ph.D.
Arts and Technology Coordinator
Bayside School for the Arts and Creative
    Technology
San Mateo, California

Carolyn Sollman
Art Teacher
Eminence School
Eminence, Indiana

Sylvia Thompson
Art Educator
Cammack Middle School
Huntington, West Virginia

PERFORMING ARTS HANDBOOK CONTRIBUTORS

Joan Boyett
Executive Director
Music Center Education Division
The Music Center of Los Angeles County

Melinda Williams
Concept Originator and Project Director

Susan Cambigue-Tracey
Project Coordinator

Arts Discipline Writers:
    Dance—Susan Cambigue-Tracey
    Music—Rosemarie Cook-Glover
    Theatre—Barbara Leonard

STUDIO LESSON CONSULTANTS

Acknowledgements: The authors wish to express their gratitude to the following art coordinators and specialists who participated in the field test of the studio lessons.

Janette Alexander, Denver City Junior High, Denver City, TX; Nan Ball, Camp Creek Middle School, College Park, GA; Lydia Bee, Junction Middle School, Palo Cedro, CA; Debra Belvin, Bearden Middle School, Knoxville, TN; Judy Buckman, Helfrich Park Middle School, Evansville, IN; Wendy Bull, Colonial High School, Memphis, TN; Isabelle Bush, Crabapple Middle School, Roswell, GA; Ann Campoll, Sauk City, WI; Pam Carsillo, Floyd Middle School, Marietta, GA; Kellene Champlin, Fulton County Art Supervisor, Fulton County, GA; Michael Chapman, Treadwell Junior High School, Memphis, TN; Fay Chastain, Hilsman Middle School, Athens, GA; Greg Coats, Havenview Junior High School, Memphis, TN; Rebecca Crim, Holcomb Bridge Middle School, Alpharetta, GA; Jeannie Davis, Hallsville Junior High, Hallsville, TX; Lane Dietrick, Freedom Junior High School, Freedom, WI; Jean Carl Doherty, Sandy Springs Middle School, Atlanta, GA; Joan Elsesser, Beaver Dam, WI; Linda Eshom, Corpus Christi Intermediate School District, Corpus Christi, TX; Eva Fronk, Hales Corners, WI; Kay Godawa, Savannah Country Day School, Savannah, GA; Gale Gomez-Bjelland, David A. Brown Middle School, Wildomar, CA; Dr. Nadine Gordon, Scarsdale High School, Scarsdale, NY; Jim Gunter, Baldwin Junior High, Montgomery, AL; Thomas Healy, Canutillo Middle School, El Paso, TX; Garlan Hodgson, Tapp Middle School, Powder Springs, GA; Joy Jones, Chisholm Trail Middle School, Round Rock, TX; Florence Kork, Harold Wiggs Middle School, El Paso, TX; David Long, Akron Central School, Akron, NY; Nellie Lynch, Duval County Art Supervisor, Jacksonville, FL; Kelly Mann, All Saints Episcopal School, Lubbock, TX; Theresa McDaniel, Towson High School, Towson, MD; Mary McDermott, Valleywood Middle School, Kentwood, MI; Barbara Merritt, Canyon Hills Middle School, El Paso, TX; Bunyan Morris, Marvin Pittman Laboratory School, Statesboro, GA; Jimmy Morris, Clarke County Fine Arts Supervisor, Clarke County, GA; Perri Ann Morris, Jenkins County High School, Millen, GA; Mary Lee Nance, Harris Middle School, Shelbyville, TN; Jackie Norman, East Middle School, Tullahoma, TN; Charles Osten, Whittle Springs Middle School, Knoxville, TN; Susan R. Owens, Haynes Bridge Middle School, Atlanta, GA; Catherine Pate, Sneed Middle School, Florence, SC; Cynthia Pate, McGary Middle School, Evansville, IN; Robert M. Perry, Jr. Paxon Middle School, Jacksonville, FL; Eunice Plieseis, West Allis, WI; Dr. Marilyn Ragaty, Burney-Harris-Lyons Middle School, Athens, GA; A. P. Register, Bassett Middle School, El Paso, TX; M. Joi Roberts, Stanton High School, Jacksonville, FL; Julia Russell, Art Supervisor, Memphis City Schools, Memphis, TN; Karen Sandborn, Metter High School, Metter, GA; Wandra Sanders, Mandarin Middle School, Jacksonville, FL; Russ Sarasin, Green Bay, WI; Dr. Barbara Shaw, Cobb County Art Supervisor, Marietta, GA; Linda W. Smith, Jenkins County Elementary School, Millen, GA; Ellen Stanley, All Saints Episcopal School, Lubbock, TX; Linda Strong, La Pietra School, Honolulu, HI; Sylvia Thompson, Cammack Middle School, Huntington, WV; Ola Underhill, Chula Vista Academy of Fine Arts, Corpus Christi, TX; A. Villalobos, Guillen School, El Paso, TX; Carol Vinson, Holston Middle School, Knoxville, TN; C. Waites, Guillen School, El Paso, TX; Shirley Yokley, Tennessee Visual Arts Consultant, TN; Barbara Zelt, Reistertown, MD.

TABLE OF CONTENTS ILLUSTRATION

Lisa Pomerantz/Deborah Wolfe, Ltd.

CONTENTS

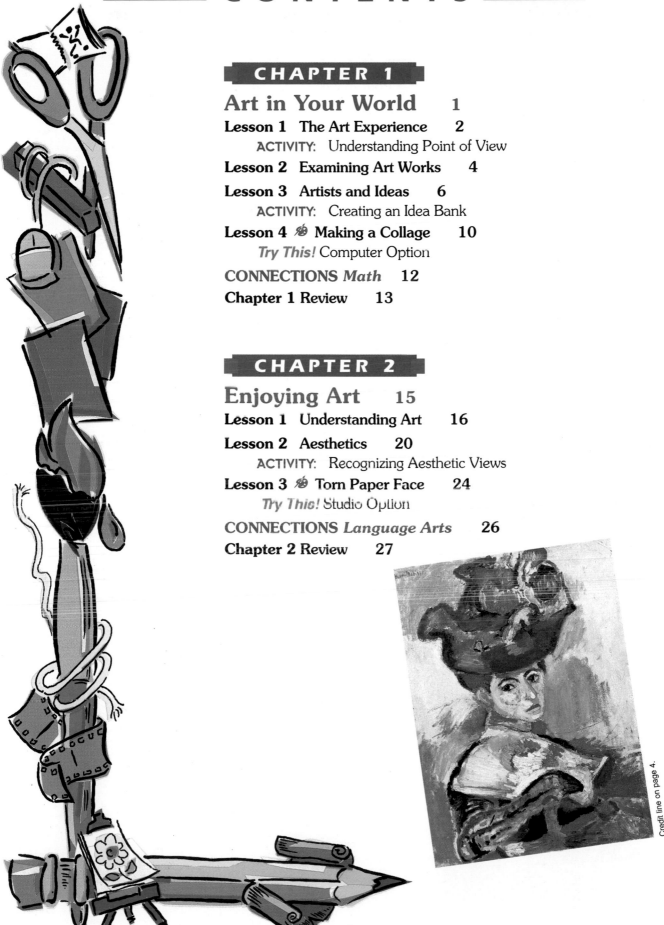

Credit line on page 4.

Credit line on page 81.

Credit line on page 94.

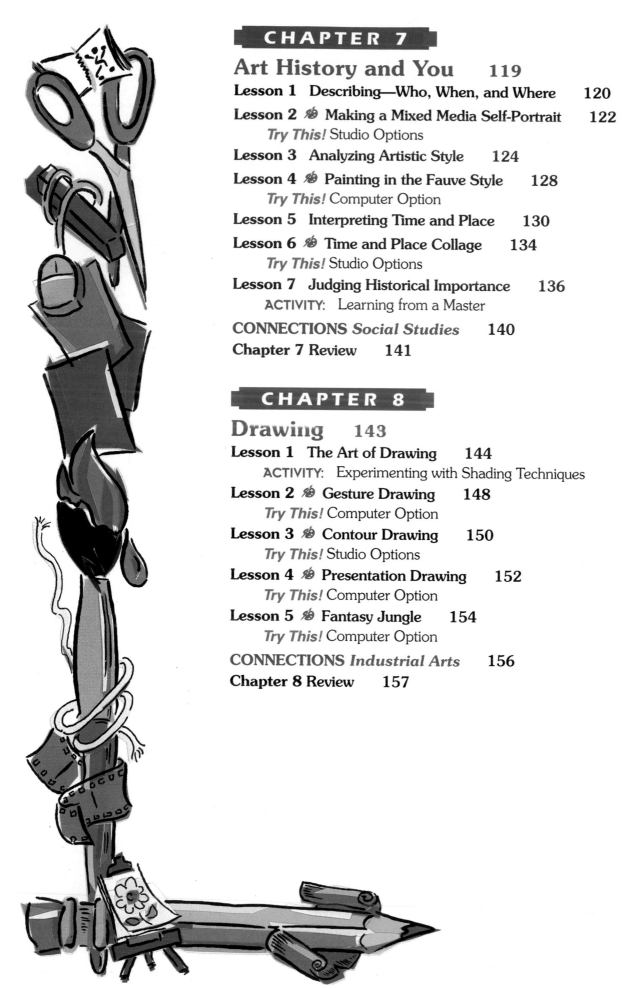

Credit line on page 161.

Credit line on page 180.

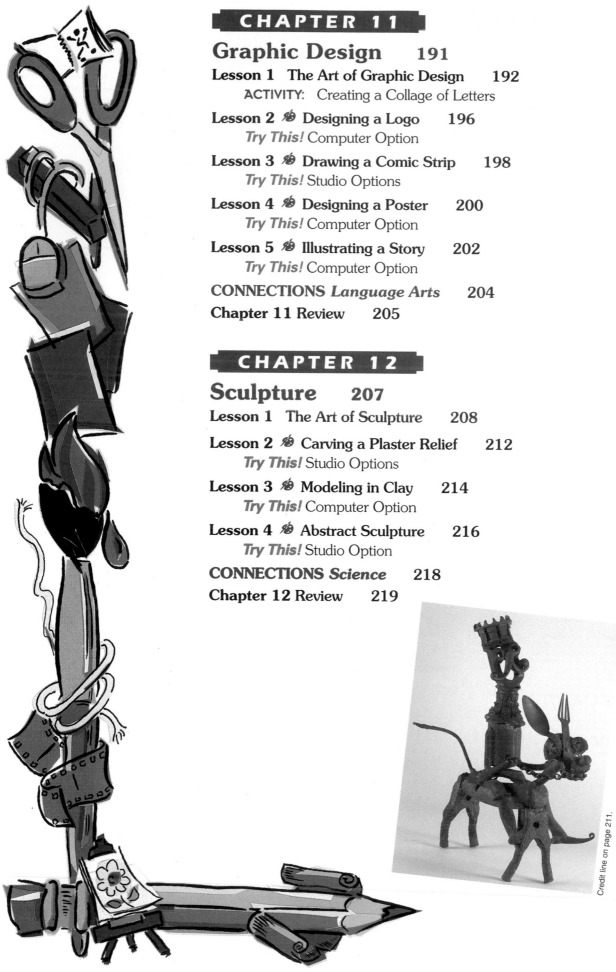

Credit line on page 211.

Credit line on page 232.

Credit line on page 240.

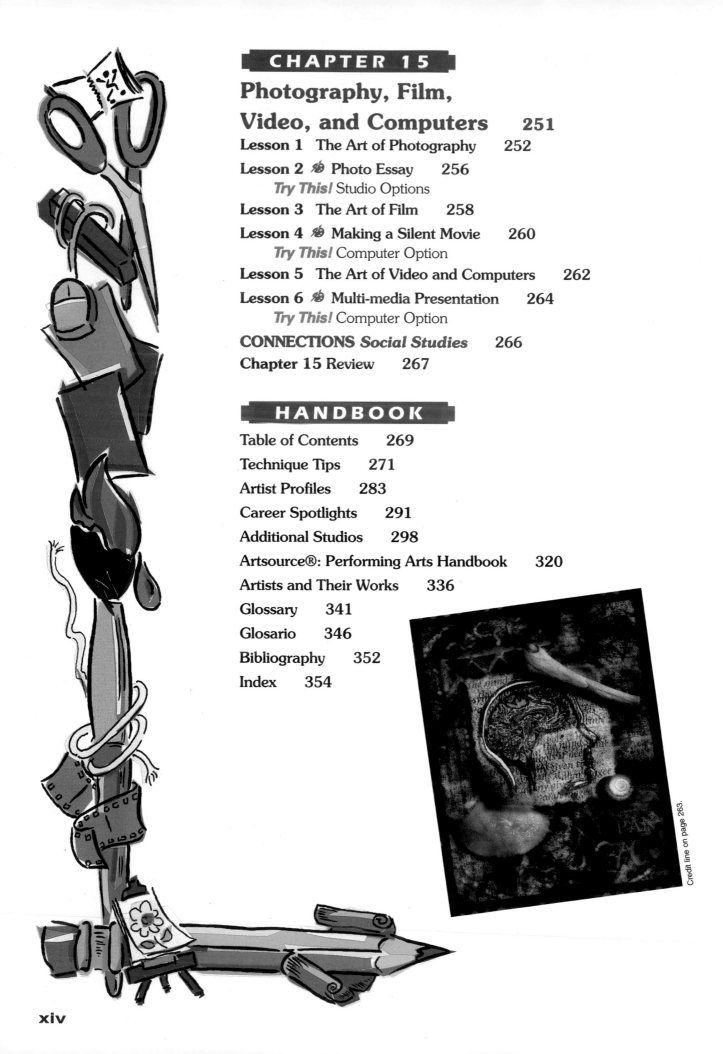

Credit line on page 263.

LISTING OF STUDIO LESSONS BY MEDIA/TECHNIQUE

▲ Artists often look to nature for inspiration. How does this artist make you appreciate the struggle for survival in the animal world?

Melissa W. Miller. *Salmon Run.* 1984. Oil on linen. 228.6 x 152.4 cm (90 x 60"). Gerald Peters Gallery, Dallas, Texas.

CHAPTER 1

Art in Your World

You are about to begin a journey to an interesting and exciting place. This is a place where your curiosity and creativity will be stirred. It is a place where you will be invited to make discoveries and share feelings and ideas. It is the world of art.

Throughout your journey you will see many works of art like the one at the left. What makes this picture art? What makes the person who created it an artist? In the pages that follow you will find answers to these and many other questions.

OBJECTIVES

After completing this chapter, you will be able to:
- Explain what can be learned by looking at art made by others.
- Explain what it means to perceive.
- Define the term *artist*.
- Name sources of ideas that artists might use.
- Make a collage.

WORDS YOU WILL LEARN

applied art
artists
collage
fine art
patrons of the arts
perceive
point of view
portfolio

PORTFOLIO IDEAS

Keep your art work in a portfolio. A **portfolio** is *a carefully selected collection of art work kept by students and professional artists.* Make sure each entry includes the following.
- Your name and the date you completed the art work.
- A summary or self-reflection of the assignment.
- Any additional information requested by your teacher.

Throughout the book, watch for other "Portfolio Ideas." Professional artists do similar types of exercises for their own portfolios.

LESSON 1

The Art Experience

Can you imagine what it would be like to play a new game without first learning the rules, or to read a story in a language that is not familiar to you? Neither of these activities can be carried out automatically. Both, and especially the reading, demand that you have some knowledge beforehand. Both require you to be prepared.

The same is true of art. Understanding art takes more than just looking at an object. It takes knowing *how* to look to find meaning. It takes truly seeing, or perceiving the object. To **perceive** is *to become aware through the senses of the special nature of objects.*

On your journey through the world of art, you will learn how to "see" art. You will learn how to perceive artistically.

A FIRST LOOK AT ART

You will begin your journey with the painting below (Figure 1–1). Look at this painting. If you were asked to write a description of what you see, what would you write? You might note that this is a skillfully made painting of two ducks. You might add that the ducks are flying above a stormy sea.

▲ Figure 1–1 Where would you have to be to view this scene? What has the artist done to link the two ducks? Notice the different shades of gray. What mood or feeling is expressed by the painting?

Winslow Homer. *Right and Left.* 1909. Canvas. 71.8 x 122.9 cm (28¼ x 48⅜"). National Gallery of Art, Washington, D.C. Gift of the Avalon Foundation.

So far, so good. But this description only begins to scratch the surface. There is much more going on in this painting. Look again, and you will notice something strange about the duck on the right. Namely, it seems to be plunging downward into the sea. Searching for clues to explain this odd behavior, you might notice the boat in the picture. It is partly hidden by the feet and tail feathers of the other duck. Looking more closely still, you might see the red flash and smoke above the boat. There is a hunter in the boat, and he is shooting at the ducks. The duck on the right has been hit. Now, for the first time, you notice the small white feather floating nearby. It was set free when a shotgun blast struck the duck.

Curiosity mounts as you realize the flash you are now seeing is the second shot. (The first has already found its target.) Try to imagine that you can hear the noise of the gun. Will the duck on the left, its wings beating wildly, escape? Will it become the hunter's next victim?

Far from just a picture of ducks, this is an action-packed glimpse of a dramatic event. Notice, by the way, where the artist has placed you, the viewer. What point of view has the artist used? **Point of view** is *the angle from which the viewer sees the scene.* Are you watching this drama unfold through the eyes of the hunter? No, you are staring, like the hunter's targets, down the barrels of the shotgun.

LEARNING FROM ART

Art, as you have just seen, has the power to challenge our minds and stir up our feelings. The ability to see the kinds of things just described can be learned with practice. This book will prepare you to use your eyes and mind to understand many different kinds of art. As each new art experience unfolds, your ability to see or perceive art will increase.

You will also learn, through looking at art by others, ways of making your own art. Looking at art created by others will develop your powers of creative thinking. It will help you find fresh and exciting ideas and reveal different ways of expressing those ideas. It will highlight the many kinds of tools and techniques you can use. Studio activities, like the one above, will give you a chance to practice what you have learned.

✔ CHECK YOUR UNDERSTANDING

1. What is meant by the term *perceive?*
2. What are some of the things to be gained by looking at art made by others?
3. Define *point of view.*

LESSON 2

Examining Art Works

When you see a great movie, do you keep the experience to yourself or do you tell friends all about it? This eagerness to share experiences and feelings with others is a typically human trait. It is also a reason why artists like to make art. **Artists** are *people who use imagination and skill to communicate ideas in visual form*. These ideas may represent experiences, feelings, or events in the artist's life.

Artists are creative thinkers. They combine a knowledge of art materials, tools, and methods with a rich imagination and deep sensitivity. They use this combination to present their reactions to the world around them.

ARTISTS AND THEIR WORK

All works created by artists are made to be viewed. Some are created with an added purpose; they are meant to be *used*. People who study art have a separate term for each of these two kinds of art. *Art made to be experienced visually* is called **fine art**. *Art made to be functional as well as visually pleasing* is called **applied art**.

Fine Art

A phrase sometimes used for fine art is "art for art's sake." This means the only use for fine art is to communicate the artist's feelings or ideas.

Fine art can be made from a number of different materials. Figures 1–2 and 1–3 show examples of these types. Figure 1–2 is a painting. Do you know what kind of fine art is shown in Figure 1–3?

◀ **Figure 1–2** How would you describe the expression on this woman's face? How does this painting make you feel?

Henri Matisse. *Femme au Chapeau (Woman with a Hat)*. 1905. Oil on canvas. 80.6 x 59.7 cm (31¾ x 23½"). San Francisco Museum of Modern Art. Bequest of Elise S. Haas.

▲ Figure 1–3 How did the artist create interest in the surface of this carving?

Allan Houser. *Waiting for Dancing Partners.* 1980. Tennessee marble. 76.2 x 53.3 cm (30 x 21"). Museum of the Southwest, Midland, Texas.

Applied Art

Applied arts are usually found in our everyday lives. Objects of applied art may be either made by hand or with machines. What other kinds of applied art can you name?

Sometimes the small differences between applied art and fine art become confused over a period of time. Look, for instance at the ornate chair in Figure 1–4. The elaborate decorations on the chair tell us that it was designed for a special person. Today, this chair is enjoyed as an example of fine art because of its great beauty.

✔ CHECK YOUR UNDERSTANDING

1. What is an artist?
2. Name the two basic kinds of art.
3. What is fine art? What are two types of fine art shown in this chapter?
4. What is applied art?

◄ Figure 1–4 Compare this chair with Figures 1–3 and 1–4. In what ways do the three pieces of art work seem alike? In what ways do they seem different?

Armchair of Satamon, sister of Tutankhamen. From the tomb of Youya and Thouyou. Thebes, Egypt. c. 1365 B.C. Archaeological Museum, Cairo, Egypt.

LESSON 3

Artists and Ideas

What do you see when you look at a blank sheet of paper? An artist will look at the blank sheet and see a challenge. That challenge—to come up with an idea—may be one of the toughest an artist faces.

Through the ages artists have answered the challenge of finding ideas, or sources of inspiration, in different ways. In this lesson you will learn about some of these ways.

WHERE ARTISTS GET IDEAS

The ancient Greeks routinely prayed to special goddesses called Muses (**myooz**-uhz)

to send them inspiration for ideas. They even built shrines to honor the Muses.

In more recent times artists in search of ideas have looked elsewhere for sources of inspiration. Here are some of the resources they have explored:

• **The world of myths and legends.** Some artists borrow ideas from famous works of literature. The artist of Figure 1–5 has brought to life characters from one of these literary works. Do you know these characters? Do you know the legend surrounding them?

▲ **Figure 1–5**   How did the artist tell you about Ichabod Crane's terror? Look at the colors and the shapes.

William John Wilgus. *Ichabod Crane and the Headless Horseman.* c. 1855. Canvas. 53.3 x 76.7 cm (21 x 30¼"). National Gallery of Art, Washington, D.C. Gift of Edgar William and Bernice Chrysler Garbisch.

- **The world of imagination.** Everyone has dreams and fantasies. Artists have the creative ability to turn dreams, and even nightmares, into the illusion of reality. Look at Figure 1–6. What message about the world of dreams might the artist be giving us?
- **Their own hearts and minds.** Personal beliefs, or feelings, are often a source of ideas for art. Sometimes artists will express those feelings in their work. Can you think of a good example of this kind of painting?
- **Real-world events and people.** People and events often turn up in art. Figure 1–7 offers a rare glimpse of Wild West hero Buffalo Bill Cody.

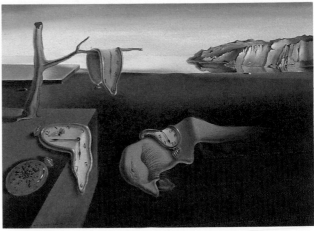

▲ **Figure 1–6** Has the artist painted a happy place or a forlorn, lonely place? What might he be telling us about time in the land of dreams?

Salvador Dali. *Persistence of Memory.* 1931. Oil on canvas. 24.1 x 33 cm (9½ x 13"). Museum of Modern Art, New York, New York. Given anonymously.

◀ **Figure 1–7** The artist did this painting of Buffalo Bill when he came to France to visit her.

Rosa Bonheur. *Buffalo Bill on Horseback.* 1889. Oil on canvas. 47 x 38.7 cm (18½ x 15¼"). Buffalo Bill Historical Center, Cody, Wyoming. Given in memory of Wm. R. Coe and Mai Rogers Coe.

▲ **Figure 1–8** A story, such as this one from the Bible, can be shown in many ways. In Figures 1–8 and 1–9, both artists put the story into their own times and dress.

Bartolomé Esteban Murillo. *Return of the Prodigal Son.* 1667/70. Oil on canvas. 236.3 x 261 cm (93 x 102¾"). National Gallery of Art, Washington, D.C. Gift of the Avalon Foundation.

- **Ideas commissioned by employers.** Many artists are hired by individuals or companies to create works of art. In the past such employers of artists were called patrons. **Patrons of the arts** are *sponsors, or supporters, of an artist or art-related places and events.* For example, the Catholic Church, as you will see, was at one time a major patron of the arts. It employed artists to create paintings and sculptures illustrating stories from the Bible.

- **Artists of the past.** Art is not made in a vacuum. Artists of a particular period of time often influence each other. Artists also learn from and build on the work of artists who came before them. Sometimes artists base works directly on earlier pieces. Look closely at both Figures 1–8 and 1–9. Read the credit lines and identify which art work was created first. Can you see the influence of this artist on the more recent work?

▲ Figure 1–9 **What period of American history does this painting depict?**

Mary Ann Willson. *The Prodigal Son Reclaimed.* c. 1815. Pen and black ink and watercolor. 49.4 x 41.4 cm (19⁹/₁₆ x 16⅝"). National Gallery of Art, Washington, D.C. Gift of Edgar William and Bernice Chrysler Garbisch.

IDEAS FOR YOUR OWN ART

In the coming chapters, you will be asked to come up with ideas of your own. Like all other artists, you may at times find yourself stuck. At such moments, an idea bank may be just the answer. It may help boost your powers of creative thinking.

The following studio activity will explain how to make an idea bank for your classroom.

Creating an Idea Bank

Find four envelopes. Label one *Noun*, one *Adjective*, one *Verb*, and one *Adverb*. Think up words for each part of speech. Use a dictionary for help. Avoid proper nouns (those beginning with capital letters). Write each of your words on a separate slip of paper. Place your slips in the correct envelope. Take turns choosing four slips, one from each type of envelope. Share envelopes with other class members to get more variety in the word combinations. These envelopes will be your idea bank for future art projects.

When you have a word combination that you like, arrange the slips on a table in this order: adjective-noun-verb-adverb. Make the words form an interesting idea.

On a sheet of white paper, 9 x 12 inches (23 x 30 cm), sketch your idea. The sketch should show the thing or object (noun) described doing the action (or verb) named.

PORTFOLIO

Change just one of the four words in your word form and make a new sketch. Is your new sketch silly, clever, serious, or scary? Compare it to your first sketch and decide which one you like better. Be sure to write the four words in each word combination next to the appropriate sketch. Keep your comparisons in your portfolio.

✔ CHECK YOUR UNDERSTANDING

1. What are patrons of the arts?
2. List and describe four sources artists use for inspiration.

LESSON 4
Making a Collage

This work of art by Lois Dvorak is made with handmade paper. Called a **collage** (kuh-**lahzh**), this is *art work arranged from cut or torn materials pasted to a surface*. The lizards are native to the New Mexico desert where she lives. (See Figure 1–10.)

WHAT YOU WILL LEARN

You will create a collage using a combination of drawn and found materials. You will combine natural materials that you find in your environment with your own drawings of insects and other small creatures from your local environment. (See Figure 1–11.)

► **Figure 1–10** **A lizard is hidden among the leaves, just as it would hide in nature. Can you find it? What materials were used to make this collage?**

Lois Dvorak. *The Lizards.* (Detail.) Handmade paper assemblage. 81.3 x 101.6 cm (32 x 40″). Private collection.

WHAT YOU WILL NEED

- Pencils and sketch paper
- Small pieces of white paper
- Watercolor markers
- Natural, found materials such as leaves, twigs, pebbles, dirt, bark, wild flowers, and grasses
- White glue
- White paper, 9 x 12 inch (23 x 30 cm)

WHAT YOU WILL DO

1. Brainstorm with your classmates for ideas of what insects, spiders, frogs, and lizards you might find outdoors in your area. Look for pictures of these creatures in the library, and in science books. Notice the difference in body structure between insect and spider.
2. Collect natural materials from your outdoor environment. Look for leaves, twigs, grasses, bark, dirt and sand, wild flowers, and pebbles. If you live in a city, the florist might have old leaves and ferns to give away.
3. Make some rough sketches of the creatures. Then make finished drawings with pencil on white paper of the creatures for your work. Decide whether you want your creatures to contrast with the background or to blend in to the colors. Color them with watercolor markers.
4. Arrange your found objects with the creatures you drew. When you are satisfied with the composition glue everything down.
5. Display your work. Can you find similarities and differences?

▲ Figure 1–11   Student work. A content collage.

Try This!   COMPUTER OPTION

■ Look through available Clip art files. Import or Copy the creatures you want to use in a collage into a computer art program. Increase or decrease the size according to your design. Add color and textures to blend the creatures into the collage or to add contrast. Title, Save, and Print. Cut out and arrange the creatures with found materials.

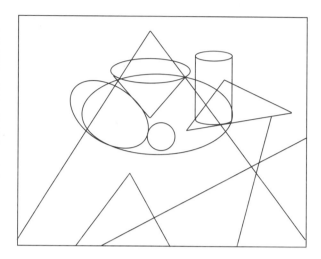

Paul Cézanne. *Apples and Oranges.* Oil on canvas. 74 x 92 cm (29⅛ x 36⅝"). Museé d'Orsay, Paris, France.

How Do Artists Use Geometry?

If you look carefully, you can see geometric shapes all around you. For example, the sun, moon, and planets are spherical. Some evergreen trees are shaped like a cone. A shoe box is a rectangular solid and a soft drink is a cylinder. However, did you know that the first use of geometry was a practical one? The word itself comes from Greek words meaning "earth" and "measure." The concept of geometry was originally used by Egyptian surveyors in the fourteenth century B.C. Every year, the Nile River had severe flooding. People who lived close to the river often lost land when the flooding stopped. Surveyors used geometry to reestablish the boundaries of the fields near the river.

Yet people have also been creating geometrically shaped objects for thousands of years. They appear in ancient pottery, cave paintings, and buildings. The ancient Egyptian pyramids are an example of a geometric shape used to create an architectural form. Over the years, the meaning of geometry has changed and expanded. For artists, geometry is often a source of ideas.

In *Apples and Oranges,* Paul Cézanne painted many objects that have natural geometric shapes. The line drawing above shows some of these shapes and forms. In addition to these objects, the overall composition of the painting shows a geometric arrangement. As a result, the painting has a sense of completeness.

MAKING THE CONNECTION

- Identify the geometric shapes and forms that Cézanne used in this painting.
- How did Cézanne create a sense of geometry in the overall composition of this work?
- Why do you think Cézanne called art works such as this "constructions after nature"?

INTERNET ACTIVITY

Visit Glencoe's Fine Arts Web Site for students at:

http://www.glencoe.com/sec/art/students

C H A P T E R 1
REVIEW

◤ BUILDING VOCABULARY

Number a sheet of paper from 1 to 8. After each number, write the term from the list that best matches each description below.

applied art	patrons of the arts
artists	perceive
collage	point of view
fine art	portfolio

1. To become aware through the senses of the special nature of objects.
2. The angle from which viewers see the scene in a painting.
3. People who use imagination and skill to share ideas in visual form.
4. Art made purely to be experienced visually.
5. Art made to be both looked at and used.
6. Art made up of cut and torn materials pasted to a surface.
7. Sponsors, or supporters, of an artist or art-related places and events.
8. A carefully selected collection of art work kept by students and professional artists.

◤ REVIEWING ART FACTS

Number a sheet of paper from 9 to 16. Answer each question in a complete sentence.

9. What are some of the things people can learn by looking at art?
10. Name two kinds of fine art.
11. Name a type of applied art.
12. What were Muses? How did the ancient Greeks use the Muses?
13. Name six sources to which artists turn for ideas.
14. What are patrons of the arts? What is the connection between art patrons and artists?
15. How can an idea bank expand your creative thinking?
16. When Dvorak created her collage, *The Lizards*, where did she turn for her idea?

? THINKING ABOUT ART

On a sheet of paper, answer each question in a sentence or two.

1. **Extend.** Based on what you learned in this chapter, how would you define *art?*
2. **Analyze.** Write a description of some object in the art room without naming it. Mention as many details as you can. See whether anyone in your class can identify the object.
3. **Analyze.** Name three examples of applied art in your home. Tell how useful you find each of the objects.
4. **Extend.** Do you think makers of applied art and fine art turn to the same sources for ideas? Explain your answer.

─ MAKING ART CONNECTIONS ─

1. **Science.** Using books and field guides, try to identify the kind of ducks shown in Winslow Homer's painting, *Right and Left*, on page **2**. In what parts of the world can this species be found? Can you tell what time of year it is? Reading about migration might help to answer the question.

2. **Language Arts.** Read the fairy tale "Little Red Riding Hood." Rewrite the story from the wolf's point of view. Share your new version with other students who also rewrote the story. Does the new point of view make the story more interesting? Why or why not?

▲ Schapiro's painting offers delightful shapes and splashes of colors. How many times does she repeat the shape of the fan?

Miriam Schapiro. *My Fan Is Half a Circle.* 1994. Acrylic, fabric, and cut paper on canvas. 203.2 x 114.3 cm (80 x 45"). Courtesy of the Steinbaum Krauss Gallery, New York, New York.

CHAPTER 2

Enjoying Art

Imagine you were in the museum where the painting at the left hangs. You might overhear someone say that he or she doesn't like the painting because it does not look like a real person. That might even sum up your own feelings about the painting.

Yet, is this all there is to say about a painting? Does art succeed as art *only* because of lifelike details? Are there any other ways of looking at—and evaluating the success of—an art object? In this chapter you will find out.

PORTFOLIO IDEAS

Often, you will begin an art work in a sketchbook. A **sketchbook** is *a pad of drawing paper on which artists sketch, write notes, and refine ideas for their work.* Think about a work of art you know and like. In your sketchbook, describe the work's subject, composition, and content. Date this entry. In the future, you can use this written entry as a source of inspiration for one of your own art works.

OBJECTIVES

After completing this chapter, you will be able to:
- Explain how subject, composition, and content relate to works of art.
- Define the term *aesthetics*.
- Discuss three schools of thought on what is important in art.
- Make a torn paper face showing a mood.

WORDS YOU WILL LEARN

aesthetics
aesthetic views
composition
content
credit line
non-objective
subject
super-realism
work of art

Understanding Art

To praise a job well done, people sometimes borrow a term from art. That term is *work of art*. A well-cooked meal might be described as "a work of art." So might a neatly arranged clothes closet.

In the study of art, the term **work of art** has a specific meaning. It is *any object created or designed by an artist*. Works of art, however, are not all equally successful.

▶ **Figure 2–1** The opera and the theatre were often subjects of art work. Why do you think this is so?

Mary Stevenson Cassatt. *At the Opera*. 1879. Oil on canvas. 80 x 64.8 cm (31½ x 25½"). Museum of Fine Arts, Boston, Massachusetts. Hayden Collection.

▲ **Figure 2–2** An elegy is a speech or song of sorrow. How is sorrow expressed in this painting?

Robert Motherwell. *Elegy to the Spanish Republic 108*. 1966. Oil and acrylic on canvas. 213.4 x 373.4 cm (84 x 147″). Museum of Art, Dallas, Texas. © 1998 Dedalus Foundation/Licensed by VAGA, New York, NY

THE WORK OF ART

Works of art may be defined by three basic properties, or features. These properties are subject, composition, and content.

Subject

The subject answers the question "What do I see when I look at this art work?" The **subject** is *the image viewers can easily identify*. The subject may be a person or persons. It may be a thing, such as a tree. It may be a place. It may even be an event, such as a parade. The subject of the painting in Figure 2–1 is easily recognized. It is a woman seated in a theater box gazing through opera glasses.

In recent years some artists have chosen to create non-objective artwork. **Non-objective** means *there is no recognizable subject matter in the work*. The picture in Figure 2–2 is such a work.

Composition

All art works are made up of parts known as visual elements. These elements, which you will learn more about in Chapter 4, include color, line, shape, form, space, and texture. You will also learn that artists use certain guidelines, called principles of art, to organize these elements in their work. The principles of balance, variety, harmony, emphasis, proportion, movement, and rhythm will be discussed in Chapter 5. The **composition** of an art work is *how the principles are used to organize the elements*.

Look again at the picture in Figure 2–1. With your finger, trace the line of the railing beginning at the lower left edge. Where does this line take you? It carries you upward along the woman's right arm. From there the dark straps of her hat lead you to her lightly colored face. The woman's face is the most important part of the painting. The artist has skillfully used lines to direct your attention to it. Part of the picture's composition is how the artist uses the element of line and the principle of movement.

Content

Often a work of art communicates a message, idea, or feeling. The *message, idea, or feeling* is the art work's **content.** Look once more at Figure 2–1. Notice the man in the distance, leaning out of his theater box. He is using his own opera glasses, not to watch the show, but to stare at the woman. She, too, must be spying on people in other boxes. Notice where

her glasses are pointed. Are they aimed downward, toward the stage?

Maybe the artist, Mary Cassatt, is trying to tell us something about human nature. Maybe she is saying that while we are busy looking at—and judging—others, we are being judged ourselves. This message is the painting's content.

Sometimes the content of an art work is expressed as a feeling, such as excitement or suspense. Can you identify the feeling expressed by the picture in Figure 2–3? What details of the picture give you a clue to that feeling?

▲ **Figure 2–3** How does this painting help you experience the sights and sounds of a baseball game? What has the artist done to evoke that feeling?

Jacob Lawrence. *Strike.* 1949. Tempera on masonite. 50.8 x 61 cm (20 x 24"). The Howard University Gallery of Art, Washington, D.C. Permanent collection.

Notice that even art works without recognizable subjects can show a feeling. Look again at Figure 2–2. The artist of this work depends on composition alone to express content. He uses scary dark shapes to communicate the terror and destruction of a civil war. These dark shapes overpower the brightly colored shapes behind, which stand for peace and happiness.

THE CREDIT LINE

Look once more at Figure 2–3. Do you see the name of the artist who created this work? Do you know the title of the work? Answers to these and other questions can be found in the credit line appearing alongside the work. A **credit line** is *a listing of important facts about an art work*.

Every art work in this book has a credit line. It is there to help you learn as much as you can about the work.

Reading a Credit Line

Most credit lines are made up of six facts. These facts, in the order in which they appear, are as follows:

- **The artist's name.** This information always comes first. Who is the artist of the work in Figure 2–1? Who is the artist of the work in Figure 2–2?
- **The title of the work.** Many titles give useful information about the subject or content. Some are meant to stimulate viewers' curiosity. Do you remember the title of the painting of the ducks back in Chapter 1 (Figure 1–1, page **2**)? Can you find a work in the present chapter with the title *Strike?* Who painted it?

- **The year the work was created.** Sometimes, in the case of older works, *c.* appears before the year. This is an abbreviation for *circa*, which means "around" or "about" in Latin. Which work in this lesson was created in 1966? What is its title?
- **The tools and materials used in creating the work.** Artists, as you will learn, use many different materials to create an art work. Watercolor paint is one of these materials. Pencil is another. How many works in Chapter 1 and in this chapter were made using oil on canvas?
- **The size of the work.** Size helps you imagine how the work would appear if you were standing before it. Height, in centimeters as well as in inches, is always listed first. The width is listed second. A third number refers to depth. What is the height of the painting in Chapter 1 by Bartolomé Esteban Murillo?
- **The location of the work.** Location includes the name of the gallery or museum where the work is housed and its city and state or country. Where would you go to view the painting in this chapter by Mary Cassatt? In what city is the National Gallery of Art located?

✔ CHECK YOUR UNDERSTANDING

1. What is a work of art?
2. What are three properties of art works?
3. Name four pieces of information given in a credit line.

LESSON 2

Aesthetics

When you hear a new song on the radio, what do you listen for? Are you mostly interested in the words? Do you tune in, instead, to the beat? Maybe what matters to you most is the skill of the performers.

The question of what counts most in a work is not only a concern of listeners of music. It is a major concern of viewers and creators of every kind of art. This question is one art scholars have been wrestling with since earliest times.

In this lesson you will learn some of the ways they think about works of art.

AESTHETICS IN ART

You have probably heard the saying "beauty is in the eye of the beholder." People see beauty in different ways. Pinpointing the meaning of beauty is only one goal of the branch of learning called **aesthetics,** (ess-**thet**-iks) *the philosophy or study of the nature and the value of art.*

▶ Figure 2–4 The artist is trying to fool your eye. Why do the objects in this painting look like you could touch them?

Charles Gifford Dyer. *Seventeenth-Century Interior.* 1877. Oil on canvas. 94 x 71.1 cm (37 x 28"). The Art Institute of Chicago. Gift of Henry W. King. 1902.227

The chief goal of aesthetics is finding an answer to the question "What is art?" In their search for an answer, art scholars have put forth different views on what is important in art. *These ideas, or schools of thought, on what to look for in works of art* are called **aesthetic views**.

AESTHETIC VIEWS

Today, students of art recognize three main aesthetic views. These aesthetic views are based on the properties of an artwork: subject, composition, and content. One aesthetic view has to do with an art work's subject. The second view relates to composition. The third view is tied to content.

View #1: Subject

The first aesthetic view states that art should imitate what we see in the real world. A successful work in this view is one with realistic subject matter. Look at the painting in Figure 2–4. Notice how lifelike the objects in this work look. The image of the musical instrument could pass for a photograph. Art scholars of this first school would praise this painting for being so true to life. Would you agree with them?

Modern artists have found ways of creating works with even more convincing lifelike subjects than the type found in Figure 2–4. A style of *art devoted to extraordinarily realistic works,* called **super-realism,** has come into being. Without being told, would you ever guess that Figure 2–5 is a photo of an art work and not a real person?

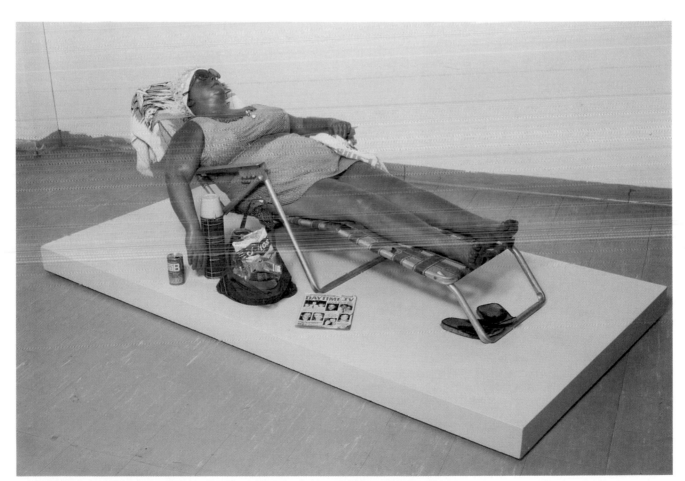

▲ **Figure 2–5** Notice the details the artist has included in this work. What message about certain American values might he be trying to express?

Duane Hanson. *Sunbather.* 1971. Polyester fiberglass polychromed in oil. Life-size. Wadsworth Atheneum, Hartford. National Endowment for the Arts/Gift of Roscoe Nelson Gray in memory of Roscoe Nelson Dalton Gray and Rene Gabrielle Gray.

View #2: Composition

The second aesthetic view or school of thought argues that what counts in art is composition. In this view a successful art work is one in which the artist has used the principles of art to skillfully combine the art elements. Look again at Figure 2–4. Supporters of this view would find much to admire in the painting. They might note the way the shapes have been arranged to balance the composition. They might explain how the contrast between light and dark emphasizes certain objects.

Some artists have paid more attention to composition than to any other feature. How would art scholars of the second school react to the work in Figure 2–6? What visual elements and principles might they refer to when discussing this work?

View #3: Content

The third aesthetic view holds that what is most important in an art work is its content. In this view a successful art work is one that sends a clear message or feeling. Look once more at Figure 2–4. Notice the work's title, *Seventeenth-Century Interior*. The artist seems to be giving us a peek at some of his most prized possessions. Note how worn some of these objects are. What feeling about favorite things might the artist be expressing? How would individuals taking this third aesthetic view react to that feeling? How do you react to it?

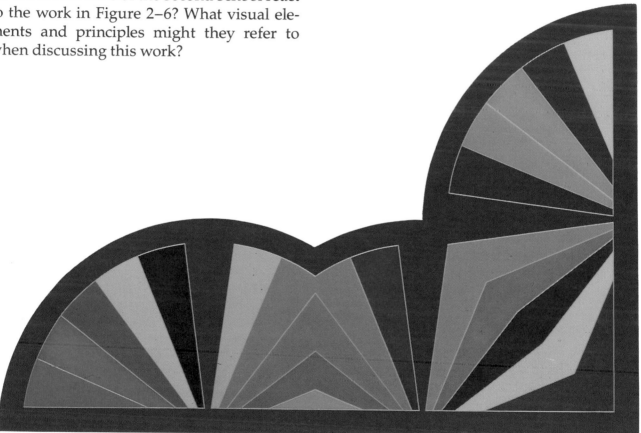

▲ **Figure 2–6   Many of this artist's works were not rectangular. He worked on a huge scale and painted designs that followed the unusual shapes of his canvases. This art work is called a "hard-edged painting." Why do you think it is called that?**

Frank Stella. *Agbatana III*. 1968. Flourescent acrylic on canvas. 305 x 457 cm (120 x 180"). Allen Art Museum, Oberlin College, Ohio. Ruth C. Roush Fund for Contemporary Art and National Foundation for the Arts & Humanities Grant, 1968.

▲ **Figure 2–7** Read the title of this painting. Does it help you understand the significance of the fancy clothes?

T. C. Cannon. *Turn of the Century Dandy.* 1796. Acrylic on canvas. 152.4 x 132.1 cm (60 x 52″). Private collection.

AESTHETICS AND THE "BIG PICTURE"

It is important to note that few students of art accept just one aesthetic view. Most believe that to achieve a full understanding of art requires keeping an open mind. How might a person with all three views react to the painting that opened this chapter? (See page 14.) Do you think the person would describe this work as true to life? Would you describe it that way? How have color, line, and shapes been used to create this work? Do you think they have been used effectively to create a unified and visually interesting design? Do you think the picture communicates a message, idea, or feeling? What might that message be? Look at the painting above. (See Figure 2–7.) Ask yourself the same questions regarding this art work.

(See page 14.)

STUDIO ACTIVITY

Recognizing Aesthetic Views

Find in a magazine a black-and-white photograph of an object seen from the front. Clip out the photo. Cut the object in half and glue half to a sheet of white paper. Use a pencil to complete the missing half of the object. Before you begin, take one of the following views:

- My drawing will be as lifelike as I can make it.
- My drawing will focus on line and shape.
- My drawing will communicate a message, idea, or feeling.

Discuss your drawing with other students in the class. How many were able to identify the aesthetic approach you took? Were you able to identify the aesthetic approach they followed?

Portfolio

Which aesthetic view appeals to you? Write a paragraph that identifies that aesthetic view and explains why you like it best. Date your writing and keep it in your portfolio. Read it several times before the end of this course and see if your opinion changes. If it does, write that on the same sheet of paper.

✔ CHECK YOUR UNDERSTANDING

1. What is the study of aesthetics? What is the chief goal of aesthetics?
2. Briefly describe the three main aesthetic views presented in this lesson.
3. What is super-realism?
4. Why do few students of art accept just one aesthetic view?

LESSON 3

Torn Paper Face

Look closely at the clown in Figure 2–8. He sits quietly with his arms folded in front of his body. He stares into space, lost in his own thoughts. Is his expression what you think a clown's expression should be? Why or why not?

If you had to describe this clown's mood, what words would you use? If you were going to create a piece of art, how would you show this mood?

WHAT YOU WILL LEARN

This studio lesson will test your skill in creating a face as seen from the front. The face will express a mood. In your work, you will focus totally on content. No effort will be made to create a real-looking face. You will exaggerate the features in your face and select colors that will communicate a mood.

You will "build" your face of torn bits of construction paper. (See Figure 2–9.)

WHAT YOU WILL NEED

- Pencil and notepad
- Scrap pieces of colored construction paper
- Sheet of construction paper, 12 x 18 inch (30 x 46 cm)
- Small brush and slightly thinned white glue

WHAT YOU WILL DO

1. Working with a partner, practice acting out different moods. On your notepad, jot down notes about which facial expressions fit which moods. What happens to

▶ **Figure 2–8 Artist Walt Kuhn painted many images of circus figures. How has he expressed a mood in this clown's face?**

Walt Kuhn. *Young Clown.* 1932. Oil on canvas. 74.6 x 62.2 cm (29⅜ x 24½"). Denver Art Museum. The Helen Dill Collection.

your eyes, for instance, when you feel anger? What happens to your mouth when you feel sadness? Decide what mood your work will show and write this on your notepad.

2. Select one sheet of construction paper for the background. Choose colors of construction paper scraps that show up clearly against one another. Keep in mind that certain colors call to mind certain moods. Red is commonly thought of as a color connected with anger. Blue might be thought of in connection with sadness. (See Figure 2–9.)

3. Begin tearing your scraps into a variety of large and small shapes to represent features of a face. Exaggerate these features to capture the mood you have chosen. To show happiness, for example, make the mouth unusually large and smiling. Position your shapes on the sheet of construction paper to form a face seen from the front. Using the brush, apply a small amount of glue to the back of each scrap. (For information on applying glue, see Technique Tip **28**, *Handbook* page **281**.) Lightly press each scrap into place.

4. When the glue has dried, display your torn paper face. Compare your work with that of your classmates. See how many of your friends can tell immediately which mood your face shows. Try to guess the moods their faces show.

EXAMINING YOUR WORK

- **Describe**   Tell whether your work reveals a front view of a face. Point to the features you exaggerated. Tell what different colors you used for your torn paper face. Explain whether they helped capture the mood of your work. Tell what mood your work shows. Discuss what reactions members of your class had toward your work.

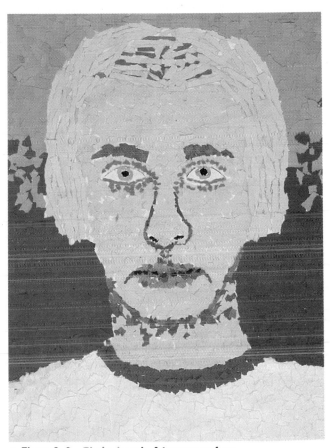

▲ Figure 2–9   Student work. A torn paper face.

STUDIO OPTION

Try This!

■ Create a non-objective picture to express another mood. Use brightly colored markers and draw a non-objective picture. Draw seven triangles, eight circles, and nine rectangles on a page. Have some of the shapes overlap. Use any colors you wish to create an interesting non-objective picture. If you choose to color the background, use only one color for contrast.

Jonathan Franklin. *Mad Hatters.* 1990. Oil on canvas. 137.2 x 228.6 cm (54 x 90"). Private collection.

What Makes a Story Come to Life?

When you were a child, did you have a favorite story? Perhaps it was *Winnie-the-Pooh* or *The Tale of Peter Rabbit.* What is your favorite book or short story now? When you think of your favorite childhood stories, what do you remember? You may remember interesting characters and exciting adventures, but when you think of children's stories, you probably also remember the illustrations. That's because a wonderful story comes to life with vivid illustrations.

Many similarities exist between stories and works of art. In this chapter you learned that artists use subject, composition, and content in their works. Writers use the same concepts, but in different ways. In a story, the subject is usually the person or persons about whom the story is written. The composition involves the combination of these characters, the setting, and the plot. The content is the message that the writer wants to convey.

Do you know the story *Alice's Adventures in Wonderland*? The title of the art work on this page, *Mad Hatters,* was inspired by that story. Do you see any similarities between this art work and the story? The artist, Jonathan Franklin, chose not to depict a scene from the book as it was written. Instead, he used the story idea as a starting point from which to express his own unique vision.

┌ MAKING THE ──── CONNECTION

✔ Explain how writers use subject, composition, and content in their work.
✔ What do you think is the subject, composition, and content of the painting called *Mad Hatters*?
✔ Find out more about the Mad Hatters in *Alice's Adventures in Wonderland.* Do you think Franklin took anything more than the title of his work from this story? Explain your answer.

INTERNET ACTIVITY

Visit Glencoe's Fine Arts Web Site for students at:

http://www.glencoe.com/sec/art/students

BUILDING VOCABULARY

Number a sheet of paper from 1 to 9. After each number, write the term from the list that best matches each description below.

aesthetics   non-objective
aesthetic views   subject
composition   super-realism
content   work of art
credit line

1. Any object created or designed by an artist.
2. The image viewers see and can easily identify in an art work.
3. How the principles are used to organize the elements in an art work.
4. The message, idea, or feeling expressed by an art work.
5. A list of facts about an art work.
6. The philosophy or study of the nature and the value of art.
7. Ideas, or schools of thought, about what to look for in art.
8. Type of art devoted to creating works with convincingly lifelike subjects.
9. Art which has no recognizable subject.

 REVIEWING ART FACTS

Number a sheet of paper from 10 to 15. Answer each question in a complete sentence.

10. List three properties of art works.

11. Which property is concerned with how the principles of a work are used to organize the elements?
12. Name five pieces of information that appear on a credit line.
13. What is the abbreviation for circa? What does this term mean?
14. What is the key question asked by people who work in the field of aesthetics?
15. Why do many students of art accept more than one aesthetic view?

 THINKING ABOUT ART

On a sheet of paper, answer each question in a sentence or two.

1. **Analyze.** Pick two works of fine art from Chapter 2 that have subjects. List the subjects found in each.
2. **Analyze.** Pick two works of fine art from Chapter 2 that you believe express a feeling. Identify the feeling of each. Explain how these feelings were shown.
3. **Compare and contrast.** In what ways is a painting like a short story or poem? In what ways is it different?
4. **Interpret.** Why do you think the final fact in a credit line includes the city and state or country in which a museum is found?

MAKING ART CONNECTIONS

1. **Drama.** Theater and television productions include the same features as works of visual art. The subject is represented by the characters, the content is represented by the script, and the composition determines how the characters and ideas are presented. Choose a play or television production that you have seen. Write a brief report identifying the subject, content, and composition.

2. **Music.** Music also has subject, content, and composition. Music may tell a story through instrumentation or through lyrics. Choose a type of music, such as rock, jazz, country, or classical and analyze the piece for its subject, content, and composition.

▲ This artist is famous for his watercolor paintings. In this work, he successfully captures the dampness of a rainy night in the city.

Frederick Childe Hassam. *Rainy Night*. c. 1895. Watercolor and gouache over graphite underdrawing on wove paper. 28.6 x 21 cm (11¼ x 8¼"). The Fine Arts Museums of San Francisco. Achenbach Foundation for Graphic Arts. Gift of Louise H. Felker and Margery H. Strass in memory of Rosalie G. Hellman. 1978.2.30

CHAPTER 3

Exploring Art Media

Every profession has its "tools of the trade." Carpenters use hammers and wood. Plumbers use wrenches and pipes. Baseball players use bats and balls.

Artists, too, have their tools of the trade. Two of these, used to create the painting at the left, are watercolor brushes and paints. Have you ever worked with these tools? If so, how did your choice of tools affect the art you created?

In this chapter you will learn more about the materials used by artists.

PORTFOLIO IDEAS

Select a favorite piece of art work that you have made. On a sheet of paper answer the following questions. Is the art work a drawing, painting, sculpture, or mixed media? How did you create the art? What materials did you use? How did your choice of materials affect the final art work? Date this paper and put it in your portfolio. Refer to it as you learn more about art. You'll be able to see how much you have learned about the way artists use media.

OBJECTIVES

After completing this chapter, you will be able to:
- Define the term *medium of art.*
- Name the different kinds of media used in drawing, print-making, painting, and sculpting.
- Experiment with drawing, printmaking, painting, and sculpting media.
- Use mixed media to create a work of art.

WORDS YOU WILL LEARN

binder
edition
freestanding
medium of art
mixed media
pigment
print
relief
reproduction
solvent
style
three-dimensional
two-dimensional

Drawing

Do you remember drawing or scribbling with crayons when you were a small child? Although you didn't know it at the time, you were using a medium of art. A **medium of art** is *a material used to create a work of art.* Crayons are one drawing medium and modeling clay is another. A computer is a third. When we talk about more than one medium at a time, we use the term *media.* Colored markers, clay, and computers are media that you may have used.

Sometimes artists combine several media to create a work of art. This is called mixed media. **Mixed media** is *the use of more than one medium.* Can you find a work of art in this chapter that is created with more than one medium?

In this lesson, you will learn about the different kinds of media used in drawing. In later lessons you will learn about media used in other areas of art. You will also get a chance to experiment with some of these art media.

THE IMPORTANCE OF DRAWING

Before a person can run or jump or pedal a bicycle, he or she must be able to stand and walk. Walking is a stepping-stone to all these other activities.

In much the same way, drawing is a stepping-stone to almost all types of art production skills. Fashion designers make drawings of a design before patterns can be made for cutting fabric (Figure 3–1). Architects need to draw sketches and blueprints before the actual building of a house can begin (Figure 3–2). Some painters make drawings before they put a brush to canvas. Figure 3–3 shows a drawing made by Janet Fish, who uses drawings to plan her paintings.

▶ **Figure 3–1 Drawing is an important step in many designing professions. How many careers can you think of that might require drawing?**

◀ Figure 3–2 Architects have to be careful and precise in their work. How do they use math and drawing skills?

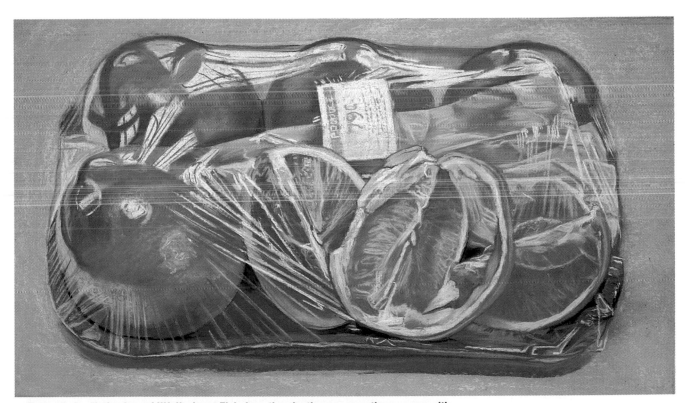

▲ Figure 3–3 Notice how skillfully Janet Fish drew the plastic wrap over the oranges with her pastels.

Janet Fish. *Oranges*. 1973. Pastel on sandpaper. 55.5 x 96.5 cm (21⅞ x 38"). Allen Memorial Art Museum, Oberlin College, Oberlin, Ohio. Fund for Contemporary Art, 1974. 74.6

THE MEDIA OF DRAWING

The media of drawing are many. You have already looked at some. Some others are shown in Figure 3–4. How many of these can you name? How many of them have you used?

Drawing media are used for planning a work of art and sometimes they are used to create a finished work of art. The drawing in Figure 3–5 is such a work.

Throughout this book you will have the opportunity to practice your drawing skills. Experiment with different drawing media to achieve the results you want. Learning to draw, like other skills, takes practice and concentration.

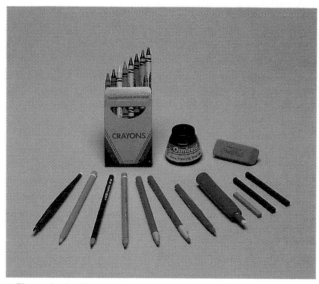

▲ Figure 3–4   There are many kinds of drawing media. This picture shows a few. Can you name other media?

▲ Figure 3–5   Pencils are not just for sketching. Notice how Chernow smoothly blended tones in this drawing using a pencil and eraser.

Ann Chernow. *Lady of L.A.* 1984. Pencil on paper. 52.7 x 80 cm (20¾ x 31½"). National Museum of Women in the Arts, Washington, D. C. Gift of Mr. & Mrs. Edward P. Levy.

▲ Figure 3–6   Student work. Leaf drawing.

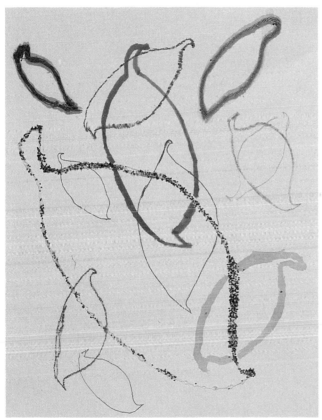

▲ Figure 3–7   Student work. Leaf drawing.

STUDIO ACTIVITY

Making Leaf Drawings

Find and bring in interesting leaves. Select two that interest you and view them from various distances, then draw several versions of each one. You might view the leaves under magnifying glasses if possible. Also take close, unmagnified views, arm's length views, and views from a distance of several feet. (See Figures 3–6 and 3–7.)

When finished with your drawings, show your work to another student and describe how the changes in distance affected what you saw and how you drew. Display the finished drawings for study by the class. Does everyone's work look the same? Why or why not?

Portfolio

Write a short paragraph describing how distance changed your perception of the leaves and affected the way you drew them. Date your paragraph and keep it in your portfolio with the drawings.

✔ CHECK YOUR UNDERSTANDING

1. What is a medium of art?
2. Name three media that are used in drawing.
3. How is drawing used by an architect?
4. How is drawing used by a painter?

LESSON 2

Printmaking

Have you ever made a fingerprint? A fingertip is pressed on an inked pad, and ink is transferred to the raised ridges of the skin. Then the fingertip with the ink on it is pressed on clean white paper. The print on the paper shows the pattern of lines made by the raised ridges of that finger.

An art print can be made in a similar way. Special printing ink is applied to a prepared surface. Then paper or fabric is pressed against the inked surface. An original art **print** is *an image that is transferred from a prepared surface to paper or fabric.* An artist who makes prints is known as a printmaker.

THE IMPORTANCE OF PRINTMAKING

Like other types of art, printmaking allows artists to produce an image on various surfaces. In printmaking, though, an artist can produce multiple copies of the original work. Each print is signed by the artist.

Notice that a print is not the same as a reproduction of an art work, such as those you see on these pages. A **reproduction** is *a photograph of a print.* Confusing original prints with a reproduction of an art work is a mistake many people make.

The printmaker uses a number of tools and materials in making a print. These are shown in Figure 3–8. How many of these media can you name? How many have you used?

THE STEPS OF PRINTMAKING

In making a print, the printmaker follows three basic steps. The first step is to make a plate. The printmaker creates a printing plate by altering a surface to create an image. Next, the printmaker applies ink to, or inks, the plate. Finally, the printmaker transfers the ink to the paper or cloth by pressing the paper or cloth against the plate. Then the paper or cloth is pulled off the plate.

▲ Figure 3–8   This picture shows printmaking media and tools. What are some of the similarities in drawing and printmaking? What are some of the differences?

This set of steps may be repeated many times for a given plate. *A series of prints that are all exactly alike* is called an **edition**. The printmaker signs his or her name, usually in pencil in the bottom margin, and writes the title on each print of an edition. He or she also writes on each print a number that has this form: 10/20. The second number tells how many prints there are in the edition. The first number tells which print you are viewing. A print labeled 10/20 means that you are looking at the tenth of 20 prints that were made from one plate.

THE PRINTMAKER'S MEDIA

Plates in printmaking are usually made of wood, stone, or metal. Sometimes, however, other materials are used. Often prints are done in color. To make a print with more than one color, the printmaker must use a separate plate for each color.

The final appearance of a print will depend on the media, colors, and techniques the printmaker used. Different combinations will give different results. When inked and printed, lines etched in metal will look different from lines drawn with grease crayon. Figures 3–9 and 3–10 show some of these differences.

◄ **Figure 3–9** A "drypoint" is made by scratching lines into a metal plate with a sharp pointed tool. When it is printed, a drypoint looks like a drawing. The difference is that the lines in the drypoint will be raised where the paper has been pressed into the scratches.

Mary Cassatt. *Maternal Caress.* 1891. Drypoint, soft ground etching and aquatint printed in color. 36.5 x 26.8 cm (14⅜ x 10⁹⁄₁₆"). Metropolitan Museum of Art, New York, New York. Gift of Paul J. Sacks, 1916.

▲ **Figure 3–10**   **This print is made with four colors. Can you tell which ones?**

Henri de Toulouse-Lautrec. *La Gitane.* 1900. Lithograph. 160 x 65 cm (63 x 25⅝″). Los Angeles County Museum of Art. Gift of Dr. & Mrs. Kurt Wagner.

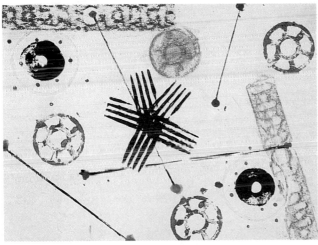

▲ Figure 3–11   Student works. Gadget prints.

STUDIO ACTIVITY

Making Gadget Prints

Gather small items with different shapes that might be dipped into paint to make a gadget print. Some possibilities are paper clips, erasers, clothespins, spools, cork, and buttons. Be as imaginative as you can. Brush tempera paint on each gadget, and press the gadget firmly on a sheet of white paper. Exchange gadgets with your classmates. (See Figure 3–11.)

Once the paint has dried, select one of the gadgets, and place it underneath the paper near a printed image of the same gadget. Make a crayon rubbing of the gadget. (See Technique Tip **25,** *Handbook* **280.**) Discuss your work with your classmates. Do the rubbings look like the prints? Why or why not?

P o r t f o l i o

Make a simple chart to compare and contrast the prints to the rubbings. List "Ways They are the Same" and "Ways They are Different." Refer to the technique you used as well as the media. Include a brief statement telling which you prefer and why.

✔ CHECK YOUR UNDERSTANDING

1. How does an original print differ from a reproduction?
2. Summarize the three basic steps in printmaking.
3. What is an edition? What is the meaning of the numbers an artist will write on a print?
4. Name two materials that can be used to make plates in printmaking.

Painting

You have probably worked with paints at one time or another. The paints may have been the kind that you smear on wet paper with your fingers or paints you mix with water. These are just two of the media used in painting. In this lesson you will learn about others.

CHARACTERISTICS OF PAINTS

Painting is the process of covering a surface with color using a brush, a painting knife, a roller, or even fingers. Sometimes paint is made into a mist by being blown onto a surface with an airbrush. Some paints dry fast, some look bright, and some blend easily. Different effects can be achieved by using different types of paints.

THE PAINTER'S MEDIA

Like other artists, painters use a wide variety of tools and materials. Some of these are shown in Figure 3–12. How many of these can you identify? How many have you used?

Before a painter begins a work, he or she chooses a type of paint and an appropriate surface on which to work. The surface is the material to which the paint is to be applied. Canvas, paper, or silk are three examples. The look of a finished painting has much to do with the combination of media the artist chooses. A painting made by putting oil paint on canvas with a knife has a look very different from a painting made by putting watercolor on paper with a soft brush.

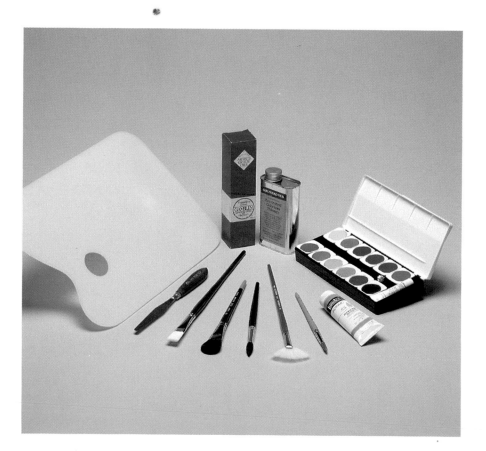

▶ Figure 3–12 Paints, brushes, solvent, a computer, and a palette are some painting tools and media. What other media can you think of that are not shown here?

All paints used in art are made up of three basic ingredients:

- **Pigment** is *a finely ground, colored powder that gives paint its color*.
- **Binder** is *a liquid to which the dry pigment is added*. The binder makes it possible for the pigment to stick to a surface. Linseed oil is the binder for oil paints. Gum arabic (**ar**-uh-bik) is the binder for watercolors.
- **Solvent** is *a liquid that controls the thickness or thinness of the paint*. Turpentine is the solvent in oil paints. Water is the solvent in watercolors. Solvents are also used to clean brushes.

STYLES OF PAINTING

When painters finish works of art, they usually sign their names to them. In a way, the signature of the artist is already there, in his or her individual style. **Style** is *an artist's personal way of expressing ideas in a work*. Style is like a snowflake or a fingerprint. No two are exactly alike, just like no two people have exactly the same handwriting. Two artists may start off with exactly the same media and end up with works that look totally different. Compare Figures 3–13, 3–14, and 3–15. In what ways are these three works alike? In what ways are they different? How do you think the thickness of the paint affected each work? How might you describe the style of each artist?

▲ **Figure 3–13**   **This artist experimented with many different styles of art before he came up with his own style. How would you describe that style? Explain your answer.**

Wassily Kandinsky. *Improvisation Number 27: The Garden of Love*. Oil on canvas. 120.3 x 140 cm (47⅜ x 55¼"). Metropolitan Museum of Art, New York, New York. The Alfred Stieglitz Collection, 1949.

▲ Figure 3–14   Henri-Charles Manguin was known as an open-air painter. This means that he did most of his work outdoors. He is best known for scenes that are near water.

Henri-Charles Manguin. *Port Saint Tropez, le 14 Juillet.* 1905. Oil on canvas. 61.3 x 50.2 cm (24⅛ x 19¾"). The Museum of Fine Arts, Houston, Texas. The John A. & Audrey Beck Collection.

✔ CHECK YOUR UNDERSTANDING

1. What are the three types of ingredients found in every type of paint?
2. What is pigment?
3. What is an artist's style?

STUDIO ACTIVITY

Experimenting with Media

Gather an assortment of school acrylics and thick tempera paints, tools for applying paint, and white paper. Besides different types of brushes, painting tools might include painting knives and twigs with the ends bunched together into a brushlike effect. Try one combination and then another, noting the effects of each. What kind of brush stroke do you get, for example, with a dry brush that has been dipped in thick paint? What happens when you use a wet brush dipped in the same paint? Does thinning the paint with water change its look on paper?

Portfolio

Make a chart that labels each paint sample with the media and technique you used to achieve the visual effect. Keep the chart in your portfolio and add more media samples to it in the future!

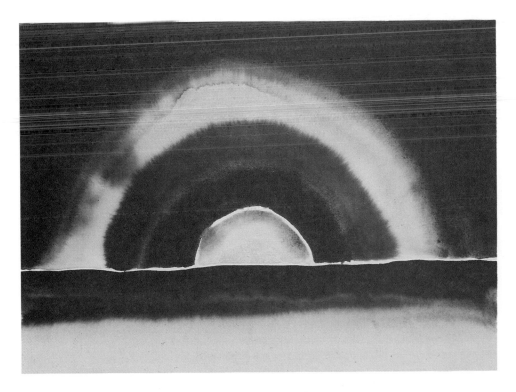

◀ **Figure 3–15   O'Keeffe "simplified" nature. Here she used a few wet watercolor shapes to capture the idea of sunrise over a desert.**

Georgia O'Keeffe. *Sunrise.* 1917. Watercolor. 22.5 x 30.2 cm (8⅞ x 11⅞"). Collection of Barney A. Ebsworth.

 **LESSON 4**

Experimenting with Pigment

Look again at the painting in Figure 3–15 on page **41** and at Figure 3–16 on this page. These were done by American artists, Georgia O'Keeffe and Edward Hopper. Notice from the credit lines that each painter used watercolor on paper. Yet the paintings look as if they were done with completely different media. In this studio lesson you will learn how one medium can be used to give such different results.

WHAT YOU WILL LEARN

You will be making a painting using watercolors on paper. You will experiment with changing the amount of solvent which, for watercolors, is water. Through this experiment, you will learn about the different effects painters are able to create using a single medium. (Figure 3–17 shows an experiment of this kind carried out by a student.)

WHAT YOU WILL NEED

- Watercolor paints and water
- Pencil and sheet of white paper, 9 x 12 inch (23 x 30 cm)
- Two watercolor brushes, one large and one small
- Tray or flat board larger than paper
- Paper towels and sponges

▲ **Figure 3–16** Edward Hopper painted this scene in watercolor. What emotion do you feel when you look at this painting? Hopper is noted for the loneliness portrayed in his work.

Edward Hopper. *Cottages at North Truro, Massachusetts.* 1938. Watercolor. 51.3 x 71.4 cm (20³⁄₁₆ x 28⅛"). Collection of Barney A. Ebsworth.

WHAT YOU WILL DO

1. Wet each cake of paint in the set with a few drops of water. This will allow the paint to begin to soften.
2. Write your name on the back of your paper with a pencil.
3. Using your large brush, wet the back of the paper with clear water. Make sure to wet the entire surface. Place the wet side of the paper on your tray or board. Now brush water on the front side of the paper. Be thorough, but do not let puddles form.
4. Load your small brush with color by rubbing it against one of the cakes of paint. Take time to dissolve the pigment. Then touch the paper in several places with the brush to make dots. What happens to the paint dots?
5. Clean your brush by swishing it around in the water. Blot it on a paper towel and load your brush with a second color. Draw lines on an unused wet area of the paper. What happens to the paint?
6. As your paper dries, add other colors to unused dry areas where the paint will not run. Concentrate on making some of your lines thick and some of them thin. (See Technique Tip **14**, *Handbook* **275**.) After a time, you will be able to paint over areas you have already painted since they have had time to dry.
7. When your paper is completely dry, share your work with your classmates. Discuss the different effects you have created.

- **Describe**   Point out areas in your work where the color is very weak. Describe the condition of the paper when you made these dots and lines. Point out dots and lines in your work where the color is very strong. Describe the condition of the paper when you made these dots and lines. Identify areas of your work where you painted over other colors.
- **Explain**   Tell what effect changing the amount of solvent will have in a painting. Tell how you think the artists of the works in Figures 3–15 and 3–16 arrived at such different results using the same medium.

▲ **Figure 3–17   Student work. Watercolor painting.**

Try This! COMPUTER OPTION

■ If your computer art program has liquid brushes and water effects, explore Brush widths, colors, and water effects. Try rough or smooth papers if your program offers these choices. Explore the opaque and transparent color settings. Record combinations that you like. Title, Save, and Print your best example of liquid watercolor effects.

Sculpture

Have you ever made a sand castle or a snowman? If you have, then you have worked in sculpture. Sculpture is art that is made to occupy space. Sculpture is three-dimensional. **Three-dimensional** means *that an object has height, width, and depth*. (See Figure 3–18.) This is one way in which sculpture is different from the other kinds of art you have looked at so far. Although objects in a drawing or painting can look quite real, the work is flat, or two-dimensional. **Two-dimensional** means *that the work has height and width but not depth*.

▶ **Figure 3–18 This artist often uses "found" objects as the basis for her art. Name some of the found objects you see in this sculpture.**

Nancy Stevenson Graves. *Zaga.* 1983. Cast bronze with polychrome chemical patination. 182.9 x 124.5 x 81.4 cm (72 x 49 x 32"). Nelson-Atkins Museum of Art, Kansas City, Missouri. © 1998 Estate of Nancy Graves Foundation/Licensed by VAGA, New York, NY

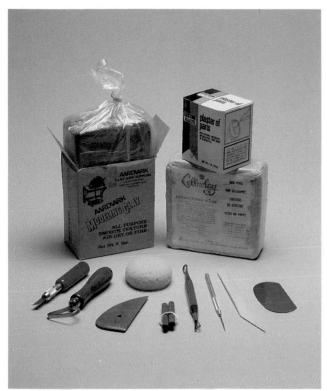

▲ Figure 3–19   There are many kinds of sculpture tools and media. Can you name some other kinds not shown in this picture?

THE MEDIA OF SCULPTURE

An artist who works in sculpture is called a sculptor. Sculptors work with a great many materials and tools. One sculpture medium that you have probably used is modeling clay. Some others are shown in Figure 3–19. How many of these can you name? How many have you used?

Most sculpture is freestanding, or in the round. **Freestanding** means *surrounded on all sides by space.* Statues of people are examples of freestanding sculptures. Every side of a freestanding sculpture is sculpted and finished. In order to see the work as the sculptor meant it to be seen, you have to move around it. The boy in Figure 3–20 is a freestanding sculpture.

▲ Figure 3–20   This ancient Chinese figure of a young boy was cast in bronze with carved jade birds. Note how serious he looks.

Unknown artist. *Figure of Standing Youth.* 400–300 B.C. Bronze and jade, Chinese eastern Zhou Dynasty. 30 cm (11¾") high. Museum of Fine Arts, Boston, Massachusetts. Maria Antoinette Evans Fund.

In addition to freestanding sculpture, there is relief sculpture. **Relief** is *a type of sculpture in which forms and figures are projected from the front only.* It is flat along the back. You can see large reliefs on buildings and small reliefs on items such as jewelry.

► **Figure 3–21** Käthe Kollwitz produced powerful treatments of well-known subjects such as poverty and sorrow. She made social statements with her work. This is a self-portrait she executed when she was 69 years old.

Käthe Kollwitz. *Self-Portrait*. 1936. Bronze on marble base. 36.5 x 23.1 x 28.7 cm (14⅜ x 9⅛ x 11⅜"). Hirshhorn Museum, Smithsonian Institution, Washington, D.C. Joseph H. Hirshhorn, 1966.

▼ **Figure 3–22** What is the center of interest in this work?

Marisol Escobar. *Poor Family I*. 1987. Wood, charcoal, stones, plastic doll. 198.1 x 396.2 x 213.4 cm (78 x 156 x 84"). Sidney Janis Gallery, New York, New York. © 1998 Marisol Escobar/ Licensed by VAGA, New York, NY

SCULPTING METHODS

There are four basic methods for making sculpture. These are:

- **Carving.** In carving, the sculptor starts with a block of material and cuts or chips a shape from it. Often a hard material like stone is used.
- **Casting.** In casting, the sculptor starts by making a mold. He or she then pours in a melted-down metal or some other liquid that will later harden. See Figure 3–21 for an example of bronze sculpture.
- **Modeling.** In modeling, the sculptor builds up and shapes a soft material. Clay and fresh plaster are two such materials.
- **Assembling.** In assembling, also known as constructing, the sculptor glues or in some other way joins together pieces of material. The sculpture in Figure 3–22 was made by assembling pieces of wood, charcoal, stones, and a plastic doll. This sculpture shows both additive and subtractive methods.

Modeling and assembling are known as additive methods of sculpting. In the additive method, the artist adds together or builds up the material. Carving is a subtractive method. In the subtractive method, the artist takes away or removes material.

STUDIO ACTIVITY

Creating a Freestanding Sculpture

Using pieces of scrap plastic foam from beverage containers, trays, and packing materials, work in teams to create a freestanding sculpture. You may use both the additive and subtractive techniques to create this work. Use slots and tabs to hold the smaller pieces of your construction together. Straight pins, strings, and other joining devices can help you hold the larger pieces together. The size of these constructions depends upon the limits of your art room and the supplies you can collect. You can carve large packing materials with scissors and utility knives. For small sculpture pieces, cut the cups and trays with scissors into a variety of shapes.

P o r t f o l i o

Take photographs of the sculpture for your portfolio. Include front, back, and side views. Then write a credit line that includes your name, title of art work, date, media, size, your school, city, and state.

✔ CHECK YOUR UNDERSTANDING

1. What is another term that has the same meaning as freestanding?
2. Name two media used by sculptors.
3. Briefly describe the four basic methods for making sculpture.
4. What is meant by the term *additive* as it is used in sculpture? Which two basic methods of making sculpture are additive?
5. What is meant by the term *subtractive* as it is used in sculpture? Which basic method of making sculpture is subtractive?

Creating with Mixed Media

The young artist who created the mixed media work in Figure 3–23 was creating a work of art which represented his life. He included objects and symbols that were important to him. The daffodil represents a summer spent studying art at the Daffodil Farm. The tiny figure of Pinocchio is from a drawing that his kindergarten teacher had framed for him. Near the center of the work there is a checkerboard. What do you think this might represent? Can you recognize any other symbols that give you more information about this young man?

He used different types of media to create this work. For example, graphite, colored pencil, and markers are some of the media he used. What others can you identify?

WHAT YOU WILL LEARN

You will create a mixed-media picture that represents something about your life. You may include a photo or sketch of yourself, but do not have it take up the whole work. As you create your work of art, experiment with a variety of media.

▲ Figure 3–23   The artist worked on this mixed media piece for a year. It shows symbols of important events in his life. Can you identify some of the symbols?

Herbert Andrew Williams. *A Year in the Life of Herbert*. 1988. Mixed media. Private collection.

WHAT YOU WILL NEED

- Pencil and sketch paper
- Sheet of white paper, 12 x 18 inch (30 x 46 cm)
- Variety of media, including markers, paints, colored pencils
- Magazine, newspaper, and wallpaper scraps

WHAT YOU WILL DO

1. Make a list of people, places, objects, and events that symbolize you and your life. Make rough sketches of these items. You may also add words. Notice that you can find the artist's name in Figure 3–23, but it is slightly hidden.
2. Look through several magazines and newspapers for pictures and words that represent your interest, skills, and cultural background. If you decide to cut out a shape, cut neatly around the edge of the shape. Do you see the brown hand near the center of Figure 3–23? Notice how it has been carefully cut and outlined with colored pencil and black ink.
3. Select from the pieces you have cut and decide on the sketch you will use. Draw your final plan on the white paper.
4. Glue down the cut objects. Use any other media, including drawings, paintings, photographs, and found objects, to finish your work. (See Figure 3–24.)
5. Place your work on display with your classmates. Can you recognize your friends by the symbols they used?

- **Describe**   List the media that you used in this work. List the symbols you included and explain how each symbol relates to you. Identify the media that you enjoyed working with and explain why. Identify any media that did not produce the results you wanted. Explain why.

▲ Figure 3–24   Student work. Mixed media.

Try This! STUDIO OPTIONS

■ Select one medium that gave you the most successful results. Determine a theme for your composition, such as a sporting event, school activity, or family celebration. Plan the composition and complete it using the medium of your choice.

■ Create a mixed-media work that represents your school, city, or country.

The Importance of Art Restoration

Statue of Liberty. Liberty Island, New York Harbor.

The Statue of Liberty is an impressive sculptural symbol of our national heritage. It towers over the harbor at New York City, representing freedom and democracy. Like many art works, however, the Statue of Liberty had become damaged over time. If it had not been restored, future generations might not be able to enjoy it in the same way we can today.

The first step in a restoration process is to identify which media and materials the artist used to create the work. These media and materials change slowly over long periods of time. For example, an environmental factor such as sunlight may cause the color in paint to change. Extreme temperatures and moisture may cause materials to wrinkle, warp, or crack. Air pollution also causes serious damage, especially to architecture and outdoor art works.

The goal of art restoration is to repair art work to its original condition. Besides knowing what media and materials were used, the restorer must determine what factors caused the damage. The restoration process may include removing layers of dirt covering an oil painting. It may involve repairing cracks in a marble sculpture. In the case of the Statue of Liberty, the iron framework had rusted and was replaced with one made of stainless steel. After the art is restored, it is preserved to help prevent further damage.

MAKING THE CONNECTION

- How would a photograph of the original Statue of Liberty aid in the restoration process?
- Why should an art restorer obtain as much information as possible about an art work *before* starting restoration?
- Look for more information about the Statue of Liberty. What media were used to create it? When did restoration take place? What processes were used to restore the statue?

INTERNET ACTIVITY

Visit Glencoe's Fine Arts Web Site for students at:

http://www.glencoe.com/sec/art/students

BUILDING VOCABULARY

Number a sheet of paper from 1 to 13. After each number, write the term from the list that best matches each description below.

binder
edition
freestanding
medium of art
mixed media
pigment
print
relief
reproduction
solvent
style
three-dimensional
two-dimensional

1. A material used to create an art work.
2. An image that is transferred from a prepared surface to paper or fabric.
3. Work that has height, width, depth.
4. A finely ground powder that gives paint its color.
5. Surrounded on all sides by space.
6. Use of more than one medium in art.
7. A work that has height and width.
8. A type of sculpture in which the image projects from only the front.
9. A photograph of a print.
10. An artist's personal way of expressing ideas in a work.
11. A liquid to which dry pigment is added.
12. A liquid that controls the thickness or thinness of the paint.
13. A series of prints all exactly alike.

 ## REVIEWING ART FACTS

Number a sheet of paper from 14 to 18. Answer each question in a complete sentence.

14. Name two drawing media.
15. What is the first step in printmaking?
16. What is a group of identical prints called?
17. How is freestanding sculpture meant to be seen?
18. What type of sculpture is flat on the back?

THINKING ABOUT ART

On a sheet of paper, answer each question in a sentence or two.

1. **Summarize.** Look again at the watercolor painting by Hassam on page **28**. How does the artist's choice of medium contribute to the success of his art work?
2. **Compare and contrast.** Compare the styles of the prints in Figures 3–9 and 3–10. Find at least three differences.
3. **Analyze.** Sculptors, like other artists, develop individual styles. How would you describe the styles of the sculptors for Figures 3–18 and 3–20?
4. **Analyze.** What method of sculpture would you be using if you whittled a tree branch? What method would you be using if you built a tower of building blocks that snapped together?

MAKING ART CONNECTIONS

1. **Language Arts.** Carefully study the Cassatt print in Figure 3–9. Try to imagine the mood of the event and what is happening in the painting. Describe the place and people shown. Use words such as color, line, shape, form, space, and texture. Write a few paragraphs about what is happening in the painting.
2. **Communication.** Find three examples of printmaking in your daily activities.

Think about how this art form has developed into an important medium for communicating ideas. Share your examples with the class.
3. **Social Studies.** In 1440 a German printer named Johannes Gütenberg invented a printing press with movable type. The effect of this invention was profound. Trace the development of the printing industry from 1440 through the present.

▲ This artist is noted for the way he uses everyday objects as sources of inspiration. How do the colors in this painting make the desserts look real?

Wayne Thiebaud. *Display Rows.* 1989. Watercolor. 27.9 x 22.9 cm (11 x 9"). Courtesy of the Campbell-Thiebaud Gallery, San Francisco, California.

CHAPTER 4

The Elements of Art

When creating a work of art, an artist is faced with a number of questions. Look at the painting at the left. Think about how the artist answered the following questions:

- What colors will I use?
- Will the painting as a whole appear to be smooth or rough to the touch?
- Will the objects in the painting look flat and two-dimensional, or will they appear deep and realistic?

How an artist answers these and other questions determines how the finished work will look.

PORTFOLIO IDEAS

Each entry in your portfolio should be marked clearly for identification. This will help you keep them in order. Make sure each piece includes your name and the date you completed the art work. Any notes about the assignment are valuable too. Make it a point to use the names of the elements of art as you write about your art work. That way you will demonstrate your growth as an artist and communicate to your readers in the language of art.

OBJECTIVES

After completing this chapter, you will be able to:
- Name the six elements of art.
- Identify the three properties of color.
- Name the different kinds of line.
- Explain the difference between shapes and forms.
- Explain how we experience texture.
- Experiment with the elements of art.

WORDS YOU WILL LEARN

analogous colors
color wheel
complementary colors
form
hue
intensity
line
line quality
line variation
monochromatic colors
motif
shape
space
texture
value

The Language of Art

When you talk to someone or write a letter, you communicate. You share your ideas and feelings. You use words—either spoken or written—to get a message across.

Artists do the same thing. They do not express their thoughts and feelings in ordinary words, however. Instead, artists use visual images—things that we can see and sometimes touch—to "speak" to us.

In this lesson you will learn about the special "language" artists use when they communicate. You will also begin to see that an artist's success in communicating depends partly on his or her skill in using this language.

THE VISUAL LANGUAGE

Since earliest times people have used the language of art to speak to each other. This is clear from the discovery of cave paintings like the one in Figure 4–1. Such early art works show that humans were writing in pictures some 12,000 years before the invention of the alphabet.

You have probably heard it said that a picture is worth a thousand words. In a very real sense, this saying is true. To understand the relationship between words and pictures, first read the following paragraph:

The frightened mother was locked in a terrible struggle with the phantom, who greedily eyed her child. "No!" the mother's wide eyes protested. "No—you can never have him!" As her heart raced wildly, the mother clutched her little boy to her body with the strength of 10 men. But no matter how hard she fought, little by little she felt her grip weaken. Slowly—ever so slowly—the child was slipping from her fingers. In the end, she was no match for the phantom. Death, she knew in that awful final instant, would soon claim another helpless victim.

Now look at Figure 4–2 with the title *Death and the Mother*. Notice the look of sheer terror on the mother's face. Notice the power in her

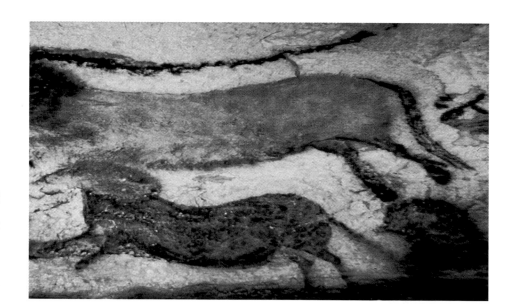

▶ **Figure 4–1** Long ago, humans painted pictures of animals on cave walls and ceilings. What reasons can you imagine they had for creating this art?

Horses. Cave painting. Lascaux. Dordogne, France. 15,000–10,000 B.C.

bulging arm as she holds fast to her child. What it took the writer 100 words to say, the artist has said in a single look!

▲ **Figure 4–2** How would you describe the look on the woman's face? Why is she terrified? Can you tell what she is clutching in her arms?

Käthe Kollwitz. *Death and the Mother.* 1934. Lithograph. Private collection.

THE VOCABULARY OF ART

You know that every language has its own word system, or vocabulary. Before a person can speak the language, he or she must know at least some of the words in its vocabulary.

The language of art, too, has a vocabulary all its own. Instead of words, however, the vocabulary of art is made up of six visual elements. An **element of art** is a *basic visual symbol an artist uses to create visual art.* These are color, line, shape, form, space, and texture. In much the way we put words together to form a sentence, the artist puts the visual elements together to make a statement.

▲ **Figure 4–3** Why might the artist have chosen to make the man so thin and angled?

Alberto Giacometti. *Man Pointing.* 1947. Bronze. 179.1 x 103.5 x 41.6 cm Base 30.5 x 33.1 cm (70½ x 40¾ x 16⅜" Base 12 x 13¼"). The Museum of Modern Art, New York, New York. Gift of Mrs. John D. Rockefeller III.

It is often hard to tell one element from another when you look at a work of art. When you look at Figure 4–3, for instance, you do not see the elements of line (long) and texture (rough). Instead, you see the sculpture as a whole. Your eye "reads" the elements of line and texture together. And yet, it is the very blending of these elements that permits you to see the art work as the artist meant you to see it: a man pointing.

"READING" THE LANGUAGE

When you first learned to read, you did not start with a book. You began by reading a word at a time. That is how you will learn the language of art: one element at a time.

Because these elements are so important, the remaining lessons of this chapter will be devoted to a discussion of them. Once you have studied these elements you will know a good part of the art vocabulary.

✔CHECK YOUR UNDERSTANDING

1. In what way can art be said to be a language?
2. What is an element of art?
3. Name the six elements of art.

Color

Color is everywhere. It is in the orange-pink glow of the summer sky just before sunrise. It is in the rich reds and oranges of autumn leaves and in the long purple shadows that lie across the snow toward the close of a winter's day.

Color is even in our everyday language. "Green with envy," "feeling blue," and "red with rage" are English expressions that mention color.

In this lesson you will learn about the very important role color plays in art. You will learn how some artists have used color successfully. This knowledge of color can help you use it more creatively and effectively in your own art works.

TRAITS OF COLOR

Look up at the sun on a clear day and you see an almost blinding white light—or so your eye tells you. In reality, what you are looking at—but failing to see—are all the colors of the rainbow. When the sunlight shines on objects, some of the light is absorbed by the object. Some of the light bounces off. Color is what the eye sees when sunlight or some other light bounces off an object.

In the 18th century, Sir Isaac Newton organized the colors into a color wheel. The **color wheel** is *an arrangement of colors in a circular format.* See Figure 4–4. Later in this chapter you will learn more about the arrangement of the colors on the color wheel.

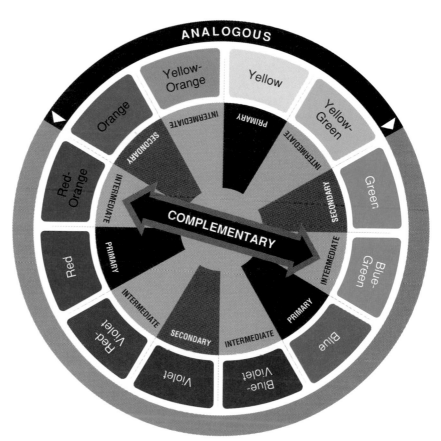

▶ **Figure 4–4   Color wheel.**

Sometimes artists use colors in bold and shocking ways (Figure 4–5). Sometimes they use them in quiet and serious ways (Figure 4–6 on page 58). To achieve different results, artists must understand the three properties or traits of color. These are hue, value, and intensity.

Hue

Hue is *a color's name*. Red, yellow, and blue are the primary hues. They are always equally spaced on the color wheel. (See Figure 4–4.) They are called primary, or first, because they can be used to mix all the other colors but cannot themselves be made by the mixing of other colors.

◄ **Figure 4–5** **What makes this painting bold? Do you think this is a successful painting? Why or why not?**

Miriam Schapiro. *High Steppin' Strutter I.* 1985. Paper and acrylic on paper. 203.2 x 138.4 cm (80 x 54½"). Bernice Steinbaum Gallery, New York. Given anonymously.

▶ Figure 4–6 Why would this be considered a quiet painting? What gives it its serious quality?

José Clemente Orozco. *Zapatistas.* 1931. Oil on canvas. 114.3 x 139.7 cm (45 x 55"). The Museum of Modern Art, New York, New York. Given anonymously.

The secondary hues are green, orange, and violet. The place of each on the color wheel — between the primary hues — tells which hues can be mixed to make it. To get orange, for example, you mix equal parts of red and yellow. Can you identify the colors that you would mix to obtain the remaining secondary hues?

Intermediate hues are made by mixing a primary hue with its neighboring secondary hue. When you mix the primary hue yellow with the secondary hue green, you get the intermediate hue yellow-green.

Value

You may have noticed that some colors on the color wheel seem lighter than others. The difference is one of value. **Value** is *the lightness or darkness of a hue*. Pale yellow is light in value and deep purple is dark in value.

You can change the value of a hue by adding black or white. In art, a light (or whiter) value of a hue is called a tint. Pink is a mixture of red and white. Pink could be called a tint. A dark (or blacker) value is called a shade. (See Figure 4–7.) Maroon is a mixture

of red and black. It could be called a shade. Be careful when using these terms. In everyday language, the word shade is often used to describe both light and dark values of a hue.

Intensity

Some hues strike the eye as bright and alive. Others appear dull or muddy. The difference is the color's intensity. **Intensity** is *the brightness or dullness of a hue*. A bright hue is said to be high in intensity. A dull hue is said to be low in intensity. Bright yellow is high in intensity. Mustard yellow is low in intensity.

Look again at the color wheel on page **56**. Notice that as you move away from green in the direction of red, the hue grows less intense. Red and green are **complementary colors,** *colors opposite each other on the color wheel*. Adding a hue's complementary color lowers the hue's intensity. (See Figure 4–7.) If you mix equal parts of two complementary colors, you get a neutral color such as brown or gray.

VALUES OF BLUE

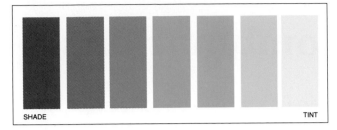

SHADE   TINT

INTENSITIES OF BLUE

HIGH INTENSITY   LOW INTENSITY

▲ **Figure 4–7** **Value and intensity scales.**

COMBINING COLORS

Colors are like musical instruments. Just as each instrument has its own special sound, so every color has its own "personality." Combining colors in just the right way can lead to striking results. The following are some common color schemes that trained artists use:

- **Monochromatic color schemes. Mono-chromatic (mahn-uh-kroh-mat-ik) colors** are *different values of a single hue.* For example, dark blue, medium blue, and light blue is a monochromatic scheme. This type of scheme tightly weaves together the parts of an art work. A danger of a monochromatic scheme, however, is that it can bore the viewer.
- **Analogous color schemes. Analogous (uh-nal-uh-gus) colors** are *colors that are side by side on the color wheel and share a hue.* Violet, red-violet, red, and red-orange are analogous colors that share the hue red. Analogous colors in an art work can tie one shape to the next.

- **Warm or cool color schemes.** Red, yellow, and orange remind us of sunshine, fire, and other warm things. For this reason, they are known as warm colors. Blue, green, and violet make us think of cool things, like ice and grass. They are known, therefore, as cool colors. When used in an art work, warm colors seem to move toward the viewer. Cool colors appear to move back and away.

✔ CHECK YOUR UNDERSTANDING

1. What are the three primary hues?
2. What is the difference between a tint and a shade?
3. What are complementary colors? Give an example.
4. What is a monochromatic color scheme?
5. Define an analogous color scheme.

 **LESSON 3**

Using Color Combinations

Artists use color schemes to create special effects in works of art. Color schemes can make a painting vibrate or make colors look brighter.

Look at Figure 4–8. Notice how Elizabeth Murray has used the red and green complementary color scheme to create this work. To give it variety she has experimented with values. Can you find a tint and a shade of red?

WHAT YOU WILL LEARN

You will create a complementary color design. You will create a motif, based on your initials. A **motif** (moh-**teef**) is *a unit that is repeated in a pattern or visual rhythm.* Plan the motif so that it touches all four edges of the paper. Then arrange the motif to form an interesting pattern. Paint all the letters with one color. Paint all the negative spaces with its complement.

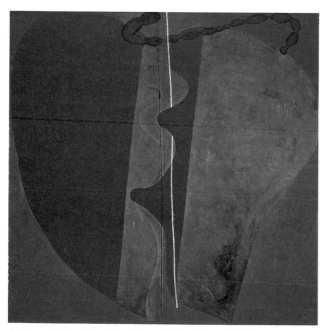

▲ **Figure 4–8** How does the artist's choice and placement of color affect the meaning of the painting?

Elizabeth Murray. *Join.* 1980. Oil on canvas. 337.8 x 304.8 cm (133 x 120″). Security Pacific Bank Collection.

WHAT YOU WILL NEED

- Pencil, sketch paper, eraser
- White paper, 4½ x 6 inch (11 x 15 cm)
- White paper, 9 x 12 inch (23 x 30 cm)
- Masking tape
- Tempera paint and two small brushes
- Paper towels

WHAT YOU WILL DO

1. Using sketch paper, draw different arrangements of your initials. In this design, an interesting shape is more important than the readability of the letters.
2. Select your best design. Using double lines, draw the letters on the smaller sheet of white paper. Be sure that the letters touch all four sides of the paper. (See Figure 4–9.)
3. Hold the paper up to a glass window with the letters facing out. You will see them backwards through the paper. Carefully draw over the lines on the back with a soft lead pencil. The lines on the back must go directly over the lines on the front. These lines will act like carbon paper.
4. You may arrange the motif any way that fits on the larger sheet of paper.
5. Place your motif on the larger sheet of paper. Hold it in place with a small piece of tape. Transfer the image by drawing over the lines of the motif. If you wish, you may flip the motif over and trace the mirror image.
6. Select a set of complementary colors. You may use primaries and secondaries, or you may use a set of intermediates such as red-orange and blue-green.

4.5"

6"

- **Describe**   Explain what set of complementary colors you selected. Did your motif touch all four sides of the paper? Describe the pattern you created with your motif. Show where you painted all the letters with one hue and all the negative spaces with its complement.
- **Explain**   Describe the effect that is created by painting the complementary colors side by side.

▲ Figure 4–9   Letter motif arrangement.

7. Use one brush and one hue to paint all the letters in your pattern. Be sure the paint is dry before you paint the second color next to it.

8. Use a second brush to paint all the negative spaces with the complement of that hue. Nothing should be left white. If you do not have two brushes, clean your brush thoroughly before using another color. (See Technique Tip **10**, *Handbook* page **273**.)

9. Put your work on display with your classmates. Do all the complements have the same exciting visual effect? (See Figure 4–10.)

▲ Figure 4–10   Student work. Motif design.

STUDIO OPTION

Try This!

■ Select a sheet of construction paper of a primary color. Cut out objects from a magazine that have the complementary color of your paper. Look for tints and shades of the primary color and its complement as well. Organize them into a design and glue them to the background paper.

Line

Think about how many times every day you see lines. You write words, numbers, and symbols with the help of lines. You use lines to draw pictures. The lines on a map help you find the best route from one place to another. You also feel lines — in the grain of a piece of wood or the veins of a leaf.

This lesson will focus on the importance of line as one of the six elements of art.

THE MEANING OF LINE

Take a pencil and move it across a sheet of paper. What happened? The moving point of the pencil made a path of connected dots on the paper. In other words, it made a line. This definition of **line** — *the path of a dot through space* — is a good one to remember. It reminds you that it takes movement to make a line. When you see a line, your eye usually follows its movement. A trained artist uses lines to control the movement of the viewer's eyes. Lines can lead the eyes into, around, and out of visual images in a work of art.

KINDS OF LINE

There are five main kinds of line: vertical, horizontal, diagonal, curved, and zigzag. When used in an art work, lines can communicate different messages or feelings to the viewer.

Vertical Lines

Vertical lines (Figure 4–11) move straight up and down. They do not lean at all. When you stand up straight and tall, your body forms a vertical line.

In art, vertical lines appear to be at attention. Artists use them to show dignity, formality, or strength.

Horizontal Lines

Horizontal lines (Figure 4–12) run parallel to the ground. They do not slant. When you lie flat on the floor, your body forms a horizontal line.

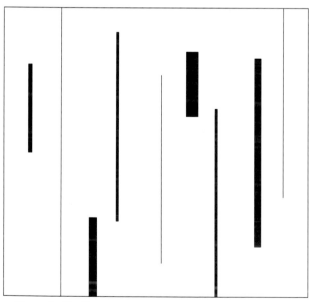

▲ **Figure 4–11** Vertical lines move straight up and down.

▲ **Figure 4–12** Horizontal lines lie parallel to the horizon.

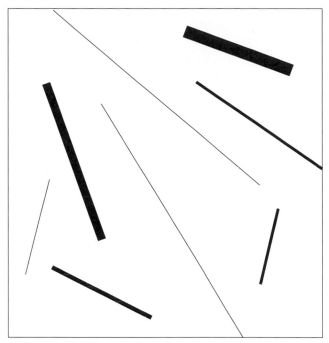

▲ Figure 4–13   Diagonal lines slant.

▲ Figure 4–14   Curved lines change direction gradually.

Horizontal lines in art seem at rest. Other words that come to mind in connection with them are quiet and peaceful. Horizontal lines make the viewer feel comfortable, calm, and relaxed.

Diagonal Lines

Diagonal lines (Figure 4–13) slant. They are somewhere between a vertical and a horizontal line. Imagine standing straight up and then, with your body stiff, falling to the floor. At any point during your fall, your body would form a diagonal line.

To the artist, diagonal lines signal action and excitement. Since they appear to be either rising or falling, diagonals sometimes make a viewer feel tense and uncomfortable. But when they meet and seem to hold each other up, as in the roof of a house, they appear firm and unmoving.

Curved Lines

Curved lines (Figure 4–14) change direction little by little. When you draw wiggly lines, you are actually linking a series of curves. Other forms that begin with curves are spirals and circles.

Like diagonal lines, curved lines, express movement, though in a more graceful, flowing way. The amount of movement in a curve depends on how tight the curve is. Notice how the painter, Vincent van Gogh suggests motion in his tree through the unusual use of curves (Figure 4–15, on page 64).

Zigzag Lines

Zigzag lines (Figure 4–16, on page 65) are made by combining different directions of diagonal lines. The diagonals form sharp angles and change direction suddenly.

Zigzag lines can create confusion. They suggest action and nervous excitement. Sometimes zigzags move in even horizontal patterns, like those at the top of a picket fence. These are less active than the jagged lines in a diagonal streak of lightning.

QUALITIES OF LINES

Lines may appear smooth or rough, continuous or broken, sketchy or controlled. The **line quality** describes *the unique character of any line.* Line quality is affected by either the tool or medium used to produce the mark, or by the particular motion of the artist's hands.

▲ **Figure 4–15   How do the lines in van Gogh's painting direct your eyes? How is van Gogh's tree different from the usual idea of a tree?**

Vincent van Gogh. *Cypresses*. 1889. Oil on canvas. 93.3 x 74 cm (36¾ x 29⅛"). Metropolitan Museum of Art, New York, New York. Rogers Fund, 1949.

▲ Figure 4–16　Zigzag lines are combinations of diagonals.

▲ Figure 4–17a　Line quality.

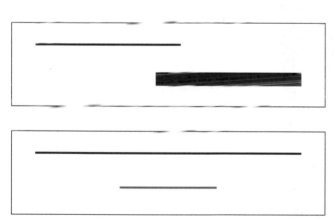

▲ Figure 4–17b　Line variation.

Lines can also be varied. **Line variation** describes *the thickness or thinness, lightness or darkness of a line.* Thick and dark lines appear to be visually heavier than thick and light lines. Look at Figures 4–17a and 4–17b and identify the different kinds of lines. What medium do you think was used to create each line?

✔ CHECK YOUR UNDERSTANDING

1. What is the meaning of the term *line* as it is used in art?
2. Name five kinds of line.
3. Describe the way each of the five kinds of line causes a viewer of an art work to feel.
4. What affects line quality?

Shape, Form, and Space

The world we live in is made up basically of two things: objects and space. Each object—a car, an apple, a book, even you—has a shape or a form. Often you are able to pick out objects by their forms or shapes alone. Sometimes you can spot a friend in the distance just by recognizing his or her shape. With your eyes closed you could feel an object and tell that it has a round form.

Shape, form, and space are all closely tied to one another. In this lesson you will learn to read the meaning of these three elements.

SHAPE

In art a **shape** is *an area clearly set off by one or more of the other five visual elements of art.* Shapes are flat. They are limited to only two dimensions: length and width. A ball's shape is a circle. A shape may have an outline or boundary around it. Some shapes show up because of color. Others are set off purely by the space that surrounds them.

Shapes may be thought of as belonging to one of two classes:

▲ Figure 4–18 An inquisition is an official investigation. Do the long vertical shapes in this painting suggest a court of law? Who is being questioned in this fantasy work?

Attilio Salemme. *Inquisition.* 1952. Oil on canvas. 101.6 x 160 cm (40 x 63"). Whitney Museum of American Art, New York, New York.

▲ **Figure 4–19** Do you like the organic shapes in this painting better than the geometric ones in Figure 4–18? Why or why not?

Arthur G. Dove. *Plant Forms*. 1915. Pastel on canvas. 43.8 x 60.6 cm (17¼ x 23⅞"). Whitney Museum of American Art, New York, New York. Purchased with funds from Mr. & Mrs. Roy R. Nueberger.

- **Geometric shapes.** These are precise shapes that look as if they were made with a ruler or other drawing tool. The square, the circle, the triangle, the rectangle, and the oval are the five basic geometric shapes. The strange world shown in Figure 4–18 is made up largely of geometric shapes.
- **Organic shapes.** These are not regular or even. Their outlines curve to make free-form shapes. Organic shapes are often found in nature. The objects in the painting in Figure 4–19 are based on organic, free-form shapes.

FORM

Like shapes, forms have length and width. But forms go a step further. They have depth. A **form** is *an object with three dimensions*. You are a three-dimensional form. So is a tree or a table.

Forms, too, are grouped as either geometric or organic. Examples of geometric forms are a baseball and a child's building block. Examples of organic forms are a stone and a cloud.

Shapes and forms are closely linked in art (Figure 4–20). The end of a cylinder is a circle. One side of a cube is a square. A triangle can "grow" into a pyramid.

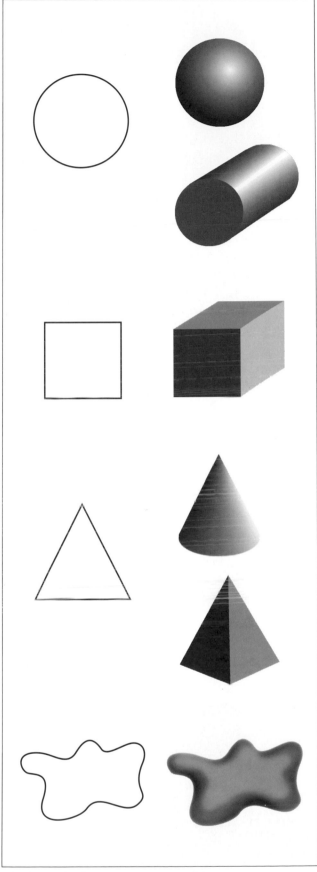

▲ **Figure 4–20** Form-shape correspondences.

▲ Figure 4–21   Does seeing this sculpture make you want to walk around it and see it from different sides?

Constantin Brancusi. *Mlle. Pogany II*. 1920. Polished bronze. 44.5 x 17.8 x 25.4 cm (17½ x 7 x 10″). Albright-Knox Art Gallery, Buffalo, New York. Charlotte A. Watson Fund, 1927.

SPACE

Space is *the distance or area between, around, above, below, and within things.* Space is empty until objects fill it. All objects take up space. You, for instance, are a living, breathing form moving through space.

Some kinds of art are three-dimensional. You may recall from Chapter 3 that sculpture is this kind of art. When a piece of sculpture is freestanding, as in Figure 4–21, we can move completely around it and see it from different sides.

Although drawings and paintings are created in two dimensions, they can be made to appear three-dimensional. Artists have developed techniques for giving the feeling of depth in paintings and drawings. These include:

- **Overlapping.** Having one shape cover part of another shape.
- **Size.** Making distant shapes smaller than closer ones.
- **Focus.** Adding more detail to closer objects, less detail to distant objects.
- **Placement.** Placing distant objects higher up in the picture, closer ones lower down.
- **Intensity and value.** Using colors that are lower in intensity and lighter in value for objects in the distance.
- **Linear perspective.** Slanting lines of buildings and other objects so they seem to come together in the distance.

Creating Space

Imagine that the room you are sitting in is a painting. Look around the room. Be on the alert for the use of techniques that lead to a feeling of deep space. For example, which objects, if any, overlap? Which objects appear to be smaller than others? Now make a sketch of the room, replacing some real objects with ones from your imagination. Make sure that your new objects follow the same rules of space as the old ones. When you have finished, discuss your drawing with other members of the class. Can they identify all the space-creating techniques in your work?

P o r t f o l i o

List the space-creating techniques you used in your sketch. Evaluate your sketch with these questions. Did I use all of the techniques correctly? What did I do best? How could I improve? Keep your evaluation with your sketch in your portfolio. You may want to sketch the room again at a later date.

✔ CHECK YOUR UNDERSTANDING

1. What is shape?
2. What are the two types of shape? Give an example of each type.
3. What is form?
4. What are the two types of form? Give an example of each type.
5. Name two techniques that artists use for creating a feeling of space.

LESSON 6

Paper Sculpture Forms

Study the work in Figure 4–22. From the credit line, you can tell what media the artist, Frank Stella, used. You can also tell the size of the piece. Try to imagine a work of this size in your classroom. Do you think it could have been made with paper? In this studio lesson you will explore some of the ways that paper can be used to make sculpture forms.

WHAT YOU WILL LEARN

You will alter a flat two-dimensional shape of paper into a three-dimensional form. You will use paper sculpture techniques to create an interesting paper sculpture form.

WHAT YOU WILL NEED

- Scrap paper for experimenting
- Pencil and ruler
- Sheets of construction paper, 12 x 18 inch (30 x 46 cm)
- Scissors, knife, stapler
- White glue

WHAT YOU WILL DO

1. Using scrap paper, experiment with a variety of paper sculpture techniques. (See Technique Tip **21**, *Handbook* **278**.) This will show you some ways of working with paper. These techniques can be used for your paper sculpture.

▶ **Figure 4–22 Frank Stella's art was often displayed by attaching it to walls with heavy bolts.**

Frank Stella. *St. Michael's Counterguard*. 1984. Aluminum, fiberglass and honeycomb. 396.2 x 342.9 x 274.3 cm (156 x 135 x 108"). Los Angeles County Museum of Art. Gift of Anna Bing Arnold.

2. Using your large sheet of paper, begin your design. As you work, you may have to alter your plan to get the effect you desire. Include three paper sculpture techniques in your design.
3. You may cut into the paper, but do not cut it into two pieces. Use staples or glue to hold the paper in place.
4. Keep turning your sculpture so that it looks interesting from every point of view.
5. Display your paper form. (See Figure 4–23.)

EXAMINING YOUR WORK

- **Describe** Tell what paper sculpture techniques you used.
- **Explain** Tell how your two-dimensional shape was altered into a three-dimensional form. Tell how you used the paper sculpture techniques to complete your design.

▲ Figure 4–23　Student work. Paper sculpture.

▲ Figure 4–24　Student work. Paper sculpture.

Try This!　## COMPUTER OPTION　

■ Explore a variety of colors and lines on your computer program. Use different combinations of colors and line widths. Cover the page. Title, Save, and Print your page on stiff paper. (To print on both sides of the paper, put one side through the printer, then flip the paper over and put the second side through another time to print the same design on the reverse side.) Use this printed paper technique to create an interesting sculpture.

LESSON 7

Texture

Rub your fingers lightly over this page. How would you describe the way it feels? **Texture** refers *to how things feel, or look as though they might feel, if touched.* No one needs to teach you about texture. You know what is rough and what is smooth. There are certain textures you find pleasant to the touch. Other surfaces you avoid touching because you do not like the way they feel.

In this lesson you will learn about the two ways texture works as an element of art.

TWO SIDES OF TEXTURE

Sandpaper, glass, a block of concrete — each has its own special texture, or feel. Have you ever tried on a piece of clothing — perhaps a sweater — that you thought looked itchy only to find it was not? Such things are possible because we experience texture through two of our senses. We experience texture with our sense of sight. We also experience it again — and sometimes differently — with our sense of touch.

► **Figure 4–25 How does your eye see the fur and beads in this hat? How do your fingers "see" them?**

Potawatomi Turban. Wisconsin. c. 1880. Otter pelt, silk ribbon, and glass beads. 15.9 cm (6¼") high. Cranbrook Institute of Science. 3146

When you look at the photograph of fur or raffia (palm fiber) in Figures 4–25 and 4–26, you see patterns of light and dark. These patterns bring back memories of how those objects feel. When this happens, you are experiencing visual texture. The photograph is smooth and flat. It is your eyes that add the softness of the fur or the coarseness of the fiber. Actual, or real texture, on the other hand, is what you experience when you touch the object itself, not the photograph. It is the message that your fingers send to your brain.

✔ CHECK YOUR UNDERSTANDING

1. What is texture?
2. Through which two of our senses do we experience texture?
3. What is visual texture? What is actual texture?

STUDIO ACTIVITY

Experimenting with Texture

Gather an assortment of fabrics and papers with smooth and rough textures. Look through a magazine for color pictures of smooth and rough visual textures and cut them out. Arrange these actual and visual textures on a small piece of cardboard. Cover all the background with textures. Your design should show contrasts of actual and visual, as well as smooth and rough textures. Glue down your design with white glue.

Portfolio

Use a pencil on a white piece of drawing paper to sketch the texture samples. Note how you use the elements of art to make your drawing look textured. Attach your drawings to your display of textures and include both in your portfolio.

◀ Figure 4–26 Why is the visual texture of the horse different from the actual texture of the photograph?

Horse. Nagana, Japan. c. 1960. Wrapped fiber. 18.7 cm (7⅜") high. Museum of International Folk Art, Santa Fe, New Mexico. Girard Collection.

LESSON 8

Painting a Landscape

Look at the painting of a tree by the Dutch artist Piet Mondrian (peet **mawn**-dree-ahn) in Figure 4–27. Does this look like a real tree? In this painting Mondrian used line quality and line variation to express the idea of a tree. Note how the artist also used color, shape, and texture to capture the idea of a tree.

WHAT YOU WILL LEARN

You will use the elements of color, line, shape, space, and texture to paint an unusual landscape. The landscape will have trees at different places in space. It will also show the underground roots of the nearest tree, plus different layers of soil and rock. (See Figure 4–28.)

WHAT YOU WILL NEED

- Pencil and sketch paper
- Tempera paint
- Soft and stiff brushes
- Mixing tray
- Water
- Sheet of heavy paper or illustration board, 12 x 18 inch (30 x 46 cm)
- Paper towels

WHAT YOU WILL DO

1. Take a walk outside or use your imagination to think of different landscapes. On scrap paper, make several pencil sketches of landscapes with trees. Show the branches clearly, but do not draw leaves.

▶ **Figure 4–27 Are warm or cool colors used in this painting? How would you describe the lines used? Are the shapes geometric or organic? What has been done to give the work a rich texture?**

Piet Mondrian. *Blue Tree.* 1909–1910. Oil on composition board. 56.8 x 74.9 cm (22⅜ x 29½"). Dallas Museum of Art.

2. Divide your sheet of white paper or illustration board horizontally into three equal parts with light pencil lines. In the top part, redraw lightly the best of your landscape sketches. The lines of the tree branches should be designed to make an interesting pattern of shapes. (Look again at Figure 4–27 for ideas.) The branches of the nearest tree should run off the top of your paper.

3. In the center part, draw the underground roots of the nearest tree. Use your imagination. The lines of the roots should add other interesting shapes.

4. In the bottom part, draw different layers of soil and rock. Once again, be as imaginative as you can.

5. Before painting your final work, experiment on scrap paper using stiff and soft brushes to create different textures. Dip the tip of the stiff bristle brush into the paint. Dab lightly at the paper. You should see bunches of dots. Drag the same brush across the paper for a fuzzy rough effect. Dip your soft brush into the paint. Dab it onto the paper making brush prints. Experiment with other techniques and develop your individual style.

6. Using tempera paint, mix your colors with white and black and with their complements to create different values and intensities.

7. Share your work with your classmates. Look for differences and similarities between your own landscape and those of other students.

- **Describe**   Point to the trees in your painting and identify the roots of the nearest tree. Identify the different layers of rock and soil and describe how you made them different.
- **Explain**   Tell why you chose the colors you did. Show different lines, shapes, and textures in your work, and explain what media you used to create the differences. Explain how you created the illusion of space in your work.

▲ Figure 4–28   Student work. An unusual landscape.

COMPUTER OPTION

Try This!

■ Think about the mood you are in right now, the season of the year, the current weather conditions, and time of day. Use Page Setup to change the page orientation to horizontal. Explore the widths and shapes of the Brush tool. Draw an interesting leafless tree that is young, or one that is old, or perhaps one that is leaning. Draw more than one tree using a variety of straight and curved lines. Choose one tree to be the center of interest. Draw this tree larger or Select the tree and enlarge it with the Re-sizing tool or Transformation menu. Below the ground line, make a cut-away view of the roots and layers of soil beneath the ground. Choose colors that reflect your mood and details that show location and season. Add background. Add more trees by Copying, Pasting, and Re-sizing. Title, Save, and Print.

Maurits Cornelis Escher. *Day and Night.* 1938. Woodcut in black and gray, printed from two blocks. 39.1 x 67.7 cm (15⅜ x 26⅝"). © 1996. Cordon Art-Baarn-Holland. All rights reserved.

Everyday Uses of Geometry

Although you may not realize it, you use geometry every day. Geometry is the branch of math that involves the properties of space. When you draw a circle, square, or triangle, you are using geometry. Slicing a pie into equal-sized pieces requires geometry.

Geometry is also commonly employed in art. For example, artists depend on geometry when they use perspective. In addition, several of the elements of art, including line, shape, and space, concern geometry. Artists often use lines to create geometric shapes in their works. The way in which shapes occupy space in an art work also relates to geometry.

Notice how M.C. Escher used the principles of geometry in his art work *Day and Night*. In this piece he repeated a pattern of shapes to create a tessellation. A tessellation is a pattern of objects that have the same shape and meet one another to completely cover a surface area. Like a jigsaw puzzle, the parts interlock so that no spaces remain between them. In addition, the parts do not overlap one other. Squares, rectangles, and triangles will tessellate, but circles and ovals will not. Can you guess why? You have probably seen tessellations in the designs of wallpaper, fabrics, and tiles.

MAKING THE CONNECTION

✔ Which elements of art did Escher use to create *Day and Night*? Explain your answer.

✔ Why do you think that Escher chose to use only white and black as the colors in this work?

✔ Look for examples of tessellations in everyday items at home or at school. Show them to the class and describe how the patterns were created.

INTERNET ACTIVITY

Visit Glencoe's Fine Arts Web Site for students at:

http://www.glencoe.com/sec/art/students

BUILDING VOCABULARY

Number a sheet of paper from 1 to 15. After each number, write the term from the list that best matches each description below.

analogous colors
color wheel
complementary
   colors
form
hue
intensity
line
line quality
line variation
monochromatic
   colors
motif
shape
space
texture
value

1. Colors opposite each other on the color wheel.
2. An area clearly set off by one or more of the other five visual elements of art.
3. Different values of a single hue.
4. The name of a color and its place on the color wheel.
5. An object with three dimensions.
6. The brightness or dullness of a hue.
7. The lightness or darkness of a hue.
8. Colors that share a hue and are side by side on the color wheel.
9. The distance or area around, between, above, below, and within things.
10. How things feel, or look as though they might feel, if touched.
11. The path of a dot through space.
12. A unit that is repeated in a pattern or visual rhythm.
13. Arrangement of hues in a circular format.
14. The unique character of any line.
15. The thickness or thinness of a line.

 REVIEWING ART FACTS

Number a sheet of paper from 16 to 22. Answer each question in a complete sentence.

16. What is a risk of using monochromatic colors?
17. What effect can be achieved by using complementary color schemes?
18. How does a trained artist use line?
19. What are some adjectives that could be used to describe horizontal lines?
20. What is the difference between line quality and line variation?
21. What is the relationship between shape and form?
22. Describe one way you can use paints to create different textures.

THINKING ABOUT ART

On a sheet of paper, answer the following question in a sentence or two.

1. **Analyze.** Imagine that you are helping paint a mural for the new school gymnasium. You have just finished painting a happy-looking section in red. You notice a student moving toward the section carrying a jar of green paint. What words of caution about the blending of colors might you pass along to this student?

MAKING ART CONNECTIONS

1. **Science.** One way artists develop new images from subject matter is to change the distance from which they view it. As an object is viewed through the microscope, greater detail is observed and the image changes. Try drawing leaves and other objects while looking at them through a microscope.

2. **Language Arts.** Think about the color expressions used on page **56**. Explain what is meant by these expressions and why certain colors are used. List other color expressions that you can think of.

▲ How do the colors and shapes in this work make you feel? What do they remind you of?
What do you suppose the title of the work means?

Rie Muñoz. *Crane Legend*. 1977. 36.2 x 47.3 cm (14¼ x 18⅝"). Waterbased painting. Rie Muñoz
Ltd., Juneau, Alaska.

CHAPTER 5

The Principles of Art

Have you ever looked at a work of art and found yourself wondering what the point of it was? Look at the painting at the left. Can you find any "rhyme or reason" to it? Why do you suppose the artist chose the colors, the lines, or the shapes she did?

If art has at times seemed puzzling to you, that is because every work of art is a "puzzle." Its "pieces" have been carefully combined. In this chapter you will learn about the guidelines artists use to make works of art.

PORTFOLIO IDEAS

Look at some paintings in your book. Find one that seems to be "out of balance" to you. Do a quick sketch of it and then write why you think it seems to be out of balance beneath the sketch. Find a second painting that you think is balanced, sketch it, and write why you think it is balanced. Date your sketches and writings and place them in your portfolio. You will be able to refer back to these later and see how well you can recognize the principles of art.

OBJECTIVES

After completing this chapter, you will be able to:
- Define the term *principles of art.*
- Explain the three kinds of balance.
- Tell how artists use the principles of variety, harmony, emphasis, proportion, movement, and rhythm.
- Explain what unity does for an art work.
- Practice organizing elements and principles in original art works.

WORDS YOU WILL LEARN

balance
emphasis
harmony
movement
principles of art
proportion
rhythm
unity
variety

The Language of Design

You know that speakers of any language follow rules of grammar. These rules govern the way words can go together to form sentences. The language of art also has rules. They are called **principles of art**, *guidelines that govern the way elements go together*.

The principles of art are: balance, variety, harmony, emphasis, proportion, movement, and rhythm. Like the elements, the principles in a work of art are hard to single out.

In this lesson you will meet the first of the principles of art, balance.

THE PRINCIPLE OF BALANCE

When you ride a bicycle and lean too far to one side or the other, what happens? You fall over. In riding a bike, balance is important.

Balance is important in art, too. In art, **balance** is *arranging elements so that no one part of a work overpowers, or seems heavier than, any other part*. In the real world, balance can be measured on a scale. If two objects weigh the same, the two sides of the scale will balance. If they do not, one side of the scale will tip. In art, balance is seen or felt by the viewer. A big, bold splotch of color off to one side of a painting pulls the viewer's eye there. It can

▲ **Figure 5–1** What kind of feelings might the formal balance of this church suggest? In what direction does the building seem to point? Why is this important?

Monastery of Oliva. Late 12th century. Oliva, Spain.

▲ **Figure 5–2** How different would this work have been if the artist had spread the figures around the picture?

Michel Sittow. *The Assumption of the Virgin*. c. 1500. Wood; painted surface. 21.3 x 16.5 cm (8⅜ x 6½"). National Gallery of Art, Washington, D.C. Ailsa Mellon Bruce Fund.

make the work seem lopsided. It can make the viewer feel uncomfortable.

Artists speak of three kinds of balance. These are formal balance, informal balance, and radial balance.

Formal Balance

Formal balance happens when one half of a work is a mirror image of the other half (Figure 5–1). Also called symmetrical balance (suh-**meh**-trih-kuhl), formal balance is the easiest type to notice. Because it is so predictable, using formal balance sometimes makes a work seem less interesting. This is not always the case. Look at the painting in Figure 5–2. Notice how the formal balance adds a feeling of quiet dignity to the work.

Informal Balance

Informal balance happens when two different objects seem to have the same visual weight. The weight is suggested by the hues, values, intensities, and shapes of those objects. Also called asymmetrical balance (**ay**-suh-**met**-trih-kuhl), informal balance often shows up in the way the artist has used color and shape. A small shape painted bright red will balance several larger shapes painted in duller hues. (See Figure 5–3.)

▲ Figure 5–3　Which figure in this painting captures your attention first? What is there about this figure that caused you to notice her first?

William Glackens. *Family Group.* 1910–1911. Canvas. 182.9 x 213.4 cm (72 x 84"). National Gallery of Art, Washington, D.C. Gift of Mr. & Mrs. Ira Glackens.

Informal balance is often used to create more interesting compositions. Arranging objects or elements informally can be very complicated, but can create visual interest when used skillfully.

Radial Balance

Radial balance happens when elements or objects in an art work are positioned around a central point. A flower with its petals spreading outward from the center is an example of radial balance in nature. The ceremonial cloth in Figure 5–4 is an example of radial balance in art.

▲ Figure 5–4　An identical pattern is repeated in this cloth, nevertheless it holds our eye. Why?

Ceremonial Cloth (Chamba Rumal). India, Himachal Pradesh. c. 1875–1925. Cotton with colored embroidery (silk). 68.6 cm (27") diameter. Philadelphia Museum of Art. Purchased with funds contributed by Ann McPheil and anonymous donors. 1991-48-1

✔CHECK YOUR UNDERSTANDING

1. Define *principles of art.*
2. List the principles of art.
3. What is balance?
4. Describe the three kinds of balance.

 **LESSON 2**

Informal Balance Landscape

Look closely at the painting of a peaceful Chinese mountain village in Figure 5–5. Do you think this work demonstrates formal or informal balance? Notice how the picture *feels* balanced even though both sides are not evenly weighted. If this work had been formally balanced, one half would have been a mirror image of the other half. In that case, it would probably have looked unnatural and uninteresting. However, the artist, Li Shida, realized that he had to do something to give the picture a balanced feeling. He knew that without balance, his picture would be disturbing to viewers. Can you see what he did to shift the weight at the left side of the picture to the right? Did you notice how the two mountains in the background appear to be curved and leaning toward the large areas of white space at the right? This small but important detail helps balance the smaller, more complicated areas at the left with the large empty areas at the right.

WHAT YOU WILL LEARN

You will use oil pastels to create an imaginary landscape using informal balance. To give your landscape a more natural appearance, you will use at least three techniques to create the illusion of space. (See page **69** for ways to suggest the feeling of depth in paintings and drawings.)

▶ **Figure 5–5 This landscape is not formally balanced, yet it has a comfortable feeling. How did the artist accomplish that feeling?**

Li Shida. *Mountain Village on a Clear Day.* 1621. Ink and color on paper. Arthur M. Sackler Gallery, Smithsonian Institution, Washington, D.C. Gift of Arthur M. Sackler.

WHAT YOU WILL NEED

- Pencil and sketch paper
- A sheet of white or colored construction paper, 12 x 18 inches (30 x 46 cm)
- Oil pastels

WHAT YOU WILL DO

1. Imagine that you are on a space vehicle destined to land on the moon. Mechanical problems have caused your ship to drift far off course and you are forced to land on an unknown planet at the edge of our galaxy. Nervously, you open the doors to your space ship and look out on the strange planet. What do you think you will see? Use your imagination to make several pencil sketches of this unusual landscape.

2. Make certain that your landscape sketches are informally balanced and make use of several techniques for showing space.

3. Choose your best sketch and reproduce it lightly in pencil on a sheet of white or colored construction paper.

4. Use oil pastels to add a rich opaque color to your drawing. Remember that color blending is easily achieved with the fingers or by laying colors on top of one another. (See Technique Tip 3, *Handbook* page **271**, for additional oil pastel techniques.)

5. Display your finished landscape along with those completed by other students in your class. Which were the most unusual? Which landscapes could be described as beautiful and inviting? Did some appear to be gloomy and threatening?

- **Describe**   Does your landscape look like another planet? What makes it different from landscapes on earth?
- **Analyze**   Is your imaginary landscape informally balanced? What techniques did you use to give your picture a balanced feeling? Does your picture show depth? What three methods did you use to create this feeling of space?
- **Interpret**   What kinds of feelings are conveyed by your picture of an unknown planet? Did you intend to convey those kinds of feelings, or did this come about unexpectedly as you worked?
- **Judge**   Do you feel that your landscape drawing is a success? What do you feel is its best feature: the subject, the way the elements and principles of art have been used, or the ideas or feelings it communicates?

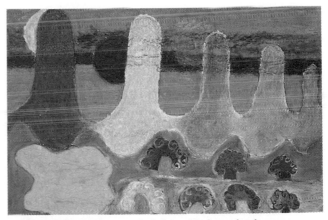

▲ Figure 5–6   Student work. Informal balance landscape.

STUDIO OPTIONS

Try This!

■ Create another fantastic landscape with oil pastels, this time using formal balance. Compare it to your first drawing using informal balance. Which is more visually pleasing?

■ Complete another oil pastel drawing of the same imaginary landscape as it might appear in the dim light of the two small moons at night. Use other techniques for showing space in this work.

Variety, Harmony, Emphasis, and Proportion

You may have heard it said that "variety is the spice of life." Variety is also the spice of art. The principle of variety and three others, harmony, emphasis, and proportion, make works of art interesting and pleasing to view. In this lesson you will learn how these principles are used by the artist to create art.

THE PRINCIPLE OF VARIETY

Imagine that you had to eat the same food every day for a whole year. Even if the food were your absolute favorite, after a while you would grow tired of it. You would long for other things to eat—even things you disliked—just for the change of pace.

▶ **Figure 5–7 Point to the different colors in this painting. How many kinds of lines can you count? How many shapes? How many textures?**

Henri Matisse. *Woman in a Purple Coat.* 1937. Oil on canvas. 81.3 x 64.1 cm (32 x 25¼"). The Museum of Fine Arts, Houston, Texas. John A. and Audrey Jones Beck Collection.

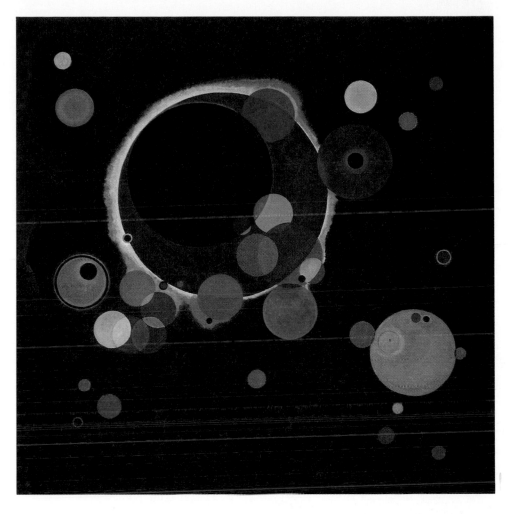

▶ Figure 5–8 Which shape brings harmony to this work?

Wassily Kandinsky. *Several Circles*. 1926. Oil on canvas. 140.3 x 141 cm (55¼ x 55⅜″). Solomon R. Guggenheim Museum, New York, New York. Gift of Solomon R. Guggenheim.

People need change to keep their lives interesting. The same goes for art. In art, **variety** is *combining one or more elements to create interest*. By giving a work variety, the artist heightens the visual appeal of the work.

Variety may be brought into play in many different ways. Light values of a color may be used to break the sameness of mostly dark values of that color. Straight lines can be a welcome change in a work made up mainly of curved lines. Which elements show variety in the work in Figure 5–7?

THE PRINCIPLE OF HARMONY

On the opposite side of the coin from variety is harmony. **Harmony** in art, as in music, is *blending elements in a pleasing way*. Harmony is uncomplicated and soothing. Often artists use a small number of the same elements again and again, or in repetition, to bring harmony to a work of art. (See Figure 5–8.)

Skilled artists use the principles of harmony and variety together in different amounts to bind the parts of a work to the whole. Too much variety and too little harmony in a work can make it complicated and confusing. Focusing only on harmony, on the other hand, can make a work humdrum and uninteresting. Notice how the artist of the work in Figure 5–8 combines harmony and variety.

THE PRINCIPLE OF EMPHASIS

When people want to call attention to an important word in a sentence, they will underline it. Underlining a word makes that word stand out from the rest of the words in the message. It gives it emphasis.

Artists also use emphasis in their messages to viewers. In art, **emphasis** is *making an element or object in a work stand out*. The use of this principle helps the artist control what part of a work the viewer looks at first. It also helps the artist control how long the viewer will spend looking at each of the different parts. Emphasis can be created by contrast, or extreme changes in an element.

In the painting in Figure 5–9 several groups of figures are shown. One of these groups seems more important than the others. Can you identify that group? Can you tell why it caught your attention?

THE PRINCIPLE OF PROPORTION

Have you ever tried on a piece of clothing and found that it made you look shorter or taller than you actually are? Perhaps the problem was one of proportion. In art, **proportion** is *how parts of a work relate to each other and to the whole*.

▲ **Figure 5–9**   Besides value contrast, what techniques call attention to the group of people that includes the girl in white?

Jean-Baptiste-Joseph Pater. *Fête Champêtre*. 1730. Canvas. 74.6 x 92.7 cm (29⅜ x 36½"). National Gallery of Art, Washington, D.C. Samuel H. Kress Collection.

Look at the painting in Figure 5–10. Notice how the artist points out the main figures in the work by making them larger than the rest.

Proportion as an art principle is not limited to size. Elements such as color can be used in differing proportions. What is the key color in the work in Figure 5–11? What do you think was the artist's reason for using this color as he did?

▲ **Figure 5–11** What has the artist done to make the element of color stand out? What one color is used most?

Alexei von Jawlensky. *Portrait of a Woman.* 1910. Oil on panel. 53 x 49.5 cm (20⅞ x 19½"). The Museum of Fine Arts, Houston, Texas. John A. and Audrey Jones Beck Collection.

✔ **CHECK YOUR UNDERSTANDING**

1. Name two ways artists can achieve variety in works of art.
2. How do artists achieve harmony in works of art?
3. What is emphasis? What two things does using this principle enable an artist to do?
4. What is proportion? How do artists use proportion?

▲ **Figure 5–10** Which figures are the largest? Why are they larger than the other figures? Who are they? Who are the figures in the "supporting roles"?

Bernardo Daddi. *Madonna and Child with Saints and Angels.* 1330. Wood. 50.2 x 24.1 cm (19¾ x 9½"). National Gallery of Art, Washington, D.C. Samuel H. Kress Collection.

Painting Using the Principles

Look at the painting in Figure 5–12. Notice how Robert Gwathmey has used the principles of variety, harmony, emphasis, and proportion. He has used a red color scheme to create harmony. Variety is introduced through different sizes and different shapes. Notice that the land, sky, and church are simple rectangles. The people are composed of geometric and free-form shapes. Hands and feet are small, arms are thin, and the shapes of the bodies vary. The painting is abstract because you recognize the subject but the shapes are not shown in a realistic way.

Notice that all the busy shapes in the foreground lead your eyes to the dark simple church on the horizon. Gwathmey emphasizes the church by isolating it and making it a different shape and a different value.

▲ **Figure 5–12**   How does the use of proportion give depth and variety to the painting?

Robert Gwathmey. *Country Gospel Music.* 1971. Oil on canvas. 101.6 x 127 cm (40 x 50"). Terry Dintenfass Gallery, New York, New York. © 1998 Estate of Stuart Davis/Licensed by VAGA, New York, NY

WHAT YOU WILL LEARN

You will create an abstract painting using the principles of harmony, variety, and emphasis. You will use a variety of lines to draw shapes that vary in size from very large to very small. You will add harmony to your work by using different light and dark values of a single hue to paint the shapes and the negative spaces. You will emphasize a center of interest by painting one small shape the complement of the hue used.

WHAT YOU WILL NEED

- Pencil and sketch paper
- Sheet of white paper, 12 x 18 inch (30 x 46 cm)
- Colored chalk, gum eraser
- Tempera paints and thick and thin brushes
- Newspaper

WHAT YOU WILL DO

1. Select a common object, such as an animal, building, vehicle, or person. Make several abstract sketches of the object on your sketch paper to plan your composition. Decide how you will use a variety of lines to divide your paper into shapes. Using several kinds of lines, vary the shape from large to small.
2. Select your best plan. Draw it, freehand, on the large white paper with a piece of colored chalk. Use the soft gum eraser to make corrections so that you don't tear the paper.

EXAMINING YOUR WORK

- **Describe**   What hue did you choose for your monochromatic color scheme? What hue was the complement of that hue? Identify the lines you used to create shapes.
- **Analyze**   How did you create variety in your painting? Tell how color was used to create harmony. Identify the object of emphasis.

3. Select one hue. Use black and white paint to create a variety of tints and shades of that hue. Select one shape to be the center of interest. Leave it white for now. Paint the rest of the shapes with your hue and tints and shades of that hue. (See Technique Tip **12**, *Handbook* page **274**.)
4. Paint the center of interest with the complement of the hue used in your painting.
5. Place your work on display with your classmates. Can you find similarities and differences in the works?

SAFETY TIP

If you experience breathing problems, do not use chalk for this lesson. Instead, use crayon or oil pastels. Always work in a room with good ventilation so you are not affected by the presence of chalk dust.

Try This! COMPUTER OPTION

■ Select a common object that is usually round. Using only the Straight Line tool, draw three or more views of the object. Another choice is to draw several round objects using straight lines. Vary the size and the line thickness to create interest and variety. Draw a frame around the shapes using the Line or Shape tool. Divide the picture into areas with three or four straight lines that go from side to side. Choose the Bucket tool and a monochromatic color scheme to create harmony. Fill the shapes with different textures in one section to create variety and emphasis. Fill all the areas with the selected hue and its tints and shades. Title, Save, and Print.

Movement and Rhythm

Have you ever thrown a rock in a pond and watched the concentric circles that followed? Have you traveled down the highway and watched the telephone lines passing by? These are two examples of movement and rhythm.

In this lesson you will learn about the principles of movement and rhythm.

THE PRINCIPLE OF MOVEMENT

You live in an age of special effects. When you go to the movies nowadays, you see strange life forms arriving from different galaxies. You see humans traveling backward in time or dancing with cartoon figures. These amazing sights and others like them are possible only through creative imaginations and special effects.

In art, special effects are nothing new. Artists have been using them for a long time. One of these effects is movement. **Movement** is *the principle of art that leads the viewer to sense action in a work or it can be the path the viewer's eye follows throughout a work.* Artists create movement through a careful blending of elements like line and shape. (See Figure 5–13.)

Through the principle of movement, the artist is able to guide the viewer's eye from one part of a painting to the next. Notice how the lines in Jean-Baptiste-Joseph Pater's painting in Figure 5–9 on page **86** carry your eye toward the girl in white. The trees and the people seem to be leaning toward her.

THE PRINCIPLE OF RHYTHM

Have you ever found yourself tapping your fingers or feet to the beat of a song? Songs can have catchy rhythms. Sometimes it seems as though we can feel these rhythms as well as hear them.

▶ **Figure 5–13   By repeating lines and shapes, the artist helps us see the movement of a speeding cyclist.**

Umberto Boccioni. *Study for Dynamic Force of a Cyclist I.* 1913. Ink wash and pencil on paper. 20.5 x 30.5 cm (8¹⁄₁₆ x 12"). Yale University Art Gallery, Connecticut. Gift of Societe Anonyme.

In art, we feel rhythms as well as see them. To the artist, **rhythm** is *the repeating of an element to make a work seem active.* Look at Figure 5–14. The artist uses rhythm to make his painting come alive. By carefully mixing shapes and colors, he gets your eye to move to the painting's "beat."

Sometimes, to create rhythm, artists will repeat not just elements but the same exact objects over and over. When they do this, a pattern is formed.

✔ CHECK YOUR UNDERSTANDING

1. What is movement?
2. What is rhythm?
3. What does an artist create by repeating an object again and again?

▼ **Figure 5–14   Which element creates rhythm? Which element does the artist incorporate with rhythm to give the painting a "beat"? How is it done?**

Jasper Johns. *Between the Clock and the Bed.* 1981. Encaustic on canvas, three panels, overall. 183.2 x 321 cm (72⅛ x 126⅜"). The Museum of Modern Art, New York, New York. Gift of Agnes Gund. © 1998 Jasper Johns/Licensed by VAGA, New York, NY

STUDIO ACTIVITY

Creating Movement and Rhythm

You can use the element of color to make a viewer's eye move around a visual image. First, find a scene filled with people and objects in a book or magazine. Make a black-and-white photocopy of the image. Use your imagination to create a wandering path through the scene that you want your viewers to follow. Trace the path lightly with a pencil. Using one brightly colored marker, color one shape on each person or object along the path. The size of the shapes may vary. Share your art work with other students.

P o r t f o l i o

Ask other students to evaluate your work. Record their comments on a sheet of paper and include it with your drawing in your portfolio.

LESSON 6

Creating Visual Movement

This painting by Rosa Bonheur has a strong sense of visual movement. To achieve that movement, the artist has used several special effects to create the feeling that the horses are moving across the canvas. (See Figure 5–15.)

First, all horses are going in the same general direction, from left to right. Notice how your eye is first attracted to the white horse in the center. The color and the position of the horse as it rears up begin the movement, which continues to the right as your eye follows the line of white horses. These horses are more active than the darker ones, creating another sense of motion.

Second, the line of trees, smaller on the left than on the right, causes your eye to move from left to right. The men in the painting also move along with the horses. However, their vertical positions balance the strong motion of the animals. This helps to give your eye a rest.

WHAT YOU WILL LEARN

You will create a construction paper design using repeated silhouettes of one action figure. You will use visual rhythm to create a sense of visual movement. Use a cool color for the background and warm colors for the figure. This color scheme will enhance the feeling of movement and provide contrast.

WHAT YOU WILL NEED

- One whole action figure cut from a magazine (sports magazines are good sources)
- Scissors and fine-tip marker
- One sheet of cool-colored construction paper, 12 x 18 inch (30 x 46 cm)
- Several pieces of warm-colored construction paper, 9 x 12 inch (23 x 30 cm)
- Pencil, eraser, and glue
- Envelope to hold cutouts, 9 1/2 x 4 inch (24 x 10 cm)

▲ **Figure 5–15 What are the elements used in repetition? How do they also provide harmony?**

Rosa Bonheur. *The Horse Fair*. 1853–55. Oil on canvas. 244.5 x 506.7 cm (96¼ x 199½"). The Metropolitan Museum of Art, New York, New York. Gift of Cornelius Vanderbilt, 1887. 87.25

WHAT YOU WILL DO

1. Look through magazines and newspapers to find a whole body of an action figure. Be sure the figure is complete with both hands and feet.
2. Using a fine-tip marker, outline the figure. Then carefully cut out the figure by cutting along the outline. You will use this figure for the motif of your design.
3. Select a sheet of cool-colored construction paper. This will be used for your background. Select several sheets of smaller pieces of warm-colored construction paper. These will be used for the figures. (See Figure 5–16.)
4. Place the magazine cutout figure on a piece of construction paper and trace around it. Conserve paper by arranging the tracing on one side of the paper and using the other half for another cutout. Cut out five, seven, or nine figures or silhouettes. Keep them in the envelope until you are ready to use them.
5. Experiment with several arrangements of the silhouettes on the background. You may want to include the original magazine cutout to create a center of interest. The figures may overlap. When you have an arrangement that shows visual movement, glue it to the background piece of construction paper.
6. Display your design. Compare the designs with those of your classmates, and look for different rhythmic beats. Which designs have a strong sense of movement?

EXAMINING YOUR WORK

- **Describe** Identify the action figure you selected. Did you cut it out carefully? What colors did you choose for the background? What colors did you choose for the cutout figures? Tell why, or why not, you chose to use the magazine cutout. Explain what kind of rhythm you created and how you achieved a feeling of visual movement.

▲ Figure 5–16 Student work. An action figure.

Try This! STUDIO OPTIONS

■ Repeat the visual movement activity above, but use complementary colors for the color scheme.

■ Using geometric shapes, create a rhythmic design that has a strong sense of movement. Use cool colors for the shapes and a warm color for the background.

LESSON 7

Unity in Art

When something breakable shatters—a vase, for example—it can never again be as it was. The pieces can be glued together, but the object will never be truly the same. The jagged seams will always be a reminder that the item is made up of separate parts.

When the pieces of an art puzzle are put together by a skilled artist, the seams do not show. The viewer cannot tell where one part ends and the next begins. The work has a oneness. It has unity.

UNITY IN ART

Unity is *the arrangement of elements and principles with media to create a feeling of completeness.* Unity in an art work is like an unseen glue. You cannot point to it as you can an element or principle, but you can sense it. You can also sense when it is missing. Look at Figure 5–17. The painting below seems to display a sense of completeness. Can you name the principles shown in this art work that contribute to that unity?

▲ **Figure 5–17** How does the artist use the elements and principle to achieve unity in this painting?

Jaune Quick-To-See Smith. *Buffalo.* 1992. Oil, mixed-media collage on canvas. 167.6 x 243.8 cm (66 x 96") diptych. Courtesy of the Steinbaum Krauss Gallery, New York, New York. Eleanor and Len Flomenhaft Collection.

DESIGN CHART	PRINCIPLES OF ART					
	Balance	Variety	Harmony	Emphasis	Proportion	Movement/ Rhythm
Color: Hue						
Intensity						
Value						
Line						
Shape/Form						
Space						
Texture						

(ELEMENTS OF ART along the side) — UNITY

Note: Do not write on this chart.

▲ **Figure 5–18   Design chart.**

PLOTTING UNITY ON A CHART

Explaining how the parts of an art work fit together can be difficult. Using a design chart (Figure 5–18) makes the task easier. Notice that the chart shows the elements along the side and the principles along the top. Think of each square where an element and principle meet as a design question. Here, for example, are some questions that might be asked about hue.

- Is the balance of the hues formal, informal, or radial?
- Do the hues show variety?
- Is a single hue used throughout to add harmony?
- Is hue used to emphasize, or highlight, some part of the work?
- Is the proportion, or amount of hue, greater or lesser than that of other elements?
- Does hue add to a sense of movement?
- Do hues repeat in a rhythmic way that adds action to the work?

Think about what questions you might ask about each of the remaining five elements.

✔CHECK YOUR UNDERSTANDING

1. What is unity in art?
2. What does a design chart help you do?

How Is Power Symbolized in Art?

Throughout the world, religion is a vital part of most social and cultural groups. In many of these religions, followers worship one or more gods, or deities. These religious deities have been the focus of art work for thousands of years. To show the power and status of these gods, artists often use the principles of art, such as proportion, in their work.

In Hinduism, the major religion of India, three gods are worshipped. Brahma is the creator of the universe, Shiva is the destroyer, and Vishnu is the preserver. Followers of Hinduism believe that the forces of good and evil are constantly battling for control of the world. Sometimes the balance of power shifts to the side of evil. When this happens, the god Vishnu is thought to come down to earth to save the world. Vishnu appears in a human form, which is known as his *avatar*. Ten of these human forms are believed to exist. Nine have already descended to earth, and the tenth has yet to come.

In *Vishnu and His Avatars,* the artist who carved the sculpture used the principles of art to portray Vishnu as a powerful figure. Can you see how proportion was used to emphasize that Vishnu is the most important figure in the work?

Vishnu and His Avatars. c. 10th Century. Red sandstone. 138.4 cm (54½") high. Museum of Fine Arts, Houston, Texas. Museum purchase with funds provided by the Agnes Cullen Arnold Endowment Fund.

MAKING THE CONNECTION

- This art work depicts Vishnu and his avatars. According to Hinduism, what is the purpose of Vishnu's avatars?
- What other principles of art, besides proportion, did the artist use in this sculpture? Explain your answer.
- Find other examples of religious figures depicted in art. Compare how the artists used the principles of art to symbolize power and status.

INTERNET ACTIVITY

Visit Glencoe's Fine Arts Web Site for students at:

http://www.glencoe.com/sec/art/students

CHAPTER 5
REVIEW

 BUILDING VOCABULARY

Number a sheet of paper from 1 to 9. After each number, write the term from the list that best matches each description below.

balance
emphasis
harmony
movement
principles of art

proportion
rhythm
unity
variety

1. The guidelines that govern how the elements of art go together.
2. What a work has when no one part overpowers any other.
3. Mixing one or more elements for contrast.
4. Blending elements in a pleasing way.
5. Making an element or object in a work stand out.
6. The way parts of a work relate to each other.
7. The principle that leads a viewer to sense action in a work.
8. The repeating of an element again and again to make a work seem active.
9. Combining elements, principles, and media into an unbroken whole.

 REVIEWING ART FACTS

Number a sheet of paper from 10 to 19. Answer each question in a complete sentence.

10. What kind of balance is shown in a work where one half mirrors the other?

11. What is another name for asymmetrical balance? For symmetrical balance?
12. Some artists think of radial balance as a complicated form of what other type of balance?
13. What can happen to a work when an artist overuses harmony?
14. What principle will an artist use to control which part of a work a viewer's eye sees first?
15. Is proportion in art limited to size of objects? Explain.
16. What principle will an artist use to carry the viewer's eye from one part of a work to the next?
17. What is a pattern?
18. What is another name for oneness?
19. What is a design chart used for?

 THINKING ABOUT ART

On a sheet of paper, answer each question in a sentence or two.

1. **Extend.** What kind of balance is demonstrated by a design viewed in a kaleidoscope?
2. **Interpret.** How might an artist give emphasis to an object by using the element of line?
3. **Compare and contrast.** What do the principles of movement and rhythm have in common? How are they different?

MAKING ART CONNECTIONS

1. **Science.** Find examples from nature that represent formal, informal, and radial balance. Draw each example. Try looking at natural objects through a microscope and draw what you see. Group your drawings according to the type of balance. Think about the different principles of art. How do they relate to the designs found in nature?

2. **Industrial Arts.** Boccioni created *Study for Dynamic Force of a Cyclist I* (Figure 5–13, page **90**) in 1913. That same year Henry Ford introduced the conveyor belt assembly line. Find out what kinds of transportation were used at that time. Use repeated lines and shapes to create your own speeding vehicle from the same period.

Judging Art Works

It is the responsibility of every judge to be fair and open-minded. This is true of judges who rule over courts of law. And it is equally true of critics who judge works of art. Neither type of judge would ever hand down a ruling without first looking at all the facts. Neither would ever pass judgment without giving reasons.

In this lesson you will learn what goes into the final step of art criticism, judging.

JUDGING ART WORKS

When you judge a work of art, you ask yourself two questions. The first of these is: "Is this a good or successful work?" The second is: "Why is it good or successful?" **Judging** means *making a decision about a work's success or lack of success and giving reasons to support that decision.*

Ways of Judging a Work

Do you remember the three aesthetic views on art that you learned about in Chapter 2? Some art scholars, you will recall, feel art should imitate the real world. For them, a work succeeds if it looks real.

Others believe that what is most important about a piece of art is its composition. For them, a work succeeds if the artist has used the principles of art to combine the elements of art into an interesting whole.

Still others hold that what counts most is the mood or feeling a work expresses. For them, a work succeeds if the viewer shares this feeling or mood when seeing it.

The judgment that an art critic makes will depend on the aesthetic view he or she accepts. Look at the painting of the telephone booths (Figure 6–13). A critic from the first aesthetic view might praise the work because it is true to life. A critic from the second aesthetic view might admire the work for the

▶ **Figure 6–13** Would you consider this painting successful? Why or why not?

Richard Estes. *Telephone Booths.* 1968. Oil on canvas. 121.9 x 175.3 cm (48 x 69"). Allan Stone Galleries, New York. Tissean-Bornemisza. © 1998 Richard Estes/Licensed by VAGA, New York, NY/Courtesy of Marlborough Gallery, New York

way the artist has created visual movement through the repetition of lines, shapes and color. A critic from the third aesthetic view might say the painting captures the existing mood of a busy city.

Not all critics limit themselves to one view of art. Many feel that accepting a single view carries the risk of missing some exciting discoveries. If a person accepts all three views, what judgments might he or she make about the sculpture in Figure 6–14? How would you personally judge the work?

JUDGING APPLIED ART

Art criticism can be applied to the study of all areas of art, not just paintings, sculptures, and other kinds of fine art. One other area that can be, and often is studied, is applied art. You may recall that **applied art** is *art made to be functional, as well as visually pleasing*. Designing details for jewelry or making decorative furniture are examples of applied art.

▲ **Figure 6–15** Does this chair's appearance make you want to sit in it? Why or why not?

Verner Panton. *Stacking Side Chair.* 1959–60 (manufactured 1967). 82.9 x 48.9 x 59.7 cm (32⅝ x 19¼ x 23½"). The Museum of Modern Art, New York, New York. Gift of Herman Miller AG.

In using art criticism for works of applied art, critics use the same four steps: describing, analyzing, interpreting, and judging. At the final step, however, the rules change. The critic no longer evaluates a work purely in terms of its appearance. It must also be judged on how well the work does its job. A chair may look beautiful, but if it is uncomfortable to sit in, it is not successful. (See Figure 6–15.)

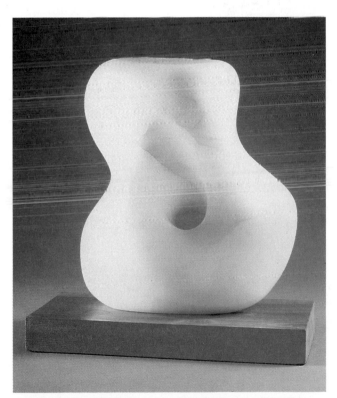

▲ **Figure 6–14** Alabaster is a beautiful soft stone. How does this sculptural form harmonize with the material?

Barbara Hepworth. *Merryn.* 1962. Alabaster. 33.0 x 29.2 x 20.3 cm (13 x 11½ x 8"). National Museum of Women in the Arts, Washington, D.C. Wallace & Wilhelmina Holladay.

✔ CHECK YOUR UNDERSTANDING

1. Define *judging*, as the term is used in art criticism.
2. What two questions do you ask yourself when you judge a work?
3. Describe briefly the three ways a critic can aesthetically view an art work.

Using Art Criticism

You have probably heard it said that experience is the best teacher. In this lesson you will discover the truth behind that saying. You will have the experience of using all four steps of art criticism on a single work.

The work you will criticize is the painting in Figure 6–16. Its title is *Christina's World*, and it was painted by an American artist, Andrew Wyeth.

DESCRIBING THE WORK

First, notice the size of the work and its medium. Try to imagine the full-size painting as it would look if it were in front of you right now. How might that affect the way you see the work?

Next, study the painting carefully. On a sheet of paper, write down every fact and detail you see. Use the following questions as a guide:

Subject

- What details about the girl's dress can you note?
- How would you describe the color and fabric of the girl's dress?
- Look at the folds in the dress. What do they tell you?
- Describe the color of the girl's belt.
- Look at the girl's hairdo. Notice the detail with which each hair is shown.
- Look closely at the girl's legs. What color are they? Is the color the same as that of her arms?
- Do you notice anything unusual about her arms or hands? Where is her left hand positioned?
- Look closely at the girl's posture. Where is all her weight resting?

Foreground

- Describe the girl's surroundings.
- In what direction do the blades of grass bend?
- How is the area where the girl is sitting different from the top of the hill?
- Describe the road.

Background

- How many buildings do you see and of what are they made?
- What facts can you gather from the background and grass? What colors are they?
- How are the buildings different?
- What color are the buildings? Do they look well-kept?
- How many chimneys do you see? Is there any smoke coming out of them?
- Do all the windows look the same?
- What color is the sky? How much of the picture is sky and how much is ground?
- What point of view do you think the artist is giving the viewer?

Design Elements

- What kinds of lines has the artist used for the buildings and for the line between the ground and sky?
- What lines are used for the girl?
- Describe the texture of the girl's dress, the grass, and the buildings.
- What kinds of colors do you see?

Try not to make guesses about the meaning of this work. Save your clues for later use.

◀ **Figure 6–16** The vast area of grass is essential to the mood of the painting. Why? Where is the emphasis? Do you feel a sense of urgency?

Andrew Wyeth. *Christina's World.* 1948. Tempera on gessoed panel. 81.9 x 121.3 cm (32¼ x 47¾"). The Museum of Modern Art, New York, New York. Purchase.

ANALYZING THE WORK

What kind of balance has the artist used? What has been done to give the work variety? How is harmony achieved? Is anything in the painting emphasized? If so, what?

How does the artist control the way your eyes move through the work? Hold a ruler along the left slope of the roof on the biggest building. Where does the line lead your eye? Does the artist use accurate proportion to represent objects?

INTERPRETING THE WORK

Reread the clues you have gathered. What might the artist be telling you about the girl and about the world she lives in? When you imagined yourself in the girl's pose, did you feel the weight on your arms? Were your legs carrying your weight?

Why do you think the artist includes such a large area of ground in the work? Why has he shown separate blades of grass? How do you think the girl feels? Why do you think she feels this way? Whose house is it?

Do you think the title is appropriate? How does it help you interpret this work? Can you think of several adjectives that describe this work? What title would you give it?

JUDGING THE WORK

Tell whether the painting succeeds. Give the reasons why you feel as you do. Does the painting make you think? Why, or why not? Does it succeed in one of the following ways?

- It is lifelike.
- It uses the elements and principles to create an unusually interesting whole.
- It communicates a feeling or mood to the viewer.

Does the work succeed in more than one of these ways? Which ones? Explain your answer.

✔ CHECK YOUR UNDERSTANDING

1. List the four steps of art criticism.
2. List the three ways a critic could aesthetically view *Christina's World.*

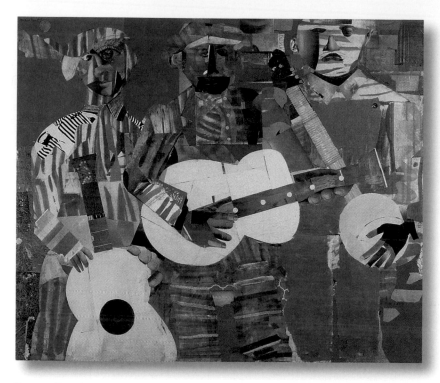

Romare Bearden. *Three Folk Musicians.* 1967. Collage on canvas on board. 127 x 152.4 cm (50 x 60"). Romare Howard Bearden Foundation, Inc. © 1998 Romare Bearden Foundation/Licensed by VAGA, New York, NY

Music: A Cultural Experience

What is your favorite type of music? Maybe you enjoy listening to rock and roll, rap, or country and western. Would you be able to explain to someone else why you like this type of music?

Like art criticism, music criticism involves more than simply liking or disliking a type of music. It means studying and understanding music in order to make informed judgments. One way to better understand music is to learn about other cultures, because particular types of music are sometimes associated with cultures or groups of people. In some cultures, certain songs and dances are an important part of ceremonies and special events. For example, special music may be connected with weddings, birthdays, or rites of passage. Knowing about these rituals can help us to comprehend and appreciate the music of that culture.

Romare Bearden's collage, *Three Folk Musicians,* conveys a sense of the African-American culture in a way that is associated with music. His lifelong interest in jazz music is a recurring theme in his paintings and collages.

MAKING THE CONNECTION

- ✔ How can learning about another culture help us better understand the music of that culture?
- ✔ What instruments are shown in *Three Folk Musicians*? What type of music might the musicians be playing? Explain your answer.
- ✔ Do you think that only one type of music could be considered "American music"? Why or why not?

INTERNET ACTIVITY

Visit Glencoe's Fine Arts Web Site for students at:

http://www.glencoe.com/sec/art/students

C H A P T E R 6
REVIEW

BUILDING VOCABULARY

Number a sheet of paper from 1 to 8. After each number, write the term from the list that best matches each description below.

analyzing   describing
applied art   interpreting
art critic   judging
art criticism   non-objective art

1. The process of studying, understanding, and judging works of art.
2. One who practices the four steps in art criticism.
3. Making a careful list of all the things you see in a work of art.
4. A work with no objects or subjects that can be readily identified.
5. Noting how the principles in a work are used to organize the elements.
6. Explaining the meaning or mood expressed by an art work.
7. Telling if and why a work of art succeeds or fails.
8. Art made to be functional as well as visually pleasing.

REVIEWING ART FACTS

Number a sheet of paper from 9 to 13. Answer each question in a complete sentence.

9. Name the four steps of art criticism.

10. In addition to describing the people, objects, and events shown in a work of art, name two other things you could identify in a description.
11. In a credit line, which is given first—the height of a work or the width?
12. Which step of art criticism answers the question "How is the work organized?"
13. In which part of art criticism does a design chart come in handy? Briefly tell how it is used.

THINKING ABOUT ART

On a sheet of paper, answer each question in a sentence or two.

1. **Analyze.** Look at Figure 6–3 on page **103.** Which aesthetic view would you use when judging this work? Explain your answer.
2. **Analyze.** Why do you think it might be important to take the size of a work into account in a criticism? Why might the medium be important?
3. **Extend.** What problems could arise if one critic used another's description in his or her criticism of a work?
4. **Interpret.** Explain how two critics using the same four steps could come up with different interpretations and judgments of a work.

MAKING ART CONNECTIONS

1. **Social Studies.** The works of Andrew Wyeth (Figure 6–16) and Milton Resnick (Figure 6–9) were produced only 11 years apart, yet they are very different from each other. Investigate this period in history to determine how each artist's work may have been influenced by current events.
2. **Language Arts.** Select an object from nature. Look at it closely and write a description of the object as if you were describing a work of art. Use each element and principle of art at least once in your description. Try reading your description to a classmate without telling what it is you are describing. Have your classmate draw the object as you describe it.
3. **Social Studies.** Use a world map to locate where each of the artists in the chapter lived. Tell when they lived and what was happening in the world at that time.

▲ This illuminated manuscript brings the story to life for the reader.

Darius and the Herdsman from the manuscript of the *Bustan* (*Garden of Perfume*) by Sa'di. Mid 16th Century. Ink, colors, and gold on paper. 29.2 x 19.7 cm (11½ x 7¾"). The Metropolitan Museum of Art, New York, New York. Frederick C. Hewitt Fund, 1911. (11.134.2)

CHAPTER 7

Art History and You

As you have seen, you can discover a lot by looking closely at works of art. When you look at the painting on the left, what do you see? You might notice the small details. You might also comment on the use of line and color.

As you look at art works, you may also have questions. For example, you may wonder whether the work is similar to others done around the same time. You may ask who created it and when. These questions are among many you will learn about in this chapter. These questions explore the whys, whens, and wheres of art.

OBJECTIVES

After completing this chapter, you will be able to:
- Define art history.
- Tell what is revealed through each of the four parts of the art historian's job.
- Define style.
- Tell how time and place influence a work of art.
- Create works of art in the styles of different art movements.

WORDS YOU WILL LEARN

analyzing
art history
art movement
collage
describing
Fauves
interpreting
judging
Madonna
Renaissance
style

PORTFOLIO IDEAS

Choose entries for your portfolio from assignments that demonstrate your knowledge and understanding of art history. Select two or more art works in this chapter and explain how time and place influenced the artists or works of art. Then briefly compare and contrast the two entries. Include any information about art movements or other artists that may have influenced the works. Summarize your findings, date them, and place in your portfolio.

Describing—Who, When, and Where

In a very real sense, no artist works totally alone. To understand any art work fully, you need to do more than just look at it. You need to look beyond it. You need to know when and where the work was done. You need to know something about the artist who did it. You need to know about his or her style of making art.

These and other kinds of information are the subject of art history. **Art history** is *the study of art from past to present*. Art history looks at changes that take place in the field of art over time. It also looks at differences in the way art is made from place to place. People who work in the field of art history are called *art historians*.

Like art critics, art historians use many different approaches when they study art. Art historians, however, go outside the art work for many of their clues. Their goal is not to learn *from* a work, as art critics do. Rather, it is to learn *about* a work.

▲ **Figure 7–1** This painting was originally done as an advertisement for the Delaware Lackawanna & Western Railroad. The artist was hired by the company's first president. Is it similar to advertisements you see today? Explain.

George Inness. *The Lackawanna Valley*. 1855. Canvas. 86.0 x 127.5 cm (33⅞ x 50¼"). National Gallery of Art, Washington, D.C. Gift of Mrs. Huttleston Rogers.

ART HISTORY

In doing their jobs, art historians may use the same four-step system you read about in the last chapter. They describe, analyze, interpret, and then judge. As you will see, however, each of these terms has a different meaning to the art historian.

In this lesson, you will look at the first of these steps.

DESCRIBING A WORK

To art historians, **describing** is *telling who did a work, and when and where it was done.* Look at the painting in Figure 7–1. To begin, the art historian would look to see whether the artist had signed the work. Check the lower left corner. What name do you see there? Suppose the historian had never heard of G. Inness. He or she would then turn to an art history book. This source would reveal that George Inness was the name of two painters, a father and a son. It would also tell that both men lived and worked in America in the 1800s.

A little further exploration might turn up these facts:

- This painting was done by the father.
- It was painted in 1855.
- The painter was 30 years old at the time.
- He had studied landscape painting on his own in both America and Europe.

The historian might also come across this one especially interesting and important detail: George Inness had been taking formal art lessons for only one month when he began work on this picture.

Now it is your turn to be an art historian. Study the painting of the child with the watering can (Figure 7–2). But before you do, cover up the credit line with your hand.

Now can you identify the artist who painted this picture? Can you find his or her name on the work? It starts with the letter *R*.

▲ Figure 7–2 Why do you suppose art historians are not lucky enough to have credit lines to help them?

Auguste Renoir. *A Girl with a Watering Can.* 1876. 100.3 x 73.0 cm (39½ x 28¾"). National Gallery of Art, Washington, D.C. Chester Dale Collection.

Can you make out the two numbers after the name? These are the last two figures of the year the work was painted. Where could you go to find out the artist's full name or to find out the century when this work was done? What other things would you try to find out?

✔CHECK YOUR UNDERSTANDING

1. What is art history?
2. What four steps do art historians use in their work?
3. Where might an art historian find details about an artist's life?

LESSON 2

Making a Mixed Media Self-Portrait

As you study art history, you will find that many artists painted portraits of themselves. These portraits are called self-portraits. By studying self-portraits, you can find out what the artist looked like, what kind of personality the artist had, and something about when and where he or she lived.

Look at the painting below (Figure 7–3). What can you tell about the artist? When and where do you think he lived? How would you describe his personality? What other things in the picture give you insight into the artist's life?

▲ Figure 7–3 How would you describe the personality of this man? Identify images in the painting that tell you something about him.

César A. Martinez. *El Mestizo*. 1987. Charcoal and pastel on paper. 73.7 x 104.1 cm (29 x 41"). Courtesy of the artist.

WHAT YOU WILL LEARN

In this lesson you will imagine you are a famous artist. You will create a self-portrait using mixed media. Your self-portrait can be realistic or abstract. You will organize colors, lines, shapes, and textures to depict your personality and interests. The self-portrait should identify when and where you live and what your interests are. You will use the principle of emphasis to call attention to your strongest personality trait.

WHAT YOU WILL NEED

- Pencil and scrap paper
- Sheet of white paper, 10 x 12 inch (25 x 30 cm)
- Found objects: buttons, string, yarn, stones, cardboard, feathers, ribbon, shells
- Scissors
- Glue
- Crayons, colored pencils, or markers

WHAT YOU WILL DO

1. On a sheet of scrap paper, write down some of your personality traits, such as outgoing, confident, shy, unpredictable, athletic, or boisterous. List traits that give you a distinctive personality.
2. Determine if you will make a realistic or an abstract self-portrait. Think about a point of emphasis in the self-portrait. For example, you may wish to emphasize your eyes because you have an expressive and warm personality. Your smile might be a point of emphasis if you have a happy, outgoing personality.
3. On another sheet of paper, if you're making a realistic portrait, sketch an outline of your face. You may use a side or front view. Think of lightweight found objects

that can be added to the picture that represent when and where you live and your interests.
4. Choose your best sketch and transfer it to the sheet of white drawing paper. Your portrait may run off the edges of your paper if you wish.
5. Take found objects and arrange them on the paper so they tell the viewer more about you. Using a small amount of glue, attach them to the paper.
6. When the glue is dry, add colors, shapes and lines using crayons, colored pencils, or felt markers.
7. Share your finished work with your classmates.

 Try This!

STUDIO OPTIONS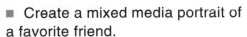

- Create a mixed media portrait of a favorite friend.

- Create a mixed media portrait of a famous person, portraying some of the skills, events, or organizations the person is noted for.

Analyzing Artistic Style

No two people have exactly the same handwriting. Their writing styles may be similar, but one may use a slightly bigger loop on the *j*'s or cross the letter *t* using a line that is slightly longer.

The same is true of artists. Each artist works in a way that is at least slightly different from any other artist. These differences are the key to stage two of the art historian's job—analyzing.

ANALYZING A WORK

You will recall that in the describing stage the art historian looks for a signature on a work. Sometimes there is no signature. Sometimes the historian does not need one because the artist's style speaks as clearly as any signature. **Style** is *an artist's personal way of expressing ideas in a work.* You may remember that many times artists develop their style by studying the work of others. *Noting the style of a work,* or **analyzing**, is what the art historian does during the next stage.

▲ **Figure 7–4   How are lines and hues combined to show depth? How does the mood in this painting differ from the mood in Figure 7–5?**

Jasper Francis Cropsey. *Autumn on the Hudson River.* 1860. Canvas. 152.5 x 274.3 (60 x 108"). National Gallery of Art, Washington, D.C. Gift of the Avalon Foundation.

▲ **Figure 7–5** **Which element do you think was most important to this artist? Which do you think was the least important?**

André Derain. *The River Seine at Carrieres-sur-Seine*. 1905. Oil on canvas. 70.7 x 110.7 cm (27⁷/₈ x 43½"). Kimbell Art Museum, Fort Worth, Texas.

Look back at the landscape by George Inness on page **120** (Figure 7–1). An art historian might note that the painting shows a lifelike, or realistic style. Which of the landscapes shown in Figure 7–4 and 7–5 also shows a realistic style? What words might you use to describe the style of the other work?

ART MOVEMENTS

Sometimes *a group of artists with similar styles who have banded together* form an **art movement**. One of these had its beginnings early in this century in France. It was known as the Fauve (**fohv**) movement. Fauves is a French word meaning "wild beasts," and artists who developed the new artistic style were known as the Fauves. **Fauve** refers to the art movement in which the artists used *wild intense color combinations in their paintings*. The Fauves were not interested in doing realistic art. Instead, they emphasized the colors in their works as a way of increasing the visual and emotional appeal. The landscape in Figure 7–5 is an example of a work in the Fauve style.

In analyzing a work, art historians will try to decide if it fits into a movement. Look at Figures 7–6 and 7–7 and be the art historian. Which of these paintings is done in the Fauve style? What details can you point to that support your decision?

▲ Figure 7–6 Compare this work with Figure 7–2 on page 121. Both paintings were done by the same artist. What similarities and differences can you find between the two works?

Auguste Renoir. *Regatta at Argenteuil*. 1874. Canvas. 32.4 x 45.6 cm (12¾ x 18″). National Gallery of Art, Washington, D.C. Ailsa Mellon Bruce Collection.

▶ Figure 7–7 Does this sailboat scene have a different feel from the one in Figure 7–6? Compare the use of elements in each painting. How do they contribute to the overall effect?

Maurice de Vlaminck. *Sailboats on the Seine*. Oil on canvas. 54.6 x 73.7 cm (21½ x 29″). Metropolitan Museum of Art, New York. Robert Lehman Collection.

Look again briefly at Figures 7–6 and 7–7. Study the work in this pair that you decided was *not* in the Fauve style. This work also came out of a movement. The movement, called Impressionism, also had its start in France in the late 1800s. This painting was done by a leader of the movement, Pierre Auguste Renoir (pee-**air** oh-**goost** ren-**wahr**).

As an art historian, how would you describe this style of Impressionist painting? What kinds of colors do you think its members liked to use? What kinds of lines do you think they liked? Can you see how they tried to show the effects of sunlight on the subject matter? Did you notice how the choppy brush strokes were used to reproduce the flickering quality of sunlight? As you practice the skills of an art historian, you can turn to your school or community library to help you find the answers.

▲ **Figure 7–8** The artist used dabs and dashes of paint in an attempt to show the flickering effect of sunlight on trees, shrubs, and other objects. Do you think the painting captures the look of a bright summer afternoon?

Claude Monet. *The Artist's Garden at Vétheuil.* 1880. Canvas. 151.4 x 121.0 cm (59⅝ x 47⅝″). National Gallery of Art, Washington, D.C. Ailsa Mellon Bruce Collection.

STUDIO ACTIVITY

Recognizing Impressionism

Study the painting in Figure 7–8. The work, by Claude Monet, is another example of the Impressionist style. Look closely at the painting. What do you notice about the use of color and of line?

Imagine that you are Monet, getting ready to do this work. Make a rough pencil sketch of a simple landscape. Use crayons, oil pastels, or chalk to color your sketch. Imitate Monet's Impressionist style by using short dashes and dabs of color. Begin in the center of the objects and work outward. Use complementary colors to make hues look dark. Compare your sketch with those of your classmates. Decide which sketches come closest to imitating the Impressionist style. Discuss what coloring techniques give the best result.

 P o r t f o l i o

Look again at Figures 7–6 and 7–8. List characteristics of these two Impressionist paintings that are similar. Look at your sketch of the Claude Monet painting. Does it contain those characteristics you listed? Put a star beside those that are found in your sketch. Keep the list and sketch together in your portfolio.

✔ CHECK YOUR UNDERSTANDING

1. Define *analyzing,* as the term is used by an art historian.
2. What is style as it relates to art?
3. Describe the features of an art work done in the Impressionist style.

Painting in the Fauve Style

Look at the painting in Figure 7–9. This was done by Henri Matisse (ahn-**ree** mah-**tees**), the leader of the Fauves whom you met in the last chapter. Notice that the room in the work is free of corners and shadows. What else can you observe from this style?

▲ **Figure 7–9** Which objects in the painting are painted in the most detail? Which are painted in the least detail? What reason might the artist have for leaving certain objects less finished than others?

Henri Matisse. *The Red Room* or *Dessert: Harmony in Red.* 1908. Oil on canvas. 180 x 220 cm (70⅞ x 86⅝"). The State Hermitage Museum, St. Petersburg/The Bridgeman Art Library, London. BAL 37552

WHAT YOU WILL LEARN

Paint an interior scene in the Fauve style of Matisse. Start with a rough sketch and choose a single bold color for the background and paint shapes in the room in other bold colors. Create harmony in your work by repeating certain line and colors throughout.

WHAT YOU WILL NEED

- Pencil and eraser
- Sheets of scrap paper
- Sheet of white paper, 9 x 12 inch (23 x 30 cm) or larger
- Watercolor paint in bold hues
- Two watercolor brushes, one large and one with very fine bristles
- Jar of water
- Paper towels

WHAT YOU WILL DO

1. On a sheet of scrap paper, do a pencil sketch of an interior scene, such as your bedroom, living room, or classroom. (Notice how much detail Matisse gives to the chair in the left foreground in Figure 7–9.) For other objects, sketch only the outline. (Notice the wallpaper on the back wall in Figure 7–9.) Do not worry about proportion or whether your shapes seem realistic.
2. Using pencil, lightly copy your sketch onto the sheet of white paper. Sign your name in pencil to the back of the paper.
3. Choose three special hues of watercolor paint. Do not use brown or black. One color is to be the background of your work. The other two are to be used for

the details. Soften the paint by adding a few drops of water to each.

4. Load your large brush with the color you have picked for the background. Using broad strokes, cover the sheet of paper with color. Do not worry about leaving streaks. Set your paper aside to dry.
5. When the paint is totally dry, begin to add objects using the remaining two colors. Use less water to make your colors as strong as possible. Use one of the colors to paint outlines. Use your small brush to make narrow lines. (See Technique Tip 4, *Handbook* page 271 for information on how to make thin lines with a brush.) Use the other color to fill in shapes. Refer to your sketch as you work.
6. Allow your painting to dry totally. Share your finished work with your classmates.

EXAMINING YOUR WORK

- **Describe**   Tell what bold hue you have used as a background color. Identify the objects you have included in your interior scene.
- **Analyze**   Tell how your use of line and color adds harmony to your work.
- **Interpret**   Identify the adjectives a viewer might use to describe the colors in your work.
- **Judge**   Tell whether you feel your work succeeds. What aesthetic view would you use to support your judgment?

Try This! COMPUTER OPTION

■ Create a landscape, cityscape, or seascape in the Fauve style. Think about the objects you will draw and the mood you want to express. Choose bright colors that are not the typical colors you would expect to see. For instance, draw a purple tree, a blue dog, or orange water. Use a variety of Brush and Shape tools to draw the scene you have chosen. Continue to use unexpected colors for the objects, sky, and background of your painting. Title, Save, and Print.

LESSON 5

Interpreting Time and Place

Our lives are shaped by when and where we live. Today we take cars and televisions for granted. People living a hundred years ago had neither of these inventions.

In art, too, time, place, and world events can have a great influence on an artist. Artists living in wartime may create works very different from those done in peacetime. Ethnic background often influences an artist's work as well. In art, time and place are central to the art historian's interpreting of works.

INTERPRETING A WORK

Do you remember the three questions art historians ask when describing a work? Two of those questions are "when?" and "where?" In stage three, art historians follow up on their answers to those questions. **Interpreting** is *noting how time and place affect an artist's style and subject matter.*

Sometimes historians interpret a work by studying the impact of time and place on its style. At other times, they focus mainly on the subject matter used. At still other times, an interpretation takes both style and subject matter into account.

Interpreting for Style

In the late 1800s a new branch of art was born. This branch was photography. Thanks to photography, familiar subjects could now be viewed from new and unusual angles.

The art of photography opened new doors for painters and other artists. Some began experimenting with new rules for making art. Figures in paintings were now pushed off to the side, as they were in photos. Parts of objects were sometimes cut off by the edges of the work. Compare the works in Figures 7–10 and 7–11. What words might an art historian use in interpreting the style of the painting?

Interpreting for Subject Matter

Today when people make news, their pictures often appear in the newspaper. If the news is big enough, their pictures may appear on television. Where do you think pictures of famous people appeared before there was photography or television?

▲ **Figure 7–10** **This photograph originally appeared in a magazine called *Camera Work*. The magazine was run by Alfred Stieglitz (steeg-luhts), an important American photographer.**

Clarence H. White. *Ring Toss*. 1903. Photograph. International Museum of Photography at George Eastman House, Rochester, New York.

◀ Figure 7–11   How would you describe the artist's use of the principle of balance? What do you think art critics at the time may have said when they saw this work?

Edgar Degas. *Four Dancers*. 1899. Canvas. 151.1 x 180.2 cm (59½ x 71"). National Gallery of Art, Washington, D.C. Chester Dale Collection.

▼ Figure 7–12   Among this painter's subjects were queens and other famous people. These days we know what leaders and famous people look like from photographs. Where else do we see their faces?

Marie-Louise-Élisabeth Vigée-Lebrun. *Theresa, Countess Kinsky*. 1793. Oil on canvas. 137.4 x 99.8 cm (54⅛ x 39⅜"). Norton Simon Art Foundation.

They appeared in paintings and other works of art. Figure 7–12 is a painting of one such person who was famous in the 1700s. The artist herself was well-known as a painter of portraits. These facts would be uppermost in the mind of an art historian interpreting this work. As an art historian, what questions might you ask about the subject in the painting? Where would you go for answers?

Portraits are not the only example of art that keeps records of people and events. Look once again at the landscape by George Inness (Figure 7–1 on page **120**). The work is a reminder of what railroads were like in the 1800s. It is also a record of an event in the artist's own life. This was the first time George Inness was paid for a painting. It marked a turning point in his career. An art historian might note both these facts in an interpretation of the painting. What other facts might an historian want to note?

Interpreting for Style and Subject Matter

A period of great awakening in the arts in Europe in the 1500s is known as the Renaissance (**ren**-uh-sahns). **Renaissance** is a *French word meaning "rebirth."* Before the Renaissance, artists were thought of as skilled craftspeople. Their work was no more important than that of carpenters or stone cutters. During the Renaissance, however, artists suddenly gained new prestige. This was partly because of the enormous talents of many of the artists of the period. You have probably heard of Michelangelo (my-kuh-**lan**-juh-loh) and Leonardo da Vinci (lee-uh-**nahr**-doh duh **vin**-chee). Both of these highly gifted artists worked during the Renaissance.

Another artist of the period whom you already met was Raphael. (In Chapter 6, you studied his painting *St. George and the Dragon* on page **104**.) Look at the painting in Figure 7–13. An art historian interpreting this work

▶ **Figure 7–13   This is thought to be the most beautiful of the many Madonnas Raphael painted. It was painted shortly before Raphael began work on *St. George and the Dragon*.**

Raphael. *The Small Cowper Madonna*. c. 1505. Wood. 59.5 x 44.0 cm (23⅜ x 17⅜"). National Gallery of Art, Washington, D.C. Widener Collection.

would notice two things. First, like most of Raphael's paintings, this one has a religious subject. Do you know the figures in the work? Reading about the Renaissance, an art historian might learn the following:

- The Catholic Church was a great patron of the arts.
- The Catholic Church hired artists to paint and sculpt scenes from the Bible.
- The art works were used to decorate churches.
- Most people living in the 1500s were unable to read.

Through these church paintings, the people were able to understand the story of Christ without reading about him.

The second thing an art historian might notice is that the painting has a religious figure as a central theme or subject. During the Renaissance, the Madonna became a theme for many works of art. A **Madonna** is *a work showing the mother of Christ*. The word madonna means "my lady." Raphael alone painted over 300 Madonnas. Figure 7–14 shows a Madonna by another Renaissance painter. Compare it with Raphael's Madonna (Figure 7–13). Notice the circles, or bands, framing the figures' heads. Do you know what these are called? How might you describe the looks on the faces of the figures? What other style features do the two works share? In what ways are the works different?

▲ **Figure 7–14** What differences do you see in the use of art elements and art principles between the two paintings shown on these two pages?

Fra Filippo Lippi. *Madonna and Child*. 1440/1445. Wood. 80 x 51 cm (31⅜ x 20⅛"). National Gallery of Art, Washington, D.C. Samuel H. Kress Collection.

✔CHECK YOUR UNDERSTANDING

1. Define *interpreting*, as the term is used by an art historian.
2. What use did portraits have in the past?
3. What is a Madonna?
4. What and when was the Renaissance? How were artists thought of before the Renaissance and during the Renaissance?

Time and Place Collage

Look at Figure 7–15. This type of art work is called a collage. A **collage** (kuh-**lahzh**) is *art arranged from cut and torn materials pasted to a surface.* Some of the materials in this collage are clues to the time and place in which it was created. Look at the piece of newspaper on the left side. Can you read any of the words? Do you know what language they are? Can you guess? Where might you go to find out when this newspaper was first printed? What would these facts reveal about when the artist worked?

WHAT YOU WILL LEARN

You will make a collage out of scrap paper (Figure 7–16). The principles of art will be used to combine the colors, textures, and shapes into a visually interesting whole. Your collage will give clues about life in America today.

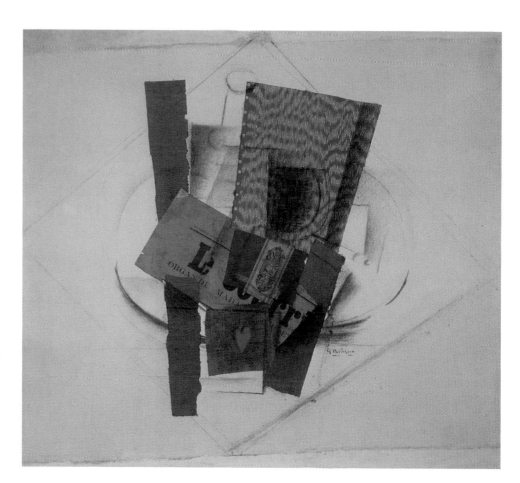

▶ **Figure 7–15** How many of the bits and pieces in this work can you identify? Do they add up to an interesting whole? Why or why not?

Georges Braque. *Le Courrier*. Charcoal, gouache and printed paper collage. 50.6 x 57.8 cm (20¼ x 22¾"). Philadelphia Museum of Art. A. E. Gallatin Collection.

WHAT YOU WILL NEED

- Magazines and newspapers
- Scissors
- Pencil and sheets of sketch paper
- Poster board
- Slightly thinned white glue
- Small brush

WHAT YOU WILL DO

1. Turn through pages of newspapers and magazines. With scissors, clip out images that might depict life in America today. Use images of different sizes. You can use pictures or words from advertisements. Be as imaginative as you can in your choices.
2. Decide what materials will fill the spaces around your images. Again, be creative in choosing visually interesting colors, textures, shapes, and sizes. Clip the pieces out and set them aside.
3. Experiment with the pieces by arranging them on your poster board using the art principles. Pieces can overlap.
4. With the thinned glue and small brush, glue the pieces of your collage in place. Set your collage aside to dry.
5. *Optional.* You may want to use watercolor or tempera paint to help unify your composition. To do this, use a thin layer of paint to cover over some parts and accent others.

EXAMINING YOUR WORK

- **Describe**   Point to the images you clipped from newspapers or magazines. Tell what colors, textures, and shapes you chose.
- **Analyze**   Tell what principles you used to organize the elements into an interesting whole.
- **Interpret**   Tell what the images you chose reveal about life in America today. Point to images that show time, place, or both. Tell what overall feeling the viewer will have when seeing your work.
- **Judge**   Tell whether you feel your work succeeds. Explain your answer.

▲ Figure 7–16   Student work. A time and place collage.

Try This! STUDIO OPTIONS

■ Make a collage about new food trends or your favorite food. Again, use magazine and newspaper clippings.

■ Make a collage of items promoting or representing your city or town.

Judging Historical Importance

What is the most important accomplishment that happened to you during the past week? What happened to you in the past month that was important? What event was an accomplishment during the past year? It is not likely your answer was the same for all three questions. For a few days doing well on a test or earning 20 extra dollars may seem like a big accomplishment. However, as days turn into months, your idea of what is important changes.

The same is true for art historians in the last stage of their work. In judging a work of art, they look at all aspects of the artist's work.

JUDGING A WORK

To art historians, judging is determining if a work of art makes a lasting contribution to the history of art. **Judging** is *deciding whether a work introduces a new style or if it is an outstanding example of an existing style*. It can also involve deciding whether a work makes a contribution to art by introducing a new style, technique, or a new medium.

Judging for Style

There are many ways in which pieces of art can make a contribution. One is by introducing a new style. Look again at Henri Matisse's painting in Figure 7–9 on page **128.** An art critic judging the painting would praise its bold colors. An art historian judging the painting would look beyond it. The historian would note how Matisse's use of bold colors influenced other artists and changed ideas about what is art. Do you remember the name of the art movement Matisse led? Do you remember what its members believed?

Look at the painting in Figure 7–17. It is a Madonna painted in the 1300s by an artist named Giotto (**jah**-toh). Is there anything in this work a historian would call new or striking? Is there any reason why the work should be judged important?

To the untrained eye today, Giotto's painting might seem stiff and awkward. To the art historian, however, there is more here than meets the eye. The historian would try to imagine himself or herself living in Giotto's time. Back then most Madonnas were like the one in Figure 7–18 on page **138.** True, this work does not look very realistic. But in the 1300s paintings seldom did. Pictures of religious figures were not meant to look real. They were painted to remind people of saints and prophets and to teach religious values. The golden lines in the drapery in Figure 7–18 were painted as a decorative pattern. No effort was made to make them look like real folds in real cloth.

The people in Giotto's day were shocked by Figure 7–17. His figures, compared with those in the typical Madonna, are lifelike. They are not flat figures painted on a gold background. They give the impression of being rounded three-dimensional forms that stand out in space.

Now look again at Figure 7–18. The child in the work does not look or act like a real child. He seems to be giving his mother a lecture. Giotto's child, on the other hand, is more believable. He holds one of his mother's fingers as a real baby might.

Consider these points and tell how an art historian might judge this work. How would you judge it?

▲ **Figure 7–17   This painting may have been one of several that were joined together to decorate the altar of a church.**

Giotto. *Madonna and Child*. c.1320/1330. Wood. 85.5 x 62.0 cm (33⅝ x 24⅜"). National Gallery of Art, Washington, D.C. Samuel H. Kress Collection.

Judging for Technique

Another way a work of art can make a contribution is by introducing new techniques. Techniques are the ways an artist chooses to use a medium. This can be explained by taking a look at Figure 7–19. This painting was done by a French artist named Georges Seurat (suh-**rah**).

You can see by looking at Figure 7–19 that the technique used here differs from the technique used by other artists. Georges Seurat took a more scientific approach by combining thousands of dots of color. This made his paintings seem to shimmer with light. This is an example of how artists who use the same medium develop individual techniques.

◄ **Figure 7–18   Paintings like this were thought to have great power. One famous Roman emperor carried one like it when he went into battle. These works were also thought to heal the sick and give sight to the blind.**

Byzantine XIII Century. *Enthroned Madonna and Child.* Wood. 131.1 x 76.8 cm (51⅝ x 30¼"). National Gallery of Art, Washington, D.C. Gift of Mrs. Otto H. Kahn.

► **Figure 7–19   Is Seurat's technique successful in portraying the scene and conveying its mood? Where did he choose to concentrate on detail? Where is lack of detail displayed?**

Georges Seurat. *Sunday Afternoon on the Island of La Grande Jatte.* 1884-86. Oil on canvas. 207.6 x 308.0 cm (81¾ x 121¼"). The Art Institute of Chicago. Helen Birch Bartlett Memorial Collection.

▲ Figure 7–20 **What do you think is most lifelike about these two figures? Would you describe them as happy or sad? Why do you think they look this way? Is there anything about them to indicate that they are the Madonna and Christ?**

Sir Jacob Epstein. *Madonna and Child.* Riverside Church, New York.

THE ART HISTORIAN AND HISTORY

The ways in which humans, animals, and objects are shown in works of art have changed over the centuries. For example, the two works in Figures 7–17 on page **137** and 7–20 both show the Madonna and Christ. However, the two artists presented this same subject differently. When Giotto painted his picture, it was admired because it looked so natural and lifelike when compared to earlier paintings of the Madonna (see Figure 7–18). The sculpture by Jacob Epstein, created 600 years after Giotto painted his picture, looks even more natural and lifelike to us today.

Art historians know that no matter how far back in time we travel to examine works of art, we will always be haunted by the feeling that there are other art forms, even further

back, that must have inspired the thoughts, emotions, and images of the artists. Epstein's moving sculpture of the Madonna has its roots in the art created not only by Giotto but the countless artists, who lived and worked before Giotto was born.

✔ CHECK YOUR UNDERSTANDING

1. Tell what the term *judging* means to an art historian.
2. What are two ways a work of art can make a contribution to the world of art?
3. How do changes in art happen?
4. Do artists learn from those who have created long before them? Explain.

George Catlin. *Catlin Painting the Portrait of Mah-to-toh-pa-Mandan.* 1857/69. Cardboard. 39.1 x 55.6 cm (15⅜ x 21⅞") oval. National Gallery of Art, Washington, D.C. Paul Mellon Collection.

How Do We Preserve History?

How do you remember important events in your life, such as a birthday, special holiday, or family vacation? Some people keep a diary in which they describe the event and their feelings about it. Other people take photographs to keep in a photo album. When they look at the album, they remember the occasion. Some people take home movies with a video camera. These are some of the many ways in which people preserve history.

Another way to preserve history is through art. Before the camera was invented, art was a way to record history for future generations. A great deal of the information we have about people and events of long ago comes from art. For example, we know about important rulers, famous battles, and notable historical events. By studying art closely, we can also learn about other characteristics of a time period, such as clothing, furniture, and architectural styles.

Catlin Painting the Portrait of Mah-to-toh-pa-Mandan is an example of how art can be an eyewitness to history. Instead of simply painting a portrait of an important historical figure, the artist preserved the "big picture." He recorded himself painting the portrait!

MAKING THE CONNECTION

- ✔ Besides diaries, photographs, videos, and art works, what are other ways in which people preserve history?
- ✔ What historical information can we learn from Catlin's painting?
- ✔ How does this painting tell us more about history than a portrait of Mah-to-toh-pa-Mandan alone would tell?

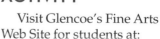

INTERNET ACTIVITY

Visit Glencoe's Fine Arts Web Site for students at:

http://www.glencoe.com/ sec/art/students

C H A P T E R 7
REVIEW

 BUILDING VOCABULARY

Number a sheet of paper from 1 to 11. After each number, write the term from the list that best matches each description below.

analyzing　　　　interpreting
art history　　　 judging
art movement　　 Madonna
collage　　　　　Renaissance
describing　　　　style
Fauves

1. The study of art from past to present.
2. Identifying who did a work of art, and when and where it was done.
3. Noting an art work's style.
4. An artist's personal way of expressing ideas.
5. A group of artists with a similar style.
6. French art movement in which artists used wild blends of strong colors.
7. Noting the way that time and place affect an artist's style and subject matter.
8. A period of great awakening in the arts in Europe in the 1500s.
9. A work showing the mother of Christ.
10. A work made up of bits and pieces of objects pasted to a surface.
11. Deciding upon a work's place in art history.

 REVIEWING ART FACTS

Number a sheet of paper from 12 to 19. Answer each question in a complete sentence.

12. In what ways is an art historian's approach to art different from an art critic's?
13. In describing a work of art, where does an art historian look first for an answer to the question "who"?
14. Why is style like a person's signature?
15. What did the Fauves believe in? When and where did they work?
16. What did the Impressionists believe in? Where did they work?
17. Where did pictures of famous people appear before the invention of photography?
18. Name two great artists of the Renaissance.
19. Name one way in which an art work might be judged as making a contribution to art history.

 THINKING ABOUT ART

On a sheet of paper, answer each question in a sentence or two.

1. **Extend.** Where else in a library besides art history books might you turn for information on an artist's life?
2. **Analyze.** Give an example of how time and place can affect style. How do time and place affect an artist's choice of subject matter?
3. **Compare and contrast.** How are describing and interpreting similar for an art historian? How are the two tasks different?

─ **MAKING ART CONNECTIONS** ─

1. **Social Studies.** Art history provides a look into the past to show us what people did, the things they used, and the clothes they wore. Look at the Renoir painting of the little girl on page **121.** What does her clothing tell you about the date this painting was made?

2. **Science.** Ask a science teacher to tell you about radiocarbon dating, a technique used by researchers to determine the age of material. Using this technique, art historians have been able to identify when an art work was made.

▲ Van Gogh's friend, Joseph Roulin, was a postal worker who often posed for the artist. Notice the texture in the coat, beard, and background. How did the artist use the element of line to create the various textures?

Vincent van Gogh. *Portrait of Joseph Roulin*. 1888. Reed and quill pens and brown ink over black chalk. 32 x 24.4 cm (12⅝ x 9⅝"). The J. Paul Getty Museum, Los Angeles, California.

CHAPTER 8

Drawing

Have you ever heard someone say, "I can't draw"? Perhaps you have said it yourself. What you may not realize is that drawing is a skill. It can be learned just as dancing or playing a sport can be learned. With practice, you can use your drawing skills to express what you see in the world.

Look at the sketch on the left. What do you think the artist saw? With nothing more than a blank sheet of paper and a few drawing media, van Gogh has created a detailed sketch. In this chapter you will find out how he made the subject of his drawing look so real.

OBJECTIVES

After completing this chapter, you will be able to:

- Name the three ways in which drawing is used in art.
- Define *shading,* and name four shading techniques.
- Make a gesture drawing.
- Make a contour drawing.
- Make a presentation drawing.

WORDS YOU WILL LEARN

blending
contour drawing
crosshatching
gesture drawing
hatching
perception
shading
stippling

PORTFOLIO IDEAS

Create an entry for your portfolio that demonstrates your skill at drawing. You might make a sketch of a favorite art work in this book, or you might attempt your own version of a drawing found in this chapter. On a separate sheet of paper, describe how your drawing uses the elements of color, line, space, shape, and texture. Explain how your choice of drawing medium affected the final art work. Put your name and date on the paper and place it in your portfolio.

The Art of Drawing

You have probably seen people doodling with a pencil. You may have done it yourself. If you have, you are not alone. Ever since you took a crayon in your hand and scribbled on paper, you have been drawing.

You can learn certain skills to help you improve your ability to draw. Look again at the drawing of the postal worker on page **142.** Notice how the artist, Vincent van Gogh, using pens, ink, and chalk, gave expression to the man's face and texture to his clothing and beard. Notice how the lines in the background add life to the drawing and create the feeling of depth.

► **Figure 8–1** Does this drawing tell you simply how these people looked? How did da Vinci perceive this group of men? How does he convey this perception?

Leonardo da Vinci. *Five Grotesque Heads.* c. 1494. Pen on white paper. Windsor Castle, Royal Library of Her Majesty the Queen.

In this lesson you will learn about some of the uses of drawing. You will also learn a few drawing techniques. In later lessons you will get a chance to use these techniques.

THE USES OF DRAWING

Drawing has many uses in art. The three important ones are to develop perception, to help plan projects, and to make a finished art work. **Perception** is *awareness of the elements of the environment by means of the senses.*

Improving Perception

To an artist, looking and seeing are not the same thing. Looking is simply noticing an object as you pass by it. Seeing, or perceiving, is really studying the object. It is picking up on every line and shadow. It is observing all the details.

Through drawing, artists become better at perceiving. Many artists use sketchbooks to record their surroundings and to study objects. They use drawing to make preliminary studies for finished works. The Renaissance artist Leonardo da Vinci filled over a hundred sketchbooks with drawings. The drawings in Figure 8–1 come from one of them.

Planning Projects

Drawing is usually the first step in completing many art works and other projects. Rough sketches, or studies, are almost always done before creating a work in another medium, such as painting or sculpture. Design drawings for this year's fashions were made long before any fabric was cut. (See Figure 8–2.) Many creative people, such as stage designers, graphic designers, and architects must show presentation drawings for a client's approval. Once the drawing is approved, work can begin on the project.

▲ Figure 8–2 Can you envision how this drawing would translate into an actual piece of clothing? What feeling do you think a viewer gets when looking at this work? Explain your answer.

LESSON 2

Gesture Drawing

Artists are able to freeze movement in a picture using a technique called gesture drawing. **Gesture drawing** is *drawing lines quickly and loosely to capture movement*. Look at Figure 8–5. This was done by the great Dutch painter Rembrandt van Rijn (**rembrant van ryn**). Notice how the lines appear to have been made quickly to catch the action of the figure.

Using gesture drawing will help you break the habit of outlining everything you draw. In gesture drawing you use your whole arm, not just your hand. (See Technique Tip 1, *Handbook* Page **271**.)

▲ **Figure 8–5**   Find the lines that suggest movement rather than define a form. Where is most of the detail concentrated?

Rembrandt van Rijn. *Jan Cornelius Sylvius, The Preacher.* c. 1644–1645. Pen and brown ink on laid paper. 13.3 x 12.2 cm (5¼ x 4¹³⁄₁₆"). National Gallery of Art, Washington, D. C. Rosenwald Collection.

WHAT YOU WILL LEARN

You will make a series of 30-second gesture drawings using charcoal, graphite, or crayon. You will focus on the *movement* of the figure, not on the likeness of the person. Then you will make a large, slower sketch of a seated figure. Select one area of this figure to emphasize with details and shading. (See Figure 8–6.)

WHAT YOU WILL NEED

- Sticks of charcoal, soft graphite, or unwrapped crayon
- Sheets of white paper, 12 x 18 inch (30 x 46 cm)
- Pencil with a sharp point, and an eraser

WHAT YOU WILL DO

1. You and your classmates will take turns acting as the model. Models should pretend to be frozen in the middle of an activity. This may be an everyday action, such as sweeping the floor, or tying a shoelace. Dancing or acting out a sport are other possibilities. Each model will hold the pose for 30 seconds.
2. Using charcoal, graphite, or a crayon, begin making gesture drawings. You can fit several sketches on one sheet of paper. Make loose, free lines that build up the shape of the person. Your lines should be quickly drawn to capture movement.
3. After many 30-second drawings, make a slower gesture drawing of a seated model. Fill a sheet of paper. Select one area of the figure to emphasize with details and shading. Try a hand, a shoe, or a sleeve. (See Figure 8–7.)
4. When you are done, display your last drawing. Did your classmates choose the same detail to emphasize?

▲ Figure 8–6 Notice how the artist emphasized the faces of the two figures and only suggested the rest of their bodies. Do you feel this technique is effective when drawing portraits? Why or why not?

Marie-Louise-Élisabeth Vigée-Lebrun. *La Princesse Barbe Gallitzin.* c. 1801. Graphite and chalk. Approximately 17.8 x 11.1 cm (7 x 4⅜"). National Museum of Women in the Arts, Washington, D.C. Gift of Wallace and Wilhelmina Holladay.

EXAMINING YOUR WORK

- **Describe**   Show the series of gesture drawings you made using charcoal, graphite, or crayon. Identify the action or pose you tried to capture in each.
- **Analyze**   Point to the loose, sketchy lines in your gesture drawings. Explain why your lines were drawn this way. Tell how movement is shown.
- **Interpret**   Explain how viewers will be able to recognize that your figures are involved in some kind of action.
- **Judge**   Tell whether you feel your drawings succeed in showing figures in motion. Explain your answer.

▲ Figure 8–7   Student work. A gesture drawing with one detailed figure.

 Try This! ## COMPUTER OPTION 💻

■ Make quick gesture drawings of your classmates as you practice the 30-second drawings described in Step 1 of the Studio Lesson. Select the charcoal Brush tool. Explore a variety of brush sizes and types of paper—smooth or soft, rough or gritty. You might also use the Bucket tool to flood-fill the page with a dark color. Choose white or light charcoal to make action drawing. Title and Save drawings you like as you practice. Select one drawing and follow the directions in the Studio Lesson.

LESSON 3

Contour Drawing

Look at Figure 8–8. Notice how lifelike the subject looks for a drawing made almost totally of line. A first step toward doing work like this is learning to do contour drawing. **Contour drawing** is *drawing an object as though your drawing tool is moving along all the edges and the ridges of the form*. This technique helps you become more perceptive. You are concerned with drawing shapes and curves.

In contour drawing, your eye and hand move at the same time. Imagine that the point of your pen is touching the edge of the object as your eye follows the edge. You never pick up your pen. When you move from one area to another, you leave a trail. Look at the model and not at the paper.

WHAT YOU WILL LEARN

You will make a series of contour drawings with a felt-tipped pen. First, you will draw different objects. Second, you will use your classmates as models. Finally, you will make a contour drawing of a classmate posed in a setting. (See Technique Tip **2**, *Handbook* page **271**.)

WHAT YOU WILL NEED

- Felt-tipped pen with a fine point
- Sheets of white paper, 12 x 18 inch (30 x 46 cm)
- Selected objects provided by your teacher

WHAT YOU WILL DO

1. Take one of the items from the collection on the display table. Place it on the table in front of you. Trace the lines of the object in the air on an imaginary sheet of glass. As you look at the object, you must concentrate and think. Notice every detail indicated by the direction and curves of the line.

▲ **Figure 8–8   Notice how the artist gives a feeling of form by changing the thickness and darkness of the line. What ways do you know of to make lines thicker and darker?**

Juan Gris. *Max Jacob.* 1919. Pencil on paper. 35.9 x 26.7 cm (14⅛ x 10½"). The Museum of Modern Art, New York, New York. Gift of James Thrall Soby.

2. Make a contour drawing of the object on a sheet of paper using a felt-tipped pen. Do several more drawings on the same sheet of paper. Turn the object so you are looking at it from a different angle. Make another contour drawing. Keep working until your drawings begin to look like the object. (See Figure 8–9.)
3. Next, exchange objects with your classmates. Do a contour drawing of your new object. Work large, letting the drawing fill the page. Do not worry if your efforts look awkward. Complete several drawings of different objects.

4. Work with a partner. Take turns posing for each other. Each model should sit in a comfortable pose. The first contour will look distorted. Remember, you are drawing the pose. Work large and let the drawing fill the page.

5. Finally, make a contour drawing of one person sitting in a setting. Include background details. (See Figure 8–10.) You may stop and peek at the drawing. When you do, do not pick up the pencil. Do not take your eyes off the model while drawing.

6. Display the final drawing. Discuss how contour drawing has improved your perception.

▲ Figure 8–9 Student work.

EXAMINING YOUR WORK

- **Describe** Show the different kinds of contour drawings you did. Identify the media you used.
- **Analyze** Compare your first contour drawing to your last. Explain how using contour drawing has changed your perception skills.
- **Judge** Evaluate your final contour drawing. Tell whether you feel your work succeeds. Explain your answer.

▲ Figure 8–10 Student work. This is an example of a contour drawing that shows background details.

Try This!

STUDIO OPTIONS

■ Make a contour drawing of a chair in your classroom using crayons.

■ Use a piece of wire that bends easily and make a three-dimensional contour "drawing" of a foot or hand.

Presentation Drawing

Sometimes artists are called upon to make presentation drawings. These drawings show a possible idea or design for a project. Figure 8–11 is a presentation drawing for a large outdoor sculpture of an ordinary clothespin. The drawing was submitted by the artist, Claes Oldenburg, as his entry in a competition for a sculpture to be placed in a square in downtown Philadelphia. Oldenburg's entry was accepted and the finished work, all 45 feet of it, was erected in 1976 (Figure 8–12).

What makes his design so unusual? Do you think it was a good choice for a city square? Why or why not? How do you think you would feel if you came across this huge sculpture of a clothespin?

Imagine you have been asked to design a set of wrought iron gates for the entrance to a zoo, botanical garden, or a playground.

WHAT YOU WILL LEARN

You will create a presentation drawing of a gate with two sides. The outside shape of the gate will be symmetrically balanced. To unify your design within the shape of the gate, create a symmetrical or asymmetrical design using lines and symbols that represent the place. Use the principles of rhythm and harmony to organize the lines.

▲ **Figure 8–12**   This giant clothespin forces viewers to look at a common object in a new way. Some are shocked while others smile in amusement. What is your reaction?

Claes Oldenburg. *Clothespin.* 1976. Cor-Ten and stainless steel. 13.7 m x 374 cm x 137.1 cm (45' x 12'3¼" x 4'6"). Centre Square Plaza, Fifteenth and Market Streets, Philadelphia, Pennsylvania.

▲ **Figure 8–11**   No one looks closely at a clothespin when hanging up laundry, but Oldenburg's design for a giant version was intended to demand attention.

Claes Oldenburg. *Late Submission to the Chicago Tribune Architectural Competition of 1922: Clothespin (Version Two).* 1967. Crayon, pencil, and watercolor on paper. 55.9 x 59 cm (22 x 23¼"). Des Moines Art Center. Partial purchase with funds from Gardner Cowles and gift of Charles Cowles, Des Moines Art Center Permanent Collection. 1972.11

WHAT YOU WILL NEED

- Sheets of scrap paper
- Sheet of white paper, 12 x 18 inch (30 x 46 cm)
- Pencil and ruler
- Colored pencils or fine-line markers

WHAT YOU WILL DO

1. Choose a theme for your gates. Make some rough sketches of designs that symbolize the theme. On scrap paper, do rough pencil sketches showing different possible outline shapes for the symmetrical gate. Choose your best design, and set it aside.
2. Do rough pencil sketches of possible designs within the shape of the gate. Will the interior part of the gate represent symmetrical or asymmetrical balance?
3. With a pencil, carefully develop your best idea. Use a ruler to make all the straight lines. (See Technique Tip 9, *Handbook* page **273**.)
4. Fill in the two sides of your gate with your best designs. Again, use the ruler when drawing straight lines. Remember that repeating symbols can produce harmony.
5. Using the colored pencils or markers, add color to your presentation drawing. Use color to help give balance to the design.
6. Display your work. Discuss different approaches to the assignment.

COMPUTER OPTION

Try This!

■ Design an entryway for your school or a public building. Use the Symmetry tool or menu and the small Brush tool to draw a balanced design. If the Symmetry option is not available, Select, Copy, Flip, and Paste parts of the design to create symmetry. Choose the Straight Line tool and Shape tools to add windows and doors. Include details that capture the mood or theme of the building—columns, pediments, sculptures, and ornaments. Title, Save, and Print your line drawing. Select colors and patterns. Use the Flood-fill tool to add color and texture to the presentation drawing. Retitle, Save, Print. Display with the black-and-white line drawing. Include a description of the place and purpose of the design.

LESSON 5

Fantasy Jungle

Look at the painting in Figure 8–13. It was done by Henri Rousseau (aan-**ree** roo-**soh**), a French painter famous for his imaginary jungles. The artist used real plants and other life forms as models in all his works.

WHAT YOU WILL LEARN

You will create your own imaginative fantasy jungle. You will study real leaves and plants as models for those in your work. Images of birds, animals, or reptiles will be based on photographs. You will do your finished work with oil pastels on colored construction paper. (See Figures 8–14 and 8–15.)

WHAT YOU WILL NEED

- Pencil and sheets of sketch paper or other plain white paper
- Sheet of colored construction paper, 12 x 18 inch (30 x 46 cm)

- White chalk and soft eraser
- Oil pastels

WHAT YOU WILL DO

1. With pencil on sketch paper, make detailed contour drawings of plants. These may be houseplants, flowers, or weeds.
2. On other sheets of sketch paper, make drawings of imaginary animals. They may be based on real birds, reptiles, and animals.
3. Using chalk, sketch the plan for your jungle on construction paper. Use the principles of harmony, informal balance, and emphasis. Pick a color of paper based on the mood your work will have. (Keep in mind differences of hue, intensity, and value.) Arrange your shapes and planned colors using informal balance. Keep other

▶ **Figure 8–13** The artist loved to spend time copying plants and animals from books. His finished works were a mixture of real-life images and images from his imagination. Which elements and techniques do you think give this painting the quality of a fantasy? Which ones display a sense of realism?

Henri Rousseau. *The Waterfall (La Cascade)*. 1910. Oil on canvas. 116.2 x 150.2 cm (45⅞ x 59"). Art Institute of Chicago. Helen Birch Bartlett Memorial Collection.

elements and principles, such as rhythm, in mind. As you draw, press lightly. That way, you will not tear the paper if you need to erase. Don't draw details so small that they can't be drawn with oil pastels.

4. **Color your jungle.** Use color contrast to create a strong center of interest or area of emphasis. Use different oil pastel drawing techniques. (See Technique Tip 3, *Handbook* page **271**.)

5. **Display your work.** Can you recognize what plants and animals your classmates used as models?

▲ Figure 8–14   **Student drawing of a fantasy jungle.**

EXAMINING YOUR WORK

- **Describe**   Identify the different plants in your fantasy jungle. Explain what real plants you used as sources. Explain what the imaginary animals were based on.
- **Analyze**   Show where you used informal balance to organize colors and shapes. Tell what principles you used to organize other elements.
- **Interpret**   Explain what kind of mood your work expresses. Tell what role background and foreground colors play in this mood. Tell whether your work has the look and feel of a fantasy jungle. Give your jungle a title.
- **Judge**   Tell whether you feel your work succeeds. Explain your answer.

▲ Figure 8–15   **Student drawing of a fantasy jungle.**

Try This!   COMPUTER OPTION

■ Choose the Pencil or small Brush tool and draw a very detailed leaf. Select, Copy, and Paste duplicates of the leaf to make a plant. Vary the sizes of the leaves and overlap them. Think of the mood of the jungle scene as you choose colors. Add harmonious colors to the leaves with the Flood-fill tool. Make other plants by using the same process—drawing one part, copying, then pasting. Include exotic flowers but select contrasting colors. Add animals, birds, or reptiles and accent the animals' patterns and textures. Invent imaginative patterns or select pre-programmed ones. Remember that it is not necessary to draw the whole animal to build interest and to make the forest look lush. Title, Save, and Print.

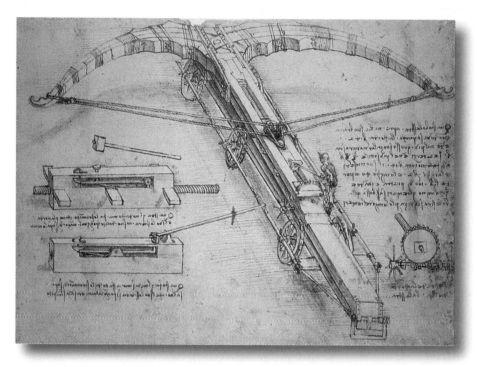

Leonardo da Vinci. *Giant Catapult.* c. 1499. Biblioteca Ambrosiana, Milan/Bridgeman Art Library, London. BAL22699

The Role of Sketches in Product Designs

Before the Industrial Revolution in the nineteenth century, craftspeople designed and created products by hand. Look at the device shown above. Imagine the time and skill required to make the catapult by hand! During the eighteenth century, the factory system and mass production replaced the handmade process. Then, in the beginning of the twentieth century, the art of industrial design was developed. This concept stressed that products should be both functional and attractive. It also emphasized products that were efficient, safe, and easy to use.

Today, industrial designers create products based on consumer needs. After studying competitive products, an industrial designer creates a design and draws sketches. When these sketches are approved, the designer creates a small model of the product as well as detailed working drawings.

Sketches have always been a useful way to present complex ideas. In the fifteenth century, Leonardo da Vinci drew sketches of his many inventions. His drawing on this page helps us understand how this machine would look and work once it was constructed.

MAKING THE CONNECTION

✔ How did the concept of industrial design help to improve consumer products in the twentieth century?

✔ Which drawing techniques did Leonardo da Vinci use to create the sketch shown on this page?

✔ Find out more about Leonardo da Vinci. What were some of the other inventions that he sketched?

INTERNET ACTIVITY

Visit Glencoe's Fine Arts Web Site for students at:

http://www.glencoe.com/sec/art/students

BUILDING VOCABULARY

Number a sheet of paper from 1 to 8. After each number, write the term from the list that best matches each description below.

blending   hatching
contour drawing perception
crosshatching   shading
gesture drawing stippling

1. The use of light and shadow to give a feeling of depth.
2. A shading technique using thin lines all running in the same direction.
3. A shading technique using lines that crisscross each other.
4. A shading technique in which dark values are added little by little.
5. A shading technique in which tiny black dots are accumulated.
6. Drawing lines quickly and loosely to show movement in a subject.
7. Drawing an object as though your drawing tool is touching the edge.
8. Awareness of the elements of the environment by means of the senses.

REVIEWING ART FACTS

Number a sheet of paper from 9 to 14. Answer each question in a complete sentence.

9. What are three main ways in which drawing is used by artists?

10. To an artist, how is looking at an object different from seeing it?
11. How does drawing help artists "see" better?
12. Name three ways in which drawing might be used to plan a project.
13. What is a name for the rough sketches an artist uses to plan a painting?
14. Name one place where drawings of finished works of art are used.

THINKING ABOUT ART

On a sheet of paper, answer each question in a sentence or two.

1. **Analyze.** Suppose someone said to you "I can't draw." How would you respond?
2. **Extend.** Why might the publishers of a book choose drawings rather than photographs as illustrations?
3. **Compare and contrast.** Which of the shading techniques you studied do you think gives the most realistic result? Which gives the least realistic result? Explain your answers.
4. **Interpret.** In what ways is using a rough or a thumbnail sketch similar to doing an outline for a piece of writing?
5. **Analyze.** Why do you think it is important to work quickly when doing gesture drawing? Why is it important to work slowly when doing contour drawing?

— MAKING ART CONNECTIONS

1. **Science.** Scientists rely on photographs and detailed drawings to record and learn about the natural world. They sketch from observation and include unique features of their subjects. Study the work of scientific illustrators shown in science books, field guides, and magazines to see the type of images they use. Would Rousseau's paintings be useful to scientists studying plant and animal forms? Why or why not?

2. **Social Studies.** Starting with a drawing of your house and school, make a contour map showing the pathway of a short imaginary journey you plan to make. Include pictorial images to represent important landmarks. Show where you turn and how many blocks or miles you travel.

▲ The artist made a series of 15 woodblock prints to show scenes from the Bible. Do you know the story of the Four Horsemen of the Apocalypse? Notice the small letter *D* inside an *A* at the bottom. Albrecht Dürer signed all his works in this way.

Albrecht Dürer. *The Four Horsemen of the Apocalypse.* 1498. Woodcut. 30.9 x 20.8 cm (12 x 8"). Reproduced by courtesy of the Trustees of the British Museum, London.

CHAPTER 9

Printmaking

Artists are curious innovators. They never tire of looking for new challenges—new ways to create. Study the picture at the left. Notice the attention the artist has paid to detail. Notice the fierce looks on the faces of the riders. Notice how the horses seem to gallop across the picture.

The work would be remarkable if the artist had drawn it. However, it was made using a technique far more technically involved than drawing with a pen or pencil. In this chapter you will learn more about the technique of printmaking and the media used in this process.

OBJECTIVES

After completing this chapter, you will be able to:

- Explain what printmakers do.
- Identify the three steps in printmaking.
- Name the four main methods for making prints and describe each of the methods.
- Make your own art work using different printmaking methods.

WORDS YOU WILL LEARN

brayer
edition
intaglio
lithograph
lithography
monoprinting
printing plate
printmaking
registration
relief printing
screen printing
serigraph

PORTFOLIO IDEAS

For your portfolio, choose two prints made in this chapter and write a comparison of the finished works. Include information about the printmaking technique used for each print. How did your choice of printmaking technique affect the final art work? Describe your use of the elements and principles of art. How well were you able to think in reverse? How many prints were made in each edition? Keep your writing with the prints in your portfolio.

The Art of Printmaking

When you think of printing, newspapers might come to your mind. But printing has its place in art, too. In art, printing, or **printmaking**, is *transferring an inked image from one prepared surface to another*. Often the surface to which a printed image is transferred is paper.

THE HISTORY OF PRINTMAKING

Printmaking is nearly 2000 years old. The Chinese were among the first people to make prints. Later the Japanese developed printmaking into a fine art. (See Figure 9–1.) The remarkable work on page **158** is a print made toward the end of the 1400s. The artist was a German named Albrecht Dürer (**ahl**-brekt **dure**-uhr).

▲ **Figure 9–1** **Do you think carving an image into wood may be more time consuming than painting it? What advantages do you think this artist may have seen in choosing wood as his medium?**

Katsushika Hokusai. *View of Mt. Fuji from Seven-Ri Beach.* 1823-29. Colored woodcut. 25.7 x 38.1 cm (10⅛ x 15″). Metropolitan Museum of Art, New York, New York. Rogers Fund.

Prints may be made with many different media and techniques. Dürer's print began as an image carved in a wooden block. Ink was applied to the block, which was then pressed onto a sheet of paper. With the invention of the printing press in 1438, block prints were used for book illustrations.

THE PRINTMAKING BASICS

All prints are made using three basic steps. These steps, in the order in which they take place, are:

- **Making a printing plate.** A **printing plate** is *a surface onto or into which the image is placed.* In making a plate, the artist makes a mirror image of the final print.
- **Inking the plate.** The artist applies ink. Often this is done with a **brayer,** *a roller with a handle.* For a multi-color print, one plate is made for each color called for in the final print.
- **Transferring the image.** The paper is pressed against the inked plate. Sometimes this is done by hand. At other times a printing press is used.

Usually more than one print is made from a given plate. *A group of identical prints all made from a single plate* is called an **edition.** The artist will determine how many prints are made in an edition.

Creating a Print Edition

As each print in an edition is made, the artist studies it carefully. Each one that meets with his or her approval is signed and numbered in pencil. The number has this form: 11/50. The number on the right tells how many prints are in the edition. The number on the left tells that this particular print is the eleventh print made.

When an edition has been completed, the artist cancels or destroys the plate. This is done by disfiguring the plate so it can no longer be used.

▲ **Figure 9–2** **This etching is one in a series of 10 prints that was inspired by Japanese woodblock prints. Notice the delicate graceful lines.**

Mary Cassatt. *The Bath.* 1891. Soft ground etching with aquatint and drypoint on paper. 31.4 x 24.5 cm (12⅜ x 9⅝"). National Museum of Women in the Arts, Washington, D.C. Gift of Wallace and Wilhelmina Holladay.

✔ CHECK YOUR UNDERSTANDING

1. Define the term *printmaking.*
2. Name the three basic steps of making a print.
3. What does the number that appears on a print mean?

LESSON 2
More About Printmaking

Printmaking is a popular art technique in today's world. Because prints are usually made in multiples, they are less expensive than paintings. People who might not be able to afford an original painting are often able to buy prints. Figure 9–3, a print by Edvard Munch, shows how stylized some prints can be.

PRINTMAKING

There are four main techniques artists use for making prints. They are relief printing, intaglio, lithography, and screen printing.

Relief Printing

You are probably already familiar with relief printing. If you have ever made a stamp print you have made a relief print. In **relief printing**, *the image to be printed is raised from a background* (Figure 9–4).

▶ **Figure 9–3   Does allowing the wood grain to show affect the feeling of the work? How? Does the title help you interpret the image?**

Edvard Munch. *The Kiss*. 1902. Woodcut, printed in grey and black, block. 46.7 x 46.4 cm (18⅜ x 18⁵⁄₁₆"). Museum of Modern Art, New York, New York. Gift of Abby Aldrich Rockefeller.

A popular medium in relief printing is carved wood. A print made by carving an image in a wooden block is called a woodcut. The print of the fierce riders on horseback on page **158** is a woodcut. Often woodcuts are done in color. When they are, a separate block, or plate, is made for each color. The blocks must be very carefully lined up during the printing process. If this is not done, the colors in the prints may overlap in the wrong places. This *careful matching up of plates in prints with more than one color* is called **registration**. How many blocks do you think were carved for the woodcut in Figure 9–3?

▲ Figure 9–4   This drawing shows a woodcut being made. In the upper left corner you will see a detail that shows where the ink contacts the paper during the printing process.

Intaglio

A second technique for making prints is, in a way, the reverse of relief printing. **Intaglio** (in-**tal**-yoh) is *a printmaking technique in which the image to be printed is cut or etched into a surface* (Figure 9–5), rather than being

▲ Figure 9–5   Look at the detail of the intaglio plate. How is it different from the woodcut detail?

raised from a background as in relief printing. In intaglio, paper is forced into the grooves that have been cut and scratched and which hold the ink. If you touch the surface of an intaglio print you can feel the buildup of the printmaking ink. One intaglio technique favored by many printmakers is engraving. In engraving, lines are scratched deep into a metal plate with an engraving tool.

Etching is another printing technique used by many artists. To make an etching, a metal printing plate is covered with a thin protective coating. The drawing is scratched through the coating with an etching needle. The plate is given an acid bath. The lines of the drawing are etched into the metal by the acid while the rest of the plate is protected by the protective covering.

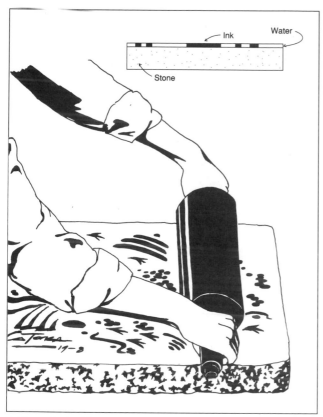

▲ **Figure 9–6** The illustration above shows a lithography stone as ink is being applied with a brayer.

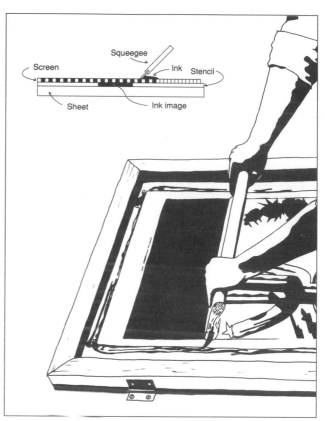

▲ **Figure 9–7** Notice the detail of a screen print. How does it differ from the other printing plate details shown in Figures 9–4, 9–5, and 9–6?

▲ **Figure 9–8** In this serigraph do you think some screens overlapped? Explain.

Doris Lee. *Untitled*. Serigraph on paper. 55.9 x 76.2 (22 x 30"). National Museum of Women in the Arts, Washington, D.C. Gift of Wallace and Wilhelmina Holladay.

Lithography

Have you ever noticed that grease and water don't mix? This fact is at the root of the printmaking technique called lithography. **Lithography** (lith-**ahg**-ruh-fee) is *a printmaking method in which the image to be printed is drawn on limestone, zinc, or aluminum with a special greasy crayon*. When the stone is dampened and then inked, the greased area alone holds the ink (Figure 9–6). Paper is pressed against the plate to make the print. *A print made by lithography* is called a **lithograph** (**lith**-uh-graf).

By using separate stones for each hue, lithographs may be printed in several colors. Lithography also allows the artist to use fine lines and blend values little by little.

Screen Printing

You have probably used lettering stencils at one time or another. The same basic idea is at work in **screen printing**, *a printmaking technique in which the artist transfers the design to the screen through various processes*. The area not to be printed is covered up with a special glue or sticky paper. (See Figure 9–7.) Ink is forced through the screen onto paper to make a print. *A screen print that has been handmade by an artist* is called a **serigraph** (**ser**-uh-graf).

Screen printing is the newest method for making prints. It was developed in the United States in this century.

To make a color serigraph, the artist makes one screen, or plate, for each color. Some serigraphs may have as many as 20 colors. How many colors can you find in the serigraph in Figure 9–8?

STUDIO ACTIVITY

Experimenting with Printmaking

One of the hardest tasks facing a printmaker is thinking backwards. The printing plate, you will recall, must be a mirror image of the final print.

Each student in the class is to select a different letter of the alphabet. Once you have chosen a letter, place a thin sheet of paper over a thick pad of newspaper. Pressing down hard, draw your letter on the thin sheet of paper. Turn the paper over, and you will see your letter in reverse. Using the image as a model, carve a stamp from a cube of modeling clay. Apply paint to your stamp with a brush. On a sheet of paper, make a pattern by pressing your stamp several times. Does each image in your pattern look the same, or do they differ? Does this make your pattern more or less interesting? Explain your answers.

P o r t f o l i o

On a separate sheet of paper, evaluate your stamp. Answer these questions: Does the stamp make the image I intended? What did I do well? What could I do better? How well did I carve the clay? Did I make a good mirror image? Keep the stamped patterns and your self-assessment together in your portfolio. Refer to it the next time you make a print.

✔ CHECK YOUR UNDERSTANDING

1. Name the four main techniques used for making prints.
2. Define the term *registration*.
3. Explain the difference between a lithograph and a serigraph.

Monoprints

Look at Figure 9–9. This is an example of a type of art print called a monoprint. **Monoprinting** is *a printmaking technique in which the image to be printed is put on the plate with ink or paint and then transferred to paper by pressing or hand-rubbing*. A monoprint plate can be used only once. The paint is absorbed into the paper, and the original image is gone.

WHAT YOU WILL LEARN

You will use a contour drawing process to make a monoprint drawing of a person. The image quality of the monoprint will help you understand the reversal process of printmaking. Create a mood within your work using the elements of line and color. The difference in line quality of a pencil line and a line made in a monoprint will become apparent. (See Figures 9–10 and 9–11.)

WHAT YOU WILL NEED

- Pencil and sheets of sketch paper
- Water-based printing ink
- Brayer
- Square of smooth vinyl flooring to be used as the printing plate
- Sheet of white paper the same size as or larger than the square of flooring

▶ **Figure 9–9   A monoprint is actually a blot. Rouault painted his clown and monkey on glass and then pressed paper on it.**

Georges Rouault. *Clown and Monkey.* 1910. Monotype, printed in color. 57.5 x 38.7 cm (22⅝ x 15¼"). The Museum of Modern Art, New York, New York. Gift of Mrs. Sam A. Lewisohn.

WHAT YOU WILL DO

1. Using pencil and sketch paper, make blind contour drawings of the model. When you are happy with your drawing, move on to the next step.
2. Squeeze ink onto the square of vinyl flooring. This is to be your printing plate. Spread the ink evenly with your brayer.
3. Place the sheet of white paper very lightly on your plate. Don't move it once it is down.
4. Supporting your hand so that it doesn't rest on the paper, use your pencil to draw a contour drawing that fills the paper. Be careful not to let anything but the pencil touch the paper. If a line looks wrong, draw it again. Do not, however, try to erase a line.
5. Starting at two corners, pull your paper carefully from the plate. Do not stop once you begin pulling. Place your paper, image side up, in a safe place to dry.
6. When the print has dried, display your work.

▲ Figure 9–10   Student work. A monoprint.

- **Describe**   Show where you used contour drawing to create an image of a person. Explain how the monoprint came out the reverse of your pencil drawing.
- **Analyze**   Explain how the quality of the monoprint line is different from a pencil line. Tell how you created contrast between the line of the print and the paper.
- **Interpret**   Tell what mood your work creates. Explain how the mood is different from one a simple line drawing would create.
- **Judge**   Tell whether you feel your work succeeds. Explain your answer.

▲ Figure 9–11   Student work. A monoprint.

Try This! STUDIO OPTIONS

■ Make an expressive drawing of a human head and face. Use a paper towel wrapped around your finger to draw this face on an inked plate. The removed ink will leave white lines on your print. Rub out solid areas for the cheeks, forehead, and chin. Make an impression of the print on a sheet of white paper.

■ Create a series of three expressive faces and repeat the steps listed above. Try the first print of the face. Check and make any corrections. When you are satisfied, continue with the other two drawings. Compare your prints to see if they work well as a series.

LESSON 4

Glue Prints

The techniques for making relief prints are almost endless. Did you know, for example, that you could make a printing plate from dried white glue? The work in Figure 9–12 was made using such a plate.

WHAT YOU WILL LEARN

You will make a printing plate from cardboard and dried glue. Lines and dots arranged in a radial design will be used. You will print an edition of three prints using water-based inks. Give your finished print a descriptive title.

▲ Figure 9–12   Student work. A glue print.

WHAT YOU WILL NEED

- White glue and newsprint
- Toothpicks and ruler
- Pencil and sheets of sketch paper
- Square of corrugated cardboard
- Water-based printing ink
- Brayer and vinyl floor square
- 3 sheets of white paper the same size or larger than the square of cardboard

WHAT YOU WILL DO

1. For practice, squeeze a thin line of glue onto a sheet of newsprint. You will notice that as it dries, it shrinks to form a line of fat dots. By pulling a toothpick from one to another, the dots can be connected again. This forms a new line. (See Figure 9–13.)
2. Using sketch paper, pencil, and ruler, plan a design with radial balance. Use straight lines and dots. Plan your design to fit your printing plate.
3. Transfer your design to the square of cardboard. Go over your lines with glue. Where your design shows lines, connect the shrinking dots to form them. Some lines may need a second coat of glue. When the glue has become clear, it is completely dry and the plate is ready to print.
4. Squeeze a small amount of ink onto a corner of the square of vinyl flooring. Roll your brayer into the ink, first in one direction, then in the other. Be sure that the brayer is well-coated and sticky with ink.
5. Transfer the ink to the cardboard print plate by rolling the brayer across your design in all directions.

6. With clean hands, place the sheet of white paper very lightly on your plate. Press it to the plate with the heel of your hand or a clean brayer. Pull the paper carefully from the plate. Set the print aside. If the plate is dry, add more ink. Make a second print, and then a third print.

7. When the prints are dry, use a pencil to write the title in the lower left corner of the white paper below the print. Sign your name in the lower right corner. In the center, record the number of the edition (3/3 means the third print in an edition of three).

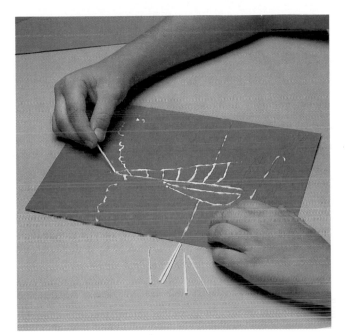

◄ Figure 9–13 The photo at the left shows the technique used to connect the dots as the glue dries.

- **Describe**   Point out the lines in your print and show what parts of the design were made with dots. Identify each print in the edition. Show where you signed and numbered each print.
- **Analyze**   Tell what kind of balance your design has. Explain how the drawing and glue print are different. Identify what is unusual about the lines and surface textures of the glue print.
- **Interpret**   Explain what your title tells others about your print. Describe what type of mood or feeling you hoped to express in your print.
- **Judge**   Tell whether you feel your work succeeds. Explain your answer.

Try This! COMPUTER OPTION

■ With a medium Brush tool, draw a plant, animal, bird, or fish that has rhythms or textures. Draw the object as large as possible on the screen. Choose a variety of tools such as the Shape, Pencil, Brush, or Bucket tool to add details and create rhythms. Include a background. Title, Save, and Print your work onto heavy stock paper. Follow the lines with glue. Allow to dry. Follow the printing directions in the Studio Lesson. If your printer will not accept thick paper, transfer a computer printout of the design to cardboard with carbon paper. Then, follow the lines with glue.

Linoleum Block Prints

Look at the print in Figure 9–14. This was done by the Spanish artist Pablo Picasso (**pah**-bloh pee-**kahs**-oh). The print was made from a relief carved in a section of linoleum. This material is softer than wood to cut. Notice the thin black lines in the gold area in the upper left corner. These show ridges left from cutting linoleum away in long strips. The artist has left them in to add to the visual interest of the work.

WHAT YOU WILL LEARN

You will create a linoleum block print using an animal as the subject. The main purpose of the print, however, will be to suggest a mood. You will use the elements of line and color to express this mood.

WHAT YOU WILL NEED

- Scrap pieces of linoleum
- Linoleum cutting tool with different sizes of blades
- Pencil and sheets of sketch paper
- Piece of linoleum, 4 x 6 inch (10 x 15 cm)
- Dark-colored marker and tape
- Carbon paper and crayon
- Inking plate and brayer
- Colored water-based printing inks
- Sheets of white paper

WHAT YOU WILL DO

1. Using a linoleum scrap, experiment with the different blades. Practice cutting thin lines and carving out large areas.
2. Using pencil and sketch paper, make rough sketches of an animal design. As you work, experiment with different moods. Remember that color and line can affect

▲ **Figure 9–14 Linoleum is softer than wood. This makes it easier to cut. Compare this work with the woodcut on page 158. What differences between the two types of print can you find?**

Pablo Picasso. *Seated Woman (After Cranach)*. 1958. Color linoleum cut, composition. 65.4 x 54.1 cm (25¹¹⁄₁₆ x 21⁵⁄₁₆″). Museum of Modern Art, New York, New York. Gift of Mr. & Mrs. Daniel Saidenberg.

mood. (See Chapter 4, Lessons 2 and 4.) Select the color ink you will use. Set aside your best design sketch.

3. Trace the outline of your linoleum block on a sheet of sketch paper. Draw your final design so that it touches all four edges of the block. Leave some shapes a solid color. Do not draw thin lines. Draw only the main lines of your animal face for now. You will add details later.

4. Hold your sketch up against a window. With a colored marker, trace over the lines you see through the page. (See Figure 9–15.) This will allow you to make a print that faces in the same direction as your drawing. Otherwise, you will end up with the mirror image of your design.

5. Place a piece of carbon paper on the linoleum. Place your design face down over the carbon paper. Trace over the lines with a pencil. Lift a corner of the carbon paper to be sure the image is transferring to the block. To keep the paper from slipping, tape the paper down.

6. Using the colored marker, color in all the areas on the linoleum that will not be cut away.

7. Using different blades, cut away the background. Remember that the background ridges can add interest to your print. As you cut, stop from time to time and make a crayon rubbing of your plate. This will help you identify areas that need further cutting.

8. Squeeze out some ink on the inking plate, and load the brayer. Roll the brayer over the linoleum block. Place the printing paper carefully on the block, and press the paper to the plate by rubbing it by hand or running it through a press.

9. Make an edition of five prints. Sign and number your prints and display one of them.

EXAMINING YOUR WORK

- **Describe**   Point out the details you used to give the idea of an animal. Identify the details you included in the background. Explain why you used these details.
- **Analyze**   Note which kinds of lines (horizontal, vertical, diagonal) and colors (warm, cool, dark, light) you used.
- **Interpret**   Identify the mood of your print. Explain how the lines and colors you used helped to express this mood.
- **Judge**   Tell whether you feel your work succeeds. Explain your answer.

▲ Figure 9–15   Student work. A linoleum print.

Try This! COMPUTER OPTION

■ Explore Brush shapes and sizes. Then draw an expressive animal. Recall how the qualities of line affect mood. Combine thick, thin, smooth, and broken lines to add details, textures, and background. Fill the page. Title, Copy, and Print. Transfer your black line drawing to a linoleum block. Follow directions in the Studio Lesson for cutting and printing.

LESSON 6

Cardboard Relief Prints

Relief printing is a method in which raised areas make the design or picture to be printed. The areas recessed from the surface will not print when the plate is inked with a roller. It is the oldest method of printing and included all types of block printing. Woodcuts, wood engravings, and linoleum blocks are the most familiar forms of relief printing. See page **163** for a picture showing how a woodcut is made, and then examine the silk screen print by Henry Napartuk in Figure 9–16.

WHAT YOU WILL LEARN

You will make a relief print of a non-objective design using a cardboard printing plate. To do this, you will glue a variety of large and small, geometric and organic cardboard shapes to the surface of a cardboard plate. You will then print an edition of three prints and number each in the manner described in Lesson 1 on page **161**.

WHAT YOU WILL NEED

- Pencil, sketch paper, and ruler
- Cardboard box, such as a shoe box, shirt box, or illustration board
- Utility knife or scissors
- White glue
- Water-based printing mix
- Brayer
- Sheets of white drawing paper, 10 x 12 inches (25 x 30 cm)

WHAT YOU WILL DO

1. Using your pencil, ruler, and utility knife or scissors, measure and cut a 5 x 7 inch (13 x 17 cm) square from a piece of cardboard to serve as your plate.
2. Trace the cut piece of cardboard several times on sheets of sketch paper. Within these drawn rectangles, draw a variety of large and small, geometric and organic shapes. Try to create interesting shapes and combinations of shapes.

▶ **Figure 9–16 A stencil was placed over silk before ink was rubbed through it to make this print.**

Henry Napartuk. *Eskimo and Beluga.* Alaska. 20th Century. Silk screen print on paper. 15.2 x 22.9 cm (6 x 9″). Mingei International Museum of World Folk Art, San Diego, California. Gift of Anna Saulsberry.

3. Select your best design and cut out the shapes. Lay these on a piece of cardboard and use your pencil to trace around the edges. Then cut out each cardboard shape.

4. Arrange your shapes on the cardboard plate to create your design and glue them in place. You are now ready to ink your plate.

5. Select a color of printing ink, squeezing some onto a separate surface, and roll it out with a brayer. When the brayer is fully coated with ink, carefully roll it over the surface of your plate.

6. Place a piece of white drawing paper on top of your inked plate and press down firmly with your hands to force the ink onto the paper. Be careful not to move the plate or the paper. When pressure has been evenly applied over the entire surface of the paper, gently pull it off. Set it aside and make a second and third print.

7. With a pencil, sign and number each print in your edition. Remember to give your edition a title.

EXAMINING YOUR WORK

- **Describe**   How many shapes did you use in your non-objective design? Did you use both geometric and organic shapes?
- **Analyze**   Did you use a variety of large and small shapes? Do you think the element of texture plays an unplanned role in your finished work?
- **Interpret**   Explain how you arrived at the title for your print edition. Do you think this title is a good one? Explain your answer.
- **Judge**   Do you think your work is visually interesting? Why or why not? If you were to do another non-objective relief print, what would you do to improve on this one?

▲ Figure 9–17   Student work. Cardboard relief print.

STUDIO OPTIONS

Try This!

■ Experiment using several different colors for the shapes in your non-objective design. Print these on white drawing paper as well as different colors of construction paper.

■ Scan your printed image into a computer Draw or Paint program and make a poster announcing an upcoming school event.

Lesson 6   *Cardboard Relief Prints*   **173**

Preserving the Natural World Through Art

John James Audubon. *The Mocking Bird.* Robert Havell, engraver. 1827. Hand-colored engraving with aquatint from *The Birds of America,* Plate XXI. National Gallery of Art, Washington, D.C. Gift of Mrs. Walter B. James. © 1996 Board of Trustees.

Have you ever seen a drawing or photograph of an animal that is extinct? Dinosaurs, for example, have been extinct for thousands of years. Through art, however, we are able to see what they looked like. All animals, plants, and other living things change over time and sometimes become extinct. Artists help us preserve and remember these inhabitants of the natural world by capturing single moments of their lives.

John James Audubon was an artist well known for his drawings of American wildlife. Audubon's approach to art was very detailed and scientific. In fact, his drawings were so realistic that many people mistook them for photographs! Although Audubon was devoted to studying all natural history, he was especially interested in American birds. In 1838, Audubon completed work on his masterpiece, *The Birds of America.* The book contained hand-colored paintings of more than 1,000 birds. Audubon and a co-author also wrote a companion book that described the birds depicted in Audubon's paintings.

The Mocking Bird on this page is a print of an Audubon drawing. After Audubon created the piece, another artist engraved it. Then it was turned into a print, making it accessible to a larger number of people.

MAKING THE CONNECTION

- How does Audubon's artistic style add to the tension in *The Mocking Bird*?
- How has Audubon preserved nature in this art work?
- Find out more about John James Audubon. What society was named after him? What is the purpose of the society?

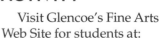

INTERNET ACTIVITY

Visit Glencoe's Fine Arts Web Site for students at:

http://www.glencoe.com/sec/art/students

REVIEW

 BUILDING VOCABULARY

Number a sheet of paper from 1 to 12. After each number, write the term from the list that best matches each description below.

brayer	printing plate
edition	printmaking
intaglio	registration
lithograph	relief printing
lithography	screen printing
monoprinting	serigraph

1. The art of transferring an inked image from a prepared surface to another surface.
2. The surface onto which an image is placed.
3. A roller with a handle.
4. A group of identical prints all made from a single plate.
5. A technique in which the image to be printed is raised from the background.
6. The careful matching of plates in prints with more than one color.
7. A technique in which the image to be printed is cut or scratched into a surface.
8. A technique in which the image to be printed is drawn on limestone with a special crayon.
9. A print made by lithography.
10. A technique in which the image to be printed is drawn on a screen made of silk.
11. A screen print that has been handmade by an artist.
12. A technique in which the image to be printed is put on the plate with ink or paint and then transferred to paper by pressing or hand-rubbing.

 REVIEWING ART FACTS

Number a sheet of paper from 13 to 18. Answer each question in a complete sentence.

13. What is inking? What tool is often used in inking?
14. What is meant by the numbers an artist writes on each print in an edition?
15. How does an artist "cancel a plate"?
16. What is a woodcut? What method of printmaking is used to make a woodcut?
17. Name one type of intaglio printing.
18. Which printmaking technique gives an edition size or number as 1?

 THINKING ABOUT ART

On a sheet of paper, answer each question in a sentence or two.

1. **Analyze.** What reasons might artists have for canceling a plate at the end of an edition?
2. **Summarize.** Why is being able to "think backwards" important to a printmaker?
3. **Extend.** What problems might there be in making a glue print with an edition of 500?

MAKING ART CONNECTIONS

1. **Social Studies.** Look at the colored woodcut by Hokusai on page **160.** Mount Fuji, a volcano in Japan, appears in many works by Hokusai and other Japanese artists. Look for other art works by Japanese artists showing volcanoes, water, and islands and share them with the class. Why do you think these images play such an important part in Japanese works of art?
2. **Science.** The printmaking technique called lithography is based on the fact that oil and water do not mix. What other substances don't mix? Find out why.

▲ Can you feel the heat of the sun as you look at this painting? How did the artist's choice of strong, bright oil paints help create that feeling?

Walter Ufer. *The Callers.* c. 1926. Oil on canvas. 128.4 x 128.4 (50½ x 50½"). National Museum of American Art, Smithsonian Institution, Washington, D.C. / Art Resource, New York.

CHAPTER 10

Painting

The goal of writers is to make their words speak to the reader. The goal of artists is to make their images "speak" to the viewer. Look at Ufer's painting at the left. Read the credit line and notice the media used. Can you identify the hues in the art work? Has the artist used any neutral colors? Has he changed the value of any hues? What is the significance of the title?

In this chapter you will learn about the many different techniques painters use. You will learn to use some of those techniques yourself.

PORTFOLIO IDEAS

Select one painting you made from this chapter for your portfolio. Evaluate it by answering the following questions:

- Did I meet the requirements of the assignment?
- How well did I use the elements and principles of art in this work?
- How does my choice of painting medium affect the finished art work?
- What do I like best about this work?
- What improvements would I make next time?

Date this entry and store it in your portfolio with your print. In the future, review it to see how you have grown as an artist.

OBJECTIVES

After completing this chapter, you will be able to:
- Name the basic ingredients of paint.
- Describe six important painting media.
- Make paintings using watercolors, school tempera, and school acrylic.

WORDS YOU WILL LEARN

acrylic
binder
encaustic
fresco
glaze
impasto
oil paint
opaque
palette
pigment
solvent
synthetic paints
tempera
transparent
watercolor

The Art of Painting

Most artists have stories about their first experiences with paint. They tell of blending beautiful, brilliant colors—and of ending up with a muddy mess! They tell of learning little by little how to make paints "behave."

In this lesson you will learn some of their secrets. You will learn to speak about color using the language of art.

THE HISTORY OF PAINTING

Do you remember reading about cave paintings in Chapter 4? Figure 4–1 on page **54** shows one such painting. Works like these date back as far as 15,000 B.C. Humans have been painting for nearly 17,000 years!

In the time since, many paint media and methods have been discovered. A large number of them are still in use.

PAINTING MEDIA

The basis of all paintings is, of course, the paint. Paint, you will recall, has three parts:

- **Pigment** is *a finely ground powder that gives every paint its color*.
- **Binder** is *a liquid that holds together the grains of pigment*.
- **Solvent** is *a material used to thin the binder*.

Every painting medium has its own unique quality. The best-known of these media are encaustic, fresco, tempera, oil paint, acrylic, and watercolor.

Encaustic

Some of the early paintings by the ancient Greeks and Romans were done using **en-caustic** (in-**kaw**-stik), *a painting medium in which pigment is mixed into melted wax*. The wax, which is the binder, is kept liquid by heat. Heat is the "solvent." Works that are painted with encaustic seem to glow with light.

Fresco

Another technique of applying paint, which also was developed long ago, is the one called fresco. **Fresco** (**fres**-koh) is *a painting medium in which pigment is applied to a wall spread with wet plaster*. The fresh plaster is applied to a small area of a wall and water-based pigments are painted quickly on the wet plaster. The paint bonds with the plaster, and when the plaster dries, the painting is part of the wall.

In fresco painting, the plaster itself is the binder. Water is the solvent. Fresco painting was refined by Italian Renaissance painters and "rediscovered" in this century by Mexican mural painters (Figure 10–1).

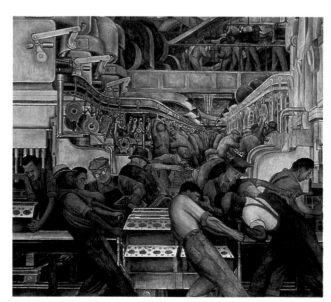

▲ **Figure 10–1** This detail is one part of a large mural. Notice how the artist used large movements of people and machines in his fresco.

Diego Rivera. *Detroit Industry*. 1923–33. Fresco. North wall central panel. (Detail.) Founders Society, Detroit Institute of the Arts, Detroit.

▲ Figure 10–2   Why do you think this artist chose tempera as his medium? How might this same image differ if he had used watercolor?

Andrew Wyeth. *Christina's World*. 1948. Tempera on gessoed panel. (Detail.) 81.9 x 121.3 cm (32¼ x 47¾"). The Museum of Modern Art, New York, New York. Purchase.

▲ Figure 10–3   What is the visual texture of this work? How do you think the artist's application of oil paint contributes to its realism?

Lavinia Fontana. *Portrait of a Noblewoman*. c. 1580. Oil on canvas. (Detail.) 115.6 x 89.5 cm (45½ x 35¼"). National Museum of Women in the Arts, Washington, D.C. Gift of Wallace and Wilhelmina Holladay.

Tempera

Another very old medium is **tempera** (**tem**-puh-ruh), *a painting medium in which pigment mixed with egg yolk and water is applied with tiny brush strokes*. Tempera does not spread easily or blend well. Because of this, **transparent**, or *clear*, layers of color must be built up little by little. This can take time. Once dry, tempera is waterproof.

Tempera allows a painter to capture the details of a subject. Look at the portion of a painting, or detail, in Figure 10–2. Note how the artist shows highlights in the hair and in the individual blades of grass.

Notice, by the way, that this use of tempera is not the same medium as the tempera paint you use in school. The paint you use in your work is a poster paint.

Oil Paint

Oil paint is *paint with an oil base*. Oil paint was first used in the 1400s and has continued to be one of the most popular mediums used today.

Linseed oil is the binder for oil paint, and its solvent is turpentine. Oil paint dries slowly. This allows artists to blend colors right on the canvas.

Oil paint can be applied in *thick, buttery layers*, called **impasto** (im-**pahs**-toh), to make interesting textures. When applied thickly, oil paint is opaque. **Opaque** (oh-**pake**) means *that it does not let light pass through*. It can also be applied in a *thin, transparent layer*, called a **glaze**. A glaze allows dry color underneath to show through. Some painters make their works glow with light by building up layers of glaze. Look at Figure 10–3. Notice how the artist has blended the colors of the face so that they seem to melt together.

Watercolor

Once used only for sketches, watercolor has become a favorite medium of serious painters. **Watercolor** is *a painting medium in which pigment is blended with gum arabic and water*. Watercolor takes its name from its solvent. For the best results, watercolors are applied to good quality white paper. Blended colors are usually mixed on a palette before painting. A **palette** can be *any tray or plate where paints are mixed before use*. A white palette allows you to see what new mixed hues will look like against white paper before painting. A piece of white scrap paper can also be used to test colors for value and intensity before painting on good quality paper.

Watercolor can give a light, misty feel to paintings or they can be intense and brilliant.

Look at Figure 10–4. The artist, Winslow Homer, was among the first to use watercolor in finished works. Notice the amount of white paper he allows to show through. How do you think this affects the look of the work?

Acrylic

Advances in technology in the twentieth century have given artists new media choices. **Synthetic paints** are *manufactured paints with plastic binders*. They came onto the scene in the 1930s. The first artist to use a synthetic paint was a Mexican mural painter. His name was David Alfaro Siqueiros (dah-**veed** al-**far**-oh see-**care**-ohs). Figure 10–5 shows a detail from one of Siqueiros's early experiments. The work was done with quick-drying duco (**doo**-koh) paint.

▲ Figure 10–4   Can you tell where the artist has allowed the white paper to show through? How does this technique affect the mood of the painting?

Winslow Homer. *Bermuda Sloop.* Watercolor on paper. (Detail.) 38.1 x 54.6 cm (15 x 21½"). The Metropolitan Museum of Art, New York, New York. Amelia B. Lazarus Fund, 1910. 10.228.3

▲ Figure 10–5   Do you find the look on this child's face troubling? Why? How do you think the medium helped the artist capture this mood?

David Alfaro Siqueiros. *Echo of a Scream.* 1937. Enamel on wood. 121.9 x 91.4 cm (48 x 36"). The Museum of Modern Art, New York, New York. Gift of Edward M. M. Warburg.

One of the most widely used paints today is acrylic (uh-**kril**-ik), *a quick-drying water-based synthetic paint.* Acrylic paint first appeared in the 1950s. Not only does acrylic offer the artist a wide range of pure, intense colors (Figure 10–6) but it also is versatile. Like oil paint, it can be applied both thickly and in thin glazes. Acrylic paints can even be thinned enough to be sprayed in a mist with an airbrush. Acrylic is less messy to use than oil paint because the solvent used for acrylic paint is water.

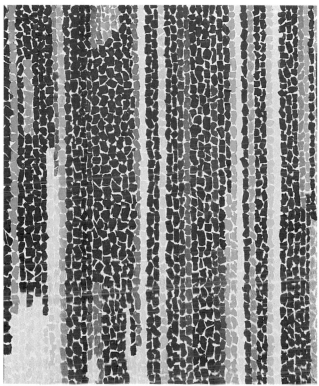

▲ **Figure 10–6** **The strong colors in the bands move up and down as well as across. Can you imagine a breeze moving across a sunlit garden when you look at this painting?**

Alma Thomas. *Iris, Tulips, Jonquils and Crocuses.* 1969. Acrylic on canvas. 152.4 x 127 cm (60 x 50"). National Museum of Women in the Arts, Washington, D.C. Gift of Wallace and Wilhelmina Holladay.

STUDIO ACTIVITY

Experimenting with Painting Media

Gather as many different kinds of paint of one hue as you can. For example, look for red watercolor, red poster paint, and red acrylic. Draw several shapes on a sheet of white paper. Draw one shape for each paint. Paint each shape with a different kind of paint. Display your results alongside those of your classmates. Discuss differences and similarities among the different paints. Compare the texture, intensity, value, and reflective quality of each paint.

Portfolio

Design a painting of one hue with the three different kinds of paint that you have sampled. Focus on subject and composition in your painting. When it is complete, write a brief evaluation of your art work using the four steps of art criticism. Keep your painting and your written self-assessment in your portfolio

✔ CHECK YOUR UNDERSTANDING

1. What are the three main parts of paint?
2. How is encaustic different from fresco? How is it different from tempera?
3. How is oil paint different from watercolor? How is it different from acrylic?
4. What is impasto? What is a glaze?
5. What is a synthetic paint? When did synthetic paints first appear?

Watercolor Painting

Look at the painting in Figure 10–7 by the artist Dong Kingman. He has captured a day in the life of an American city. Do you know what city it is? Is this just an ordinary day? How can you tell?

Take another look at the painting. What kind of paint did the artist use to create this work? What is unusual about his use of white paper?

▲ **Figure 10–7** What is the mood of this work? How does the medium help set the mood? How does the artist's attention to small details help?

Dong Kingman. *Cable Car Festival.* 1988. Watercolor on paper. 76.2 x 55.9 cm (30 x 22"). Conacher Gallery San Francisco.

WHAT YOU WILL LEARN

You will make a watercolor painting in the style of Dong Kingman. The subject will be a festival that includes people and a setting. Pick an event similar to the one in Figure 10–7. Use bright colors to emphasize some part of the event in which people are having fun. Use lines and color to create a feeling of excitement. You will leave areas of your work unpainted.

WHAT YOU WILL NEED

- Pencil and sheets of sketch paper
- Watercolor paints
- Palette for mixing colors
- Container for water
- Thin and thick watercolor brushes
- Sheet of good quality white paper, pressed board, or watercolor paper, 12 x 18 inch (30 x 46 cm)
- Paper towels

WHAT YOU WILL DO

1. Brainstorm with your classmates to develop ideas for your work. Choose a festive occasion that is important to you, your school, or your community. Think of the particular part of the festival that represents the excitement. Think of special colors tied to the occasion and how those colors add to the festive mood.
2. Make pencil sketches to plan your work. Use line movements to create excitement. Choose your best idea.
3. Remember to set up all your supplies before you begin. Watercolor is a quick-drying medium.
4. Mix a light value of a watercolor paint on your palette. (You create light values with watercolors by adding more water to the

▲ Figure 10–8   Student work. A watercolor painting.

color you choose. This will allow more white from the paper to show through.) With the thin brush, draw your final sketch onto the sheet of good white paper. (See Technique Tip **4**, *Handbook* page **271**.)

(See Technique Tip **4**, *Handbook* page **271**.)

EXAMINING YOUR WORK

- **Describe**   Identify the festive occasion you chose to paint. Tell what part of the event you focused on. Tell what colors and kinds of lines you used.
- **Analyze**   Point to areas in which bright colors are used. Explain how these colors emphasize these areas. Explain how you created contrast.
- **Interpret**   Tell what words a viewer might use to describe the mood of your painting. Explain how color and line are used to create this mood. Give your work a title based on its mood.
- **Judge**   Tell whether you feel your work succeeds. What views of art would you use to defend your answer?

5. Decide which area of your work you will emphasize and paint this area with your brightest colors. Paint other areas in contrasting dull colors. Leave large areas of the white paper showing. Do not paint in all your drawn objects. If you like, draw over some of your light lines with darker paint with a thin brush.
6. When your work is dry, display it. Discuss various ways classmates have achieved contrast and shown excitement using line and color.

Try This! COMPUTER OPTION

■ Select a festival or celebration to paint. Use the Pencil tool to make a sketch. Explore a variety of wet Brushes, transparent colors, and liquid effects. Choose smooth or rough paper, if available. Draw active lines to enhance the mood of the festivity. Apply bright colors directly by using a variety of Brushes.

Leave some spaces white or off-white to make the painting lighter in value.

Notice how Kingman included comedy in his work with the little mice in the lower right corner. Include a small, unexpected detail in your painting to create humor. Title, Save, and Print.

LESSON 3

Non-objective Painting

Look at the painting in Figure 10–9. The artist, Sonia Delaunay, believed color was the most important art element. With her artist-husband, Robert, she explored the expressive quality of color. Notice the rhythmic movement of the shapes along diagonal lines. Notice also the soft edges of the shapes.

WHAT YOU WILL LEARN

You will make a painting that, like Delaunay's, is made up of the repetition of geometric shapes. Also like hers, yours will show rhythmic movement. You will use a primary- or secondary-color scheme. The background will be painted in black. (See Figure 10–10.)

WHAT YOU WILL NEED

- Pencil, sketch paper, and ruler
- Round shapes of different sizes, such as jar lids, or pre-cut cardboard patterns
- Paper towels
- Yellow chalk
- White paper, 12 x 18 inch (30 x 46 cm)
- Tempera paints, thin and thick brushes

▶ **Figure 10–9 Does your eye start at the top of this painting or at the bottom? Is the beat of the work a fast one or a slow one? Explain your answers.**

Sonia Delaunay. *Colored Rhythm No. 698*. 1958. Oil on canvas. 114.3 x 87 cm (45 x 34¼"). Albright Knox Art Gallery, Buffalo, New York. Gift of Seymour H. Knox.

WHAT YOU WILL DO

1. Using pencil and sketch paper, plan your work. Using the ruler, draw a diagonal line across the paper from top to bottom. With the ruler, make squares and/or rectangles so that their sides rest on the diagonal. Use the circle patterns to make a series of circular shapes in different sizes. These should meet and cross the lines of the four-sided shapes. Repeating the different shapes will give a feeling of rhythm and movement to the design.

2. Using yellow chalk, draw your design on the sheet of white paper. Use the ruler and circle pattern. The edges of your shapes do not have to be perfect. Draw your design so that it touches at least three sides of the paper.

3. Choose a primary- or secondary-color scheme for the work. You may also use white. Repeat your colors in a way that adds to the sense of rhythmic movement.

4. Using the thin brush, paint the outline of each shape. Switch to the thick brush to fill in each shape with the same color you used for its outline. Since poster paints will run, be sure that one shape is dry before you paint a wet color next to it. (For more on using poster paints, see Technique Tip **13**, Handbook page **275**.)

5. When your work is dry, display it along with those made by other members of the class. Do any of the paintings look like yours? Are some completely different?

- **Describe** Identify the diagonal line that organizes the shapes in your work. Point out and name the different geometric shapes you used. Explain which color scheme you chose.
- **Analyze** Tell what colors and shapes you repeated to create rhythmic movement. Tell whether the "beat" of your work is steady or irregular. Show the path the viewer's eye follows through your work. Explain how you created contrast.
- **Interpret** Tell what mood your work expresses. Give your work a title based on this mood.
- **Judge** Tell whether you feel your work succeeds. Explain your answer.

▶ Figure 10–10 Student work. Non-objective painting.

COMPUTER OPTION

■ Choose the Straight Line tool and hold down the Shift key to draw two or three straight diagonal lines that intersect and touch the edges of the paper. Select geometric Shape tools and create a pattern by repeating the shapes using the Copy and Paste tools. Use the Transformation menu to Flip or Rotate the shapes. Title and Save. Use the Flood-fill tool to add primary and secondary colors to all open spaces. Retitle, Save, and Print.

LESSON 4

Expressive Painting

Sometimes artists use their works to speak about issues and social problems of the day. Look at the painting in Figure 10–11 called *Differing Views*. It was done in the early 1980s by a contemporary artist. Study the two people in the painting. What do their expressions and their position within the room tell you about what might just have happened in this scene? What do you think will happen next?

What statement about human relationships might the artist be making in this work? Which elements and principles has he chosen to punctuate his statement?

WHAT YOU WILL LEARN

You will learn to use social issues as content for a work of art. A social statement can be subject matter for art works. Select a social issue that faces the world today. You will paint a close-up view of people to illustrate this issue. Colors and heavy lines will be used to emphasize the mood of your work. Distorting the proportions of shapes will also add to this mood. Free-flowing, loose brush strokes will be used to show movement and add texture. (See Figure 10–12.)

WHAT YOU WILL NEED

- Pencil and sheets of sketch paper
- School acrylic paints
- Shallow tray with sides to mix paints
- Water (as a solvent)
- Bristle brushes, varied sizes
- Sheet of heavy white paper, 12 x 18 inch (30 x 46 cm)
- Water (to clean brushes) and paper towels

▶ **Figure 10–11 Would you describe the mood of this painting as happy or lonely? How does the artist help you feel that mood? How does the medium help?**

James Robert Valerio. *Differing Views.* 1980–1981. Oil on canvas. 234.3 x 261 cm (92¼ x 103¾"). Courtesy of George Adams Gallery, New York.

WHAT YOU WILL DO

1. Brainstorm with your classmates, and list social issues of the day. Some possibilities include pollution, teenage pregnancy, drug abuse, the homeless, and acid rain. Choose one that you know about and that truly concerns you.
2. Think about a way that you can create a painting that will make people think about the problem. How can you show its effect on people?
3. Make several pencil sketches for your composition. Use distortion and exaggeration to make your message strong. This is a painting, not a poster. Do not put any words in balloons for your people to speak. The visual image must carry the message. Select the best sketch.
4. Decide on a color scheme. Think about what colors will help express your feelings. How can you use strong contrast?
5. Pour a little of a light-value paint into the shallow tray. Add enough solvent to make a thin paint. Using your 1/4-inch (0.6-cm) brush draw the main shapes of your work on the sheet of white paper.
6. Paint your composition. Using your 1-inch (2.5-cm) brush, add deeper hues to the shapes. Do not try to smooth over the brush strokes. Let them show movement and create different textures. Use strong colors to emphasize the outlines of your shapes.
7. Put your work on display. Can you and your classmates read the themes in each others' statements?

EXAMINING YOUR WORK

- **Describe**   Identify the person or persons in your work. Tell what problem you chose to speak about. Tell what statement you decided to make. Identify the colors and lines used. Identify places where different textures are used.
- **Analyze**   Point to places where free-flowing, loose brushstrokes are used to show movement. Explain how the heavy lines and brush strokes add to the distortion, exaggeration, and contrast. Show where the proportions of shapes have been distorted.
- **Interpret**   Tell what mood your painting expresses. Explain how the colors you chose help express this mood. Tell how distortion adds to the mood. Give your work a title that sums up its meaning.
- **Judge**   Tell whether you feel your work succeeds in making a social statement. Tell whether it succeeds as a work of art. Explain your answers.

▶ Figure 10–12   **Student work. An expressive painting.**

Try This!

STUDIO OPTIONS

■ Carry out this project combining magazine cutouts and paint.

■ Choose one hue, and paint your work using a monochromatic color scheme.

Claude Monet. *The Water Lily Pond.* 1904. Oil on canvas. 88 x 91.4 cm (34⅝ x 36"). Denver Art Museum. The Helen Dill Collection.

How Does Light Affect What You See?

Could you see the painting above if you were in a pitch black room? Of course not! In order for humans to see, a light source must be present. We can see an object only if light travels from its source, to an object, and then to our eyes.

The appearance of objects depends on what happens when light strikes the objects. We can see through transparent objects, for example, because light passes through them. Clear glass is transparent. With opaque objects, however, we can see only the surface of the objects because light cannot pass through them. Instead, the light is either absorbed or reflected. A wooden desk is an example of an opaque object. With translucent objects, some light passes through. The light is scattered, however, so that the images behind the objects are only partially visible. Frosted glass is translucent.

The effect of light on objects has always been a source of fascination to painters, especially Impressionist painters. In *The Water Lily Pond*, the painting shown above, Claude Monet used dabs of paint to create the effect of sunlight dancing on the flowers and reflecting on the water's surface.

MAKING THE CONNECTION

- ✔ What is the difference between transparent and translucent objects?
- ✔ Which term—transparent, opaque, or translucent—describes Monet's painting? How does the medium of oil paint affect the way you see the colors he used?
- ✔ Find out more about Impressionist painters. Why were they called Impressionists? Name three other Impressionists besides Monet.

INTERNET ACTIVITY

Visit Glencoe's Fine Arts Web Site for students at:

http://www.glencoe.com/sec/art/students

REVIEW

BUILDING VOCABULARY

Number a sheet of paper from 1 to 15. After each number, write the term from the list that best matches each description below.

acrylic	palette
binder	pigment
encaustic	solvent
fresco	synthetic paints
glaze	tempera
impasto	transparent
oil paint	watercolor
opaque	

1. A finely ground powder that gives every paint its color.
2. A liquid that holds together the grains of pigment.
3. A material used to thin the binder in paint.
4. A medium in which pigment is mixed into melted wax.
5. A medium in which pigment is applied to a wall spread with wet plaster.
6. A medium in which pigment mixed with egg yolk and water is applied with tiny brush strokes.
7. Paint with an oil base.
8. Thick, buttery layers of paint.
9. Clear.
10. A thin, clear sheet of paint.
11. A painting medium in which pigment is blended with gum arabic and water.
12. Manufactured paints with plastic binders.
13. Quick-drying water-based synthetic paint.
14. Does not allow light to pass through.
15. Light colored tray where paints are mixed before they are used for painting.

REVIEWING ART FACTS

Number a sheet of paper from 16 to 20. Answer each question in a few words.

16. What are the three parts of paint? What is the purpose of each part?
17. What is the solvent in encaustic? In fresco?
18. Why is tempera paint hard to use? What is an advantage of using it?
19. What fact about oil paint allows an artist to blend colors on the canvas?
20. Name two different techniques for applying oil paint. Tell what kind of results you get with each technique.

? THINKING ABOUT ART

On a sheet of paper, answer each question in a sentence or two.

1. **Interpret.** What sort of paint do you think cave dwellers used to make their paintings? What sorts of tools do you think they painted with? Explain your answers.
2. **Analyze.** Do you think encaustic was an easy medium to use? Why or why not?
3. **Compare and contrast.** Name some problems of creating frescoes that would not be true of other painting techniques.

MAKING ART CONNECTIONS

1. **Language Arts.** Look again at *Echo of a Scream* on page **180**. Then write about a time when you felt like screaming. Use details and vivid, colorful words to describe how you felt. You might also describe seeing someone else scream.

2. **Science.** Stare at a bright shape for a minute and then look away. What do you see? It's called an afterimage, and it has the same shape and size as the one you stared at, but a different color. Read about this illusion, or ask your science teacher to help you find information, then share what you learn with the class.

▲ This artist was very careful about his work. He was even known to go into the print shops and mix his own colors.

Henri de Toulouse-Lautrec. *Jane Avril*. 1899. Color lithograph. 68.3 x 47 cm (26⅞ x 18½"). Philadelphia Museum of Art. Given by Mr. and Mrs. R. Sturgis Ingersoll.

CHAPTER 11

Graphic Design

Artists, as you have seen, work and create in many different areas. Some artists paint. Others draw or sculpt. Others make prints.

The poster at the left is an example of yet another area in which artists work. This poster was done by a famous French painter, Henri de Toulouse-Lautrec. He was the first artist to create posters for commercial use. Most of his posters were used to advertise musical performances.

Artists working in commercial art use various art media and techniques to communicate their messages. In this chapter you will learn about this field.

OBJECTIVES

After completing this chapter, you will be able to:
- Explain what graphic design is.
- Describe jobs of different graphic artists.
- Identify layout and typeface.
- Design a logo, a comic strip, a concert poster, and a story illustration.

WORDS YOU WILL LEARN

editorial designers
graphic artists
graphic design
illustrators
layout
logo
typefaces

PORTFOLIO IDEAS

Select a graphic art work from this chapter for your portfolio. Exchange the piece with a classmate for a peer evaluation. Asking for feedback from another artist helps you see different viewpoints about your work. Peers can tell you what they like and offer suggestions for revising the work. Their comments may even inspire you to change your work before it goes into your portfolio! If the peer evaluation is written, store it with the finished art work in the portfolio, and remember to include your preliminary sketches and self-reflection.

The Art of Graphic Design

There are artists at work all around you. Artists create the television commercials you view and the billboards you read. Some of the art work they create includes posters, packaging, magazine advertisements, and corporate symbols. There were even artists responsible for the graphic design of this book.

Artists who work in these areas are known as graphic artists. **Graphic artists** *work in the field of art known as graphic design.* **Graphic design** is the *field of art that uses pictures and words to instruct, or to communicate a specific message.* Look around your classroom. What graphic design symbols and images do you see?

GRAPHIC ARTISTS

Graphic artists work in a great many areas. Each area has its own special tasks and job title. Some of these areas are editorial design, illustration, advertising design, and sign making. Sometimes graphic artists work together as members of a larger creative team. Most of them use computers to create their designs.

Editorial Design

The field of graphic design flourished in the 1500s. That was when the printing press was invented, making it possible to produce multiple copies of printed material at one time. People who arranged the words and pictures were similar to today's graphic artists.

Today these people are called editorial designers. **Editorial designers** are *graphic artists who arrange words and illustrations and prepare the material for printing.* Some editorial designers work on books, while others work on magazines and newspapers.

Planning the **layout**, or *the arrangement of words and pictures on a page*, is only one task of the editorial designer. Another is selecting the **typefaces**, or *styles of lettering for the printed material.* Figure 11–1 shows a typeface design based on an early typeface used many years ago in Europe. Today's editorial designers can choose from hundreds of typefaces. How many different typefaces can you find on this page? What differences can you spot among these styles?

abcdefghijklmnopqrstuvwxyz

ABCDEFGHIJKLMNOPQRSTUVWXYZ

1234567890 [&.,:;!?"""·=¢%/$£]

▲ Figure 11–1   These letters and numbers are shown in a typeface. Can you see how the style was taken directly from a type of hand lettering called calligraphy?

▲ **Figure 11–2** Do you know this story? You may have heard it when you were small. How do illustrations like this help you visualize the personality of the characters?

Beatrix Potter. *Jemima Puddle Duck*. 1908. Pencil, pen and ink, watercolor. Frederic Warne & Co., London.

Illustration

Have you ever used step-by-step drawings to put something together? If you have, you have used the same work habits of an illustrator. **Illustrators** are *graphic artists who create printed materials that explain or teach.* Many times illustrators work closely with editorial designers.

The color wheel on page **56** of this book (Figure 4–4) was drawn by an illustrator. So were the shaded shapes on page **147** (Figure 8–4). The drawing in Figure 11–2 was made to illustrate a children's book. When you look at Figure 11–3, you see the drawing of a technical illustrator. Notice the fine details that are included in the drawing.

Did you notice that each illustration listed above used a different art medium? Illustrators may use an airbrush, pen and ink, colored pencils, or watercolors to achieve the look they want. Today illustrators often use computers and other technology to create art.

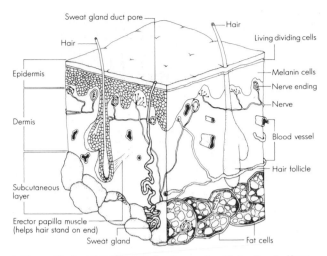

▲ **Figure 11–3** This is a drawing from a health textbook. How do drawings like this one help explain the lessons being taught?

Advertising Design

Other graphic artists specialize in advertising design. In this area the graphic artist communicates and creates a message in words and pictures to help sell or promote products or services.

Look again at the lithograph on page **190**. This was done by Henri de Toulouse-Lautrec to promote a concert by a well-known performer. Figure 11–4 shows an ad by another French printmaker of the 1800s. This one was for a company that made teas and chocolates. Notice that both artists used a combination of words and pictures. This is true of the work of graphic artists today.

Like editorial designers, advertising designers are concerned with layout and type styles. Some advertising designers work on newspaper or magazine ads. Others design commercials for television. The success of their work is measured by the impact the message has on the receiver. Can you think of an advertisement that has left an impression in your mind?

▲ **Figure 11–4** What mood does the artist convey? Is it appealing? Is it appropriate for the company he is promoting? Why?

Theophile-Alexandre Steinlen. *Compagnie Française des Chocolats et des Thés.* 1899. Color lithograph. 76.2 x 101.6 cm (30 x 40"). Metropolitan Museum of Art, New York, New York.

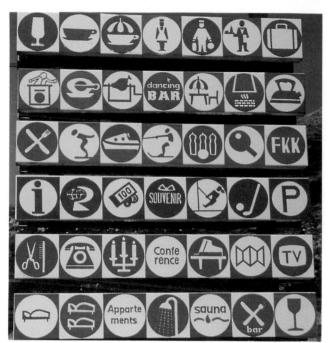

▲ **Figure 11–5** These are international signs intended to help travelers. Do the pictures quickly convey their messages? How does the artist's choice of color contribute to the sign's effectiveness?

▲ **Figure 11–6** Notice how much information the designer has packed into these few words and symbols. Could a person unable to read tell what kind of business this was?

Rendered by John Sullivan. *Tailor's Shears* (Shop sign). c. 1935. National Gallery of Art, Washington, D.C.

Sign Making

You may not think of Figure 11–5 as an art work. Yet it was someone's job to choose a type style and size for the letters. Someone had to design the figures and pick a color combination for the signs.

The "someone" behind these choices was a graphic artist with the job title of sign maker. The art of making signs traces its roots to the earliest times. The sign in Figure 11–6 imitates those made during America's Colonial period. Can you tell what this sign is made of? Can you tell what kind of business the sign advertised?

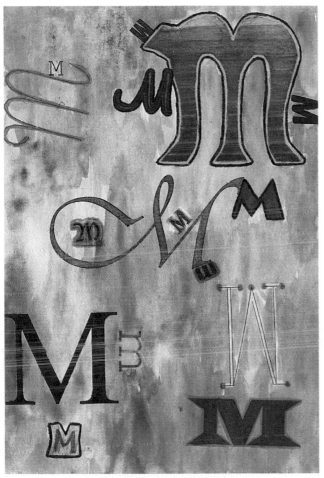

▲ Figure 11–7 Student work. Letter collage.

STUDIO ACTIVITY

Creating a Collage of Letters

Choose one of the 26 letters of the alphabet. Search through newspapers, magazines, and books. See how many different typefaces and sizes for this letter you can find. Cut examples of the letter from newspapers and magazine headlines. On a sheet of paper, make a collage based on the examples of your letter. To add interest to your collage, turn some of your letters upside down and some sideways. Try overlapping some of your letters. When you have an interesting arrangement, glue the letters to the background with white glue. If possible, photocopy your finished collage. Then add color using watercolors, crayons, or pastels. (See Figure 11–7.) (For more information on making a collage, see Technique Tip **28**, *Handbook* page **281**.)

P o r t f o l i o

Exchange your collage with a classmate for peer evaluation. Write an evaluation of the classmate's work using the steps of art criticism. Include the classmate's evaluation with your collage in your portfolio.

✔ CHECK YOUR UNDERSTANDING

1. What does an editorial designer do?
2. What is a layout? What is another term meaning "type style"?
3. What is the job title of a graphic artist who makes step-by-step drawings?
4. What are three art tools that an illustrator might use?
5. What do graphic artists who specialize in advertising do?

LESSON 2

Designing a Logo

A **logo** is *a special image representing a business, group, or product.* All logos are one-of-a-kind shapes or pictures. Some contain letters or words as well. Figure 11–8 shows some well-known logos. How many of these have you seen? Do you know the business, group, or product each stands for?

Imagine you are a graphic artist for an advertising agency. You have been asked to create a logo for a space colony on a newly discovered planet. Imagine you were also asked to come up with a name for the colony.

▲ Figure 11–8   What do you think makes a logo successful? Why? What other logos can you think of that you see often? What companies or products do they stand for?

Logos courtesy of American Red Cross, Childreach Sponsorship, and Plan International USA.

WHAT YOU WILL LEARN

Working in a small group, you will create a logo for a new space colony. The logo should contain the name of the colony (or at least the name's initials). The logo should capture the idea that the space colony is a pleasant place to live. It should create a feeling that the settlers are living in their own backyard rather than out in space. You will use a variety of colors, lines, and shapes to help show this. These elements must be arranged using either formal or informal balance. See Figure 11-9.

WHAT YOU WILL NEED

- Pencil, eraser, and ruler
- Sheets of sketch paper
- Sheet of white paper, 9 x 12 inch (23 x 30 cm)
- Watercolor markers

WHAT YOU WILL DO

1. You have been selected to design a logo. The logo must include the name or initials of the space colony. Brainstorm with the class about what life might be like on the space colony. Will the colony be divided into neighborhoods? Will the colony be under a temperature-control dome? What kinds of jobs will the people have? What will they do for entertainment? Will they have TV?
2. Working by yourself, make rough pencil sketches for your logo. Think about different ways of showing the letters you chose to use. Think about what images you might use to stand for a space colony. Choose different lines and shapes to show that life in the colony is pleasant and comfortable.

3. Working neatly, draw your best idea onto the sheet of white paper. Use a ruler to draw the straight lines.
4. Color in your logo with the watercolor markers. Use colors that suggest the spirit of adventure experienced by people living in the colony.
5. Display your work. Look for similarities and differences between your work and those of classmates.

▲ Figure 11–9 Student work. A space colony logo.

- **Describe**   Point to the image you created for your logo. Explain why you chose that image. Show where the name or initials of the space colony appear in your design. Name the colors you chose for your logo.
- **Analyze**   Point to the variety of colors, lines, and shapes used in your logo. Explain why you chose these elements. Tell what kind of balance you used. Explain why you decided to use that type of balance.
- **Interpret**   Explain how the colors, lines, and shapes in your logo suggest comfort and pleasant living conditions.
- **Judge**   Tell whether you feel your work succeeds. Identify the best feature of your design. List ways you could improve your design.

SAFETY TIP

When a project calls for the use of markers, always make sure to use the water-based kind. Permanent markers have chemicals in them that can be harmful when breathed in.

Try This! COMPUTER OPTION

■ Design a personal logo. Think about the qualities of line that best express your personality. First, choose a format for the logo. Use the Rectangular, Oval, or other Shape tool to draw a simple, open geometric shape. Within this shape draw two or three letters using the Brush, Straight Line, or Text tool.

Explore variations of Fonts, Sizes, and Styles. Use the Selection tool to Flip, Rotate, or Reverse the letters. Include simple shapes or symbols. Make several logos. Title and Save your best design. Add a variety of colors with the Flood-fill or Bucket tool to enhance the mood of the logo. Retitle, Save, and Print.

LESSON 3

Drawing a Comic Strip

Some graphic artists are storytellers. They tell their stories in connected boxes, or frames, made up of words and pictures. We know these strings of frames better as comic strips. Like a play, every comic strip has a cast of characters. When characters speak, their words often appear in outlined white spaces called balloons. (See Figures 11–10 and 11–11.)

Most "comic" strips are funny. Some, however, are not. Some are satirical, meaning that they poke fun at public figures and world events. Others are adventure stories or show suspense in some other way. Look again at Figure 11–10. Which kind of strip is this box from?

WHAT YOU WILL LEARN

You will create a comic strip made up of five or more boxes, or frames. Each box will be at least 5 inches (13 cm) square. The characters in your strip may be drawn in either a humorous or realistic way. Your strip may be funny, action-packed, or have a serious subject. If your strip is funny, the last frame should have the punch line. The lines and shapes will be used to add rhythm or movement to your strip.

WHAT YOU WILL NEED

- Notepad and pencil
- Sheets of sketch paper
- Eraser and ruler
- Sheets of white paper, 12 x 18 inch (30 x 46 cm)
- Black fine-line felt-tip marker
- Colored pencils, markers, or crayons
- Transparent tape

WHAT YOU WILL DO

1. Think about the people and situations you could include in your comic strip. Possibilities are school activities, fun with friends, or fantasy. Decide whether you will make your comic strip humorous or adventurous.

2. On your notepad, plan out your story. Identify the characters you will use. Decide what you will show them doing in the strip. Write out what you will have them say. Decide how many frames you will need to show the action.

▼ Figure 11–10 How does the illustration help you in interpreting the words?

Jeff MacNelly. *Shoe.* © 1989. Tribune Media Services, Inc.

3. Make rough pencil sketches of your characters. Use lines and shapes to show movement. Sketch the background. Practice drawing word balloons. Do a rough sketch for each one of the boxes that will be in your strip. Carefully print out the words each character will say. Number each frame.

4. Divide a sheet of paper, 12 x 18 inch (30 x 46 cm) into as many squares or rectangles as you will need. How many will you use? Will all the boxes be the same size, or will some be larger for emphasis? Use your ruler and pencil to draw the boxes. (See Technique Tip **22**, *Handbook* page **278** for information on measuring squares and rectangles.) Use extra sheets as needed. Use repetition of characters and environments to give the strip unity.

5. Working lightly in pencil, carefully draw your final sketches into the boxes. Print out your characters' words in balloons.

6. Go over all the lines and letters with the black fine-line marker. Color in your shapes with colored pencils, markers, or crayons. If you used more than one sheet, join the pages together with transparent tape.

- **Describe**   Identify the characters in your strip. Tell who they are and what they are doing. Show that you used at least five boxes. Point to the different lines and shapes.
- **Analyze**   Explain how the lines and shapes create rhythm or movement in your strip.
- **Interpret**   Identify the mood of your strip. Tell what clues help the viewer understand this mood. If your strip was humorous, was the punch line in the last box effective?
- **Judge**   Tell whether you feel your work succeeds. Explain your answer.

7. Display your work. Notice how classmates completed the assignment. Ask your classmates to read your strip. Can they understand your story? Can they recognize the theme?

▲ Figure 11–11   Student work. A black-and-white comic strip.

Try This! STUDIO OPTIONS

■ Redraw your strip. This time, instead of adding color, use different values of India Ink. Different values can be obtained by adding small amounts of water to India ink. Apply the India ink with a small brush. Does this change the mood of the work? Explain.

■ Work with all students in your class to plan a whole comic book. Each student will create one story for the book. When it is finished, protect the pages with lamination, and bind them into a book.

Designing a Poster

In music, as in art, different artists have different styles. The style of today's most popular rock group is different from that of yesterday's. Both are very different from the musical style of Mozart.

When graphic artists design concert posters for musical groups, they try to capture the musician's style. Their works often reflect one of the three views of art you have learned about. Look at the concert posters in Figure 11–12. Which of these is realistic? Which uses design composition alone to make its statement? Which expresses a feeling?

WHAT YOU WILL LEARN

You will invent a musician or musical group and choose the style of music your imaginary artist makes. Then you will design a concert poster for that artist. Decide on a title for the group. The poster will include the title of the concert and name of the artist. You will choose the medium or media to carry out the assignment. You will use the principles of balance, rhythm, and emphasis to organize the elements of colors, lines, shapes, space, and texture in your design. (See Figure 11–13.)

WHAT YOU WILL NEED

- Notepad and pencil
- Sheets of sketch paper
- Eraser and ruler
- Any or all of the following: broad-line and fine-line colored markers, crayons, collage materials (magazines, newspapers, scissors, white glue, small brush)
- Sheet of heavy white paper
- Transparent tape

▲ **Figure 11–12**   Describe the style of music of the top poster. If you were interested in rock and roll, would this poster interest you? What does the guitar symbolize to you? Explain.

(TOP) Victor Moscoso. *Junior Wells and His Chicago Blues Band.* 1966. Offset lithograph, printed in color. 50.5 x 35.6 cm (19 ⅞ x 14"). The Museum of Modern Art, New York, New York. Gift of the designer.
(BOTTOM) Ernie Friedlander Studios. 1990. Offset lithograph. 91.5 x 61 cm (36 x 24"). Portal Publications Ltd.

WHAT YOU WILL DO

1. Think of a musical style and name for your imaginary musician or group. Write the name on your notepad. Create a title for the concert poster. Write a short description of your group.
2. Create your own style or choose a style of lettering for the concert title and the artist's name. Decide where on the poster

each will appear and decide how large each will be. Sketch them in.

3. Plan how you will fill the remaining space. If you plan to use collage materials, find and clip images found in magazines and newspapers. Choose which aesthetic view of art you will take. Decide if you wish your work to look realistic, to make a statement with design alone, or to express a feeling or mood.

4. Working lightly in pencil, place your title lettering, artist's name and any other images on the poster. (See Technique Tip **5**, *Handbook* page **271**, which gives instructions on using a grid to enlarge letters and images.)

5. Using markers or crayons, color in the letters and images you have drawn. Using glue and brush, paste down any magazine or newspaper clippings you have chosen to add to your design.

6. Display your concert poster. Take a poll among your classmates. How many can tell the style of music your imaginary artist plays?

▲ Figure 11–13   Student work. Music concert posters.

Try This! COMPUTER OPTION

■ Create a compact disc cover for a musical group or soloist you enjoy. Use the Rectangular shape tool and hold down the Shift key to draw an open square. Select, Copy, and Paste a second square for the back cover. Design both covers. Choose the Text tool, a Font, Size, Style, and Color and invent a title. Select letters and Copy or use Transformation tools to Flip, Rotate, Distort, or change Size emphasizing the mood of the music. Import clip art and/or drawn images to describe the style of music. Add color with the Brushes or the Flood-fill tool to reflect the mood of the music. On the back cover include designs, letters, and colors that match the front. Use the Text tool to list individual song titles. Title, Save, and Print.

 **LESSON 5**

Illustrating a Story

Look at Figure 11–14. This painting by artist Jacob Lawrence was used as the cover of a book that he wrote. The cover art and the other illustrations in the story make the story come alive for the readers. What do you expect the story to be about?

WHAT YOU WILL LEARN

Select an action story or poem you have recently read and liked. You will paint an illustration for an incident that took place in the story or poem. Your illustration will capture the setting, mood, and style of the whole work. You will decide whether your illustration will have formal or informal balance. You will decide whether to use realistic proportions for your figures or distortion. (See Figure 11–15.)

WHAT YOU WILL NEED

- Notepad, pencil, and eraser
- Sheets of sketch paper
- Paper towels
- Sheet of white paper, 12 x 18 inch (30 x 46 cm)
- School acrylic paint
- Bristle brushes, varied sizes
- Water

▲ **Figure 11–14   This art work was used for the cover of a book called *The Great Migration*. How does it illustrate the title?**

Jacob Lawrence. *The Migration of the Negro.* (Panel #3 of 60.) 1940–41. Tempera on Masonite. 30.5 x 45.7 cm (12 x 18"). Phillips Collection, Washington, D.C. Acquired through Downtown Gallery, 1942.

▲ **Figure 11–15** Student work. A story illustration of the book *Bridge to Terabithia.*

WHAT YOU WILL DO

1. Think about a short story, novel, or poem you have read and liked. Decide what scene from this work you want to illustrate using the main characters.
2. On the notepad, describe what the characters are doing. Write down information about their expressions, moods, and actions. List ways you will use color and the other elements of art in your painting. Decide whether the proportions of your figures will be realistic or exaggerated. Decide if you will use emphasis to

- **Describe** Tell what story you have chosen to illustrate. Tell what is happening in the part of the work you have illustrated. Explain who the characters are. List the elements and principles used.
- **Analyze** Tell whether your work has formal or informal balance. Point to and describe the proportions of your figures. Tell whether these proportions were used to make these figures look realistic or cartoon-like.
- **Interpret** Explain how your illustration captures the setting, mood, and style of the story. Give your illustration a title and explain why you chose the title.
- **Judge** Tell whether you feel your work succeeds.

make a figure or object stand out. Balance your illustration using either formal or informal balance.
3. Make rough pencil sketches for your painting.
4. Lightly sketch your plan on the good paper. Use your 1/4-inch (0.6 cm) brush and a light-value paint to draw the main shapes of your illustration on the sheet of white paper. Use your larger brushes to fill in shapes. Complete your painting.
5. Display your painting. Notice similarities and differences in the way you and classmates completed the assignment. Try to guess the titles of the different stories and poems illustrated.

Try This! ## COMPUTER OPTION

■ Create a storybook for a younger class. Working with other students, choose a page from a familiar story to illustrate. Sketch with the Pencil or a variety of Brushes and colors to capture the mood of the scene. Use the whole screen for your page. Choose the Text tool and Font, Size, and Style that matches the original text. Remember to include the page number. Title, Save, and Print. Proofread to correct any errors. The pages of the story can be printed and bound as a book. Laminating will preserve the pages.

Book Illustration Through the Ages

Portrait of Chaucer and beginning of the "Tale of Melibeus," from the Ellesmere Manuscript of *The Canterbury Tales* by Geoffrey Chaucer. c. 1410. 40 x 28.3 cm (15¾ x 11⅛"). The Huntington Library, San Marino, California.

Today's graphic artists design and illustrate books using modern computer software. With the click of a mouse, artists can easily change colors and shading or create lines and shapes. When the art work is finished and a book is completed, publishers print thousands of copies.

Mass production of books has only been possible since the invention of the printing press in 1454. Before that time, each book was created and illustrated individually. To create copies of a book, an artist had to copy the drawings and lettering by hand.

Imagine being one of the artists from medieval Europe who illustrated books like the one shown on this page. These books included full-page paintings, elaborate designs in the margins, and decorated initial letters. These books were known as illuminated manuscripts. The page shown here from Chaucer's *The Canterbury Tales* is an example of an illuminated manuscript.

Over the centuries, many famous artists have illustrated books. These artists include Rembrandt, Peter Paul Reubens, and Pablo Picasso. Today, the most commonly illustrated books are those created for children. You have probably read books by Maurice Sendak and Dr. Seuss, popular twentieth-century illustrators.

MAKING THE CONNECTION

✔ How has the use of computers helped graphic artists?
✔ Look again at the page from *The Canterbury Tales*. Do you think that these illustrations were meant to help explain the story or simply to decorate the page? Explain your answer.
✔ How might the skills of a graphic artist today differ from those of a medieval book illustrator?

INTERNET ACTIVITY

Visit Glencoe's Fine Arts Web Site for students at:

http://www.glencoe.com/sec/art/students

BUILDING VOCABULARY

Number a sheet of paper from 1 to 7. After each number, write the term from the list that best matches each description below.

editorial designers   layout
graphic artists   logo
graphic design   typefaces
illustrators

1. The field of art that uses pictures and words to instruct or communicate.
2. Graphic artists who arrange words and illustrations and prepare the material for printing.
3. The arrangement of words and pictures.
4. Styles of lettering.
5. Graphic artists who create printed materials that explain, teach, or decorate.
6. A special image connected with a business, group, or product.
7. People who work in the field of art known as graphic design.

REVIEWING ART FACTS

Number a sheet of paper from 8 to 14. Answer each question in a complete sentence.

8. Name four main areas of graphic design.
9. What invention spurred the beginning of the field of graphic design?

10. Name two tasks of an editorial designer.
11. What were lithographs by artists like Toulouse-Lautrec used for in the 1800s?
12. Name two places besides TV shows where you can see the work of advertising designers.
13. What kinds of graphic artists make step-by-step drawings?
14. Besides shapes or pictures, what do logos often contain?

THINKING ABOUT ART

On a sheet of paper, answer each question in a sentence or two.

1. **Analyze.**   Make a list of products that you have seen advertised. Then indicate which ones you see advertised on television and which you see advertised in print. Which advertising media is more effective? Why?
2. **Extend.**   How do you think the invention of the printing press affected the work of the sign maker?
3. **Extend.**   In which kinds of books—science or history—do you think technical illustrations would be more useful? Explain your answer.

MAKING ART CONNECTIONS

1. **Drama.**   Find out all you can about the theme and character of an upcoming play in your school or community. Design a poster advertising the play. Develop visual images that show what the play is about. Include information such as where and when the show will be given, the name of the organization producing it, the author, and how much tickets cost.

2. **Physical Education.**   Design a logo representing your favorite sport, create a poster design advertising an upcoming event, or design a school spirit T-shirt. Learn as much about the subject as possible. Observe and draw athletes in action, cheerleaders, mascots, and equipment used. Develop original imagery. Do not use existing images.

▲ Benin artists excelled in creating bronze sculptures. The figure on horseback shown above was most likely an important person, although his true identity is not known.

Nigeria, Benin. *Horse and Rider.* Early 17th Century. Bronze. 47 cm (18½") high. The Detroit Institute of Arts. Gift of Mrs. Walter B. Ford II.

CHAPTER 12

Sculpture

Like other artists, sculptors begin new projects by asking themselves questions. Here are some questions that faced the sculptor of the work at the left.

- What medium will I use?
- Will I create by adding to or taking away from?
- Will the work be realistic?
- Will the figures appear smooth or rough?

In this chapter you will learn about the different choices sculptors have when they create their art work.

PORTFOLIO IDEAS

Prepare a portfolio entry based on a sculpture you made in this chapter. Because the art work itself is three-dimensional and may not fit conveniently in a portfolio, you have alternative methods. Include preliminary sketches, a written description of your idea for the sculpture, and photographs of the finished work. Remember to date the entries and take photographs from all points of view—front, back, and sides—so viewers can enjoy the sculpture in all dimensions.

OBJECTIVES

After completing this chapter, you will be able to:
- Name the four basic methods used by sculptors.
- Describe each method of sculpting.
- Define the terms *freestanding* and *relief.*
- Tell which sculpting methods are additive and which are subtractive.
- Create sculptures of your own using carving, modeling, and assembling.

WORDS YOU WILL LEARN

additive
assembling
carving
casting
freestanding
high relief
low relief
modeling
relief
subtractive

The Art of Sculpture

When artists work with paints, they create the illusion of space in their works. It is the job of sculptors to create their works in space. Look at the painting in Figure 12–1. The object in it seems to have roundness and depth. If you try to grasp it, however, your hand will bump up against flat canvas. The boy in Figure 12–2, on the other hand, has *real* roundness and depth. The work casts *real* shadows. It invites you to move around it. It invites you to see it from every side.

In this lesson you will learn about the many tools and methods sculptors use to create their art work. In later lessons you will use some of these tools and methods yourself.

THE BEGINNINGS OF SCULPTING

You may recall that the earliest artists, the cave dwellers, were painters. But did you know they were also sculptors? Stone, horn, ivory, and bone were some media used by these early sculptors. The sculpture in Figure 12–3, completed in 2600 B.C., is regarded by many to be one of the wonders of the world. Do you know in what country this remarkable work is found? Do you know what it is called? What medium was used to construct it?

▶ **Figure 12–1   How real does this beetle look to you? Notice the shadow it casts as it seems to walk across the page.**

Albrecht Dürer. *Stag Beetle.* 1505. Watercolor and gouache. 14.2 x 11.4 cm (5⁹⁄₁₆ x 4½"). The J. Paul Getty Museum, Los Angeles, California.

◀ Figure 12-2 **Notice how the work twists and turns in space. Does this make you want to move around the work?**

Jean Baptiste Carpeaux. *Neapolitan Fisherboy.* 1857. Bronze with light brown patina. 34.6 cm (13⅝"). Allen Memorial Art Museum, Oberlin College, Oberlin, Ohio. Gift of Charles F. Olney.

▼ **Figure 12-3** **At its highest point this sculpture is 65 feet (19.8 m) tall. The head is that of an ancient Egyptian king. The body is that of a lion. What statement could the Egyptians have been making?**

Great Sphinx, Giza. c. 2600 B.C.

LESSON 1

The Art of Crafts

Before there were machines, everything that people used was made by hand. Fabric to make clothing was woven by hand. Plates, bowls, and pots to cook with were made by hand. At that time, artists worked not only out of a wish to create, but also out of necessity. These artists considered the useful function of the item. They also considered the beauty or the aesthetic qualities of the object. In many cases, their items were works of art.

An artist who made such useful and aesthetically pleasing goods was — and still is — called a craftsperson. A **craftsperson** is *someone who has become an expert in an area of applied art. The different areas of applied art in which craftspeople work* are called **crafts**.

▶ **Figure 13–1** This quilt was created to celebrate Georgia's 250th birthday. Everything on the quilt symbolizes one part of the state. Can you tell which part by studying the symbols?

Elizabeth Garrison. *Georgia.* 1983. Quilt. 120 x 157.5 cm (48 x 63"). Private collection.

CRAFTS

Today there is a renewed interest in all types of crafts. Look at the quilt in Figure 13–1. It was not made to cover a bed. Instead, it was designed and created by a craftsperson to hang on a wall. Crafts have increased in popularity because people appreciate the one-of-a-kind, well-made product.

Today, as in the past, craftspeople use many different media. Some work in wood (Figure 13–2). Others work in metals (Figure 13–3). Still others work in fibers, fabrics, glass, and clay.

▲ **Figure 13–4** This one-of-a-kind basket is made of natural materials. How does the craftsperson create unity in the work?

Kim Keats. *Banded Tulip Basket*. 1986. Wisteria and dyed reeds. 33 x 68.6 x 35.6 cm (13 x 27 x 14″).

▲ **Figure 13–2** What makes these blocks special? How are they different from the kind made in factories?

Ann Renée Weaver and Tony Mann. *Alphabet Blocks in Case*. Brazilian Mahogany, non-toxic paints and finishes and brass hardware. Case, 7 x 41.3 x 15.2 cm (2¾ x 16¼ x 6″). Blocks, 4.8 x 4.3 x 4.4 cm (1⁷⁄₁₀ x 1⁷⁄₁₀ x 1¾″).

Weaving

Weaving is *a craft in which fiber strands are interlocked to make cloth or objects*. The basket in Figure 13–4 and the textile in Figure 13–5 are examples of the weaver's art.

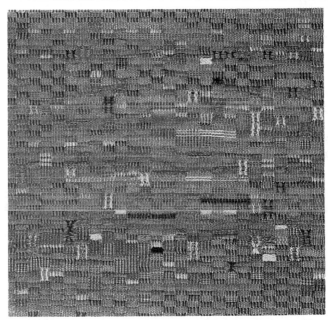

▲ **Figure 13–5** This weaver enjoyed the color and texture of her design.

Anni Albers. *Pasture*. 1958. Mercerized cotton. 35.6 x 39.4 cm (14 x 15½″). The Metropolitan Museum of Art, New York, New York. Purchase, Edward C. Moore, Jr., Gift, 1969. 69.135

▲ **Figure 13–3** How do you imagine it would feel to touch this bronze vessel? How different would it be if it were made of glass?

China. *Ritual Food Vessel (Liding)*. Shang Dynasty, 12th–11th Centuries B.C. Bronze. 19.9 x 15.7 x 15.7 cm (7⅞ x 6³⁄₁₆ x 6³⁄₁₆″). Arthur M. Sackler Gallery, Smithsonian Institution, Washington, D.C. Gift of Arthur M. Sackler.

Some weavers use yarn, rope, twigs, reeds, and grasses as fibers (Figure 13–6). **Fibers** are *any thin, threadlike materials.* Today fibers are spun from animal hairs, such as wool, plant materials, such as cotton, and manufactured materials, such as nylon.

Cloth weaving is done on a loom. A **loom** is *a frame or machine that holds a set of threads that run vertically.* These are called the warp threads. The weaver passes threads from a second set under and over the first set. These threads are called the weft. This creates a pattern and locks the threads together. Today some artists work on computerized looms. In factories, computers are programmed to control the weaving machines.

▲ **Figure 13–6** **This artist turned ordinary rope into a work of art!**

Claire Zeisler. *Tri-Color Arch.* 1983–84. Hemp and synthetic fiber. 188 cm (74") high. The Metropolitan Museum of Art, New York, New York. Gift of Peter Florsheim, Thomas W. Florsheim, and Joan Florsheim-Binkley, 1987. 1987.371

Glassmaking

The practice of melting sand to make glass is thousands of years old. So is the art of glassblowing. **Glassblowing** is *the craft of shaping melted glass by blowing air into it through a tube.* One of the most famous contemporary glassmakers is Dale Chihuly. Notice how the luminous color swirls seem to flow through the design in Figure 13–7. Are you reminded of shapes that are natural to the sea? Today glassmakers like Chihuly experiment with designs that, like much art of the day, are daring.

▲ **Figure 13–7** **Imagine the artist shaping this shell-like form while the glass is red hot!**

Dale Chihuly. *Cadmium Red Seaform Set with Obsidian Lip Wrap.* 1993. Blown glass (9 pieces). 61 x 109.2 x 81.3 cm (24 x 43 x 32"). Courtesy of the Charles Cowles Gallery, New York.

Ceramics

Ceramics is another craft. Ceramic pieces are any objects made from clay and hardened by fire. Clay is a natural material found in the ground all over the world. **Pottery** is *the craft of making objects from clay.* You may think of pottery as bowls and dishes, but it can also be statues, masks, or anything else made out of clay.

The making of clay pots goes back to ancient times. Today craftspeople use many of the same techniques that were used many centuries ago.

Making pottery starts with preparing the clay. Water is added to the clay so that it is wet enough to be worked easily. Potters have special words for the different conditions of the clay:

- **Plastic clay** is clay that is wet enough to be worked but firm enough to hold its shape.
- **Leather hard clay** is clay that is still damp but is too dry to shape. It can be carved or joined together with slip.
- **Slip** is *clay that has so much added water that it is liquid and runny*. It is used as glue to join pieces of clay together. It is also used in decorating a finished work.

When working clay by hand, there are special methods that have been developed to shape the clay. Some of these are called pinching, coiling, and slab building. In the studio lessons that follow you will have a chance to try these techniques.

Clay can also be shaped by throwing it, which means turning it on a rapidly spinning wheel called a potter's wheel. This helps make a smooth, symmetrical piece. Some works combine both methods.

After the clay is shaped, it must be **fired**, or *hardened by heating in a kiln*. A **kiln** is *a special piece of equipment used to fire ceramics*. It can get as hot as 3000° F (1650° C). Before clay

▲ **Figure 13–9   Why do you think the artist chose to glaze this piece?**

Jiangxi Province, China. *Flask*. Ming Dynasty. Early 15th Century. Porcelain painted with cobalt underglaze. 47 cm (18½") high; 35.6 cm (14") diameter. Asia Society, New York, New York. Mr. and Mrs. John D. Rockefeller.

has been fired in a kiln, it is called greenware. After it has been fired, it is called bisqueware (**bisk**-ware).

Sometimes bisqueware is **glazed**, or *coated with a mixture of powdered chemicals that melt during firing into a hard, glasslike finish*. The glaze is spread on the pottery and the item is fired a second time.

Pottery does not always have to be glazed. Some of the best pottery, like terra cotta, is unglazed (Figure 13–8). However, if it is to hold food or liquid, it must be glazed with nontoxic glazes to keep the clay from absorbing the moisture. (See Figure 13–9.)

▲ **Figure 13–8   This sculpture is terra cotta. How different would it look if the artist used a different medium?**

Mary Frank. *Swimmer*. 1978. Ceramic. 43.2 x 238.8 x 81.3 cm (17 x 94 x 32"). Whitney Museum of American Art, New York. Purchase, with funds from Mrs. Robert M. Benjamin, Mrs. Oscar Kolin, and Mrs. Michael Millhouse.

✔CHECK YOUR UNDERSTANDING

1. What is a craftsperson? Define the term *craft*.
2. What is weaving? What is the name of the machine on which cloth is woven?
3. What is glass made of? What is glass-blowing?
4. How is slip used?
5. Describe the difference between plastic and leather hard clay.
6. What is the difference between greenware and bisqueware?

Clay Bowl

Look at Figure 13–10. This is a piece of pottery that was handbuilt by Margaret Tafoya. Her work was done without the use of a potter's wheel. You also can make a container, such as a glass, mug, or bowl in the same way. Before you begin, concentrate on the form of the object. Identify the rim, body, and foot of the vase. Notice how the area lifts from the bottom to give shape and support to the container.

WHAT YOU WILL LEARN

You will make a small container by the pinch method. Make all the sides with even thickness and smooth the rim of the bowl and add a foot to the base. You may decorate it by pressing found objects into its surface. You may add pieces and coils of clay to create rhythmic, repeated patterns.

WHAT YOU WILL NEED

- Sheets of newspaper or cloth
- Clay and slip
- Container of water
- Clay and clay scoring tools
- Plastic sheet or bag
- *Optional:* found objects, such as buttons, weeds, and pieces of broken toys

WHAT YOU WILL DO

1. Spread sheets of newspaper or cloth over your work area. Pinch off a small piece of clay. Dip one finger in the water and wet the piece. Set it aside for later. It may be used for decorating.
2. Form your clay into a ball by rolling it.
3. Hollow out the ball of clay by pressing your thumbs into the center while gently squeezing the clay between your thumbs

▲ **Figure 13–10** This piece is a reflection of a Native American style. How might this vase be different if the artist created it on a potter's wheel?

Margaret Tafoya. *Jar.* Santa Clara Pueblo, New Mexico. c. 1965. Blackware. 43 x 33 cm (17 x 13"). National Museum of Women in the Arts, Washington, D.C. Gift of Wallace & Wilhelmina Holladay.

on the inside and your fingers on the outside. Form it into the shape you want your container to have.

4. Gradually thin the sides and bottom of your pot with your thumbs and fingers. Make the walls and bottom smooth and even. Fix any small cracks in the clay by pressing and smoothing it out with your fingers and thumbs.

5. Wet your fingertips or use a damp sponge to smooth the top rim of your bowl.

6. Roll out a coil, or rope, of clay about 1/2 inch (13mm) thick. Turn your bowl upside down. Join your coil to the bottom to make a foot, or stand, for your work.

7. Decorate the surface of the bowl with a rhythmic pattern while the clay is still damp. Press your found objects into the surface of the bowl to create a pattern. Use your fingers to support the inside of the bowl while you make your impression. Add a second pattern by joining some small pieces of clay to your work. (See Technique Tip **17**, *Handbook* page **275**, for hints on joining clay pieces.)

8. Cover the piece loosely with a plastic sheet or bag. This will help it dry evenly and keep it from cracking. Remove the plastic when the clay is leather hard. When your work is completely dry, it is ready to fire.

9. *Optional*: Apply glaze and fire your work a second time. Do not apply glaze to the bottom of your piece. If you do, it will stick to the shelf in the kiln.

EXAMINING YOUR WORK

- **Describe** Show that the sides of your container have an even thickness and that the rim is smooth. Point out the ring of clay you added to the bottom to create a foot. Point out the found objects and pieces of clay rope you added as a design.
- **Analyze** Describe the texture of your bowl's surface, and explain what you did to change the surface texture. Tell whether you used found objects and strips of clay to create a feeling of rhythmic repeated pattern.
- **Interpret** Tell whether your bowl is functional or a purely decorative item.
- **Judge** Tell whether your bowl succeeds as art. Explain your answer.

▲ Figure 13–11 Student work. Clay bowl decorated with found objects.

STUDIO OPTION

Try This!

■ Use the pinch method to make a clay bell. Poke a small hole in the top of the bell big enough to thread a string through. Form a small bead with a hole going through the center. Then make a thin clay clapper with a small hole at the top for the string. Dry and fire these clay pieces. Ask your teacher for assembling instructions.

Slab Container

An easy way to make ceramic objects is by using clay slabs. A **slab** is *a slice or sheet of clay*. The slab method works especially well when you are building an object with straight sides. Figure 13–12 shows a work made from slabs.

Slabs can be cut into any shape. The slab method can also be used to make cylinders. In this case, the slab must be curved while the clay is still flexible to avoid cracking. If you want to build a straight-wall rectangular box, the slabs must be dry, but not quite leather hard.

WHAT YOU WILL LEARN

You will use the slab method and proper joining techniques to make a container shaped like a cylinder. This can be used as a vase, pencil holder, or jar. You will decorate the surface of the container with designs cut from another slab. The designs may be flowers, animals, letters, or other objects made with geometric forms and shapes. (See Figure 13–13.) Be sure that the decorative designs are in proportion to the size of the container. Your container will be glazed inside and out.

WHAT YOU WILL NEED

- Sheets of newspaper or cloth
- Two guide sticks, each about 1/2 inch (13 mm) thick
- Clay and slip
- Rolling pin, pipe, or smooth jar
- Ruler
- Needle tool or open paper clip
- Container of water
- Scoring tools or fork

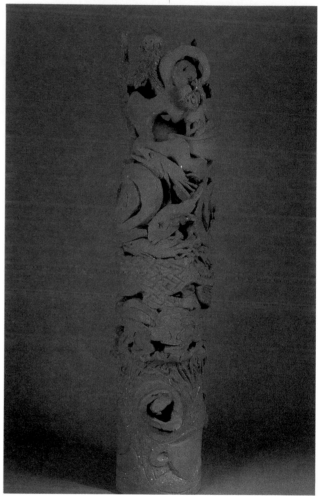

▲ **Figure 13–12   Can you tell where some of the different slabs come together?**

Jane Pleak. *Summertime Totem.* 1987. Ceramic redware. 129.5 x 35.6 x 35.6 cm (51 x 14 x 14″). Private collection.

WHAT YOU WILL DO

1. Spread sheets of newspaper or cloth over your work area.
2. Place the guide sticks on the cloth 6 inches (15 cm) apart. Place the clay between the guide sticks. Flatten it with the heel of your hand. Resting the rolling pin, pipe, or jar on the guide sticks, roll out the clay. This will help keep the thickness of the slab even.

3. Using the ruler and needle tool, measure and lightly mark two rectangles on the slab. One should be 6 x 10 inches (15 x 25 cm), the other, 5 inches (13 cm) square. Any mistakes can be wiped away with your fingers. Cut out the rectangles using the needle tool. Save the scraps. Keep them damp.

4. Bend the longer slab into a cylinder. Join the edges by scoring and using slip. (See Technique Tip 17, *Handbook* page **275**.) Wet your fingers and wipe away any cracks in the surface of the cylinder.

5. Using the needle tool, trim one end of the cylinder so it will stand straight. Stand the cylinder, trimmed end down, on the 5-inch (13 cm) square slab. With the needle tool, lightly and carefully trace around the base of the cylinder. Remove the cylinder, and cut out the circle you have drawn. Join the cylinder and circle to form your container.

6. Cut design shapes of your choice from the leftover clay slab. Using the joining techniques you used to form the cylinder, apply the slab designs to the surface of the container. Allow the container to dry slowly. When it is at the greenware stage, fire it.

7. Apply glaze to every surface but the bottom, and fire the container a second time. If you want the container to hold water, pour a small amount of glaze in the container. Swirl it around the bottom and sides. Keep turning the container as you pour the excess glaze out so that it will cover the inside completely.

EXAMINING YOUR WORK

- **Describe**   Show that the surface of your container is smooth and free of cracks. Tell whether your container is glazed inside and out. Describe the designs you added.
- **Analyze**   Point out the shapes you used to decorate your container. Tell whether your decorations are in proportion to the size of your container.
- **Interpret**   Tell how you would use the container.
- **Judge**   Tell whether your work succeeds as applied art. Explain your answer.

▲ Figure 13–13   Student work in progress. A slab container.

COMPUTER OPTION

Try This!

■ Use your computer art program to design the slab container you will create for this Studio Lesson. Explore a variety of brushes, shapes, and sizes. Sketch several views of the clay container—front, side, looking down, or looking up. Discover the tools to imitate the edges and textures of the clay. Explore shapes that you will apply to the surface of the container. Title, Save, and Print.

LESSON 4

Making a Weaving

Look at the tapestry weaving in Figure 13–14. It was woven on a floor loom. The craftsperson dyed the threads before weaving. She wanted to control the color scheme, as well as the shape and texture.

Like all work done on a loom, this one is made by interlocking fibers. *The threads attached to the loom* are known as **warp** threads. *The threads pulled across the warp* are the **weft** threads. The weft threads are passed over and under the warp threads to lock the two sets of fibers together.

WHAT YOU WILL LEARN

You will make a fabric wall hanging using a cardboard loom and yarns, strings, and found fibers. You will use a variety of textures and limit the colors to a monochromatic or analogous color scheme.

WHAT YOU WILL NEED

- Ruler, pencil, scissors, and transparent tape
- Sheet of heavy cardboard, 12 x 18 inch (30 x 46 cm)
- Spool of strong, thin thread
- Different colored yarns and strings
- Found materials that can be used as fibers, such as grass, strips of paper, and used film
- Tapestry needle
- Comb
- Wooden dowel

WHAT YOU WILL DO

1. To make your loom, hold the ruler along the top edge of your cardboard. With the pencil, mark off every 1/4 inch (6 mm).

▲ **Figure 13–14   Describe some of the elements and principles of art the artist incorporated into her weaving.**

Tommye M. Scanlin. *Cat Dreams.* 1988. Hand-dyed wool tapestry. 86.4 x 55.9 cm (34 x 22"). Private collection.

Using the scissors, make a cut about 1/2 inch (13 mm) deep at each mark. Do the same thing along the bottom of the cardboard.

2. Tape the end of your thread to the back of the cardboard. Bring the spool to the front, passing the thread through the top left notch. Pull the spool down to the bottom of the loom. Pass the thread through the bottom left notch and around to the back. Move one notch to the right. Pull the thread through and up the front

of the loom. Keep working until you reach the last notch. (See Figure 13–15.) Bring the spool to the back. Cut the thread, and tape the end.

3. Decide which color scheme you will use. Select fibers you will use for your weft. Choose textures to add interest to your wall hanging.

4. Thread one of your thinner yarns through the eye of the tapestry needle. Start to weave at the bottom of your loom. Move the yarn across the warp, passing over one thread and under the next. (Figure 13–16.) Keep working in this over-and-under manner. When you reach the end of the warp, reverse directions. If you wove over the last thread, you must weave under when you start the next line of the weft. Do not pull the weft too tight. Curve it slightly as you pull it through the warp. This is called ballooning.

5. After weaving a few rows, pack the weft threads tightly with the comb. The tighter the weave, the stronger the fabric will be. Experiment with different weft fibers.

6. Be sure to end with another inch (2.5 cm) of thin, tightly-packed fiber. Break the tabs of your loom to slip the weaving off the cardboard. Fold the weaving over the dowel and stitch your weaving together, using a long piece of yarn and a tapestry needle.

7. Make a hanging loop by tying the ends of a piece of string to each end of the dowel.

▲ Figure 13–15   Notice the series of vertical lines. These are the warp threads.

▲ Figure 13–16   These are the threads that will display your image. What are these threads called?

Try This! STUDIO OPTIONS

■ Make a table placemat for a favorite holiday. Choose the colors that best symbolize that holiday.

■ Experiment with weft and warp materials of differing textures and weights to create a wall hanging, incorporating found objects as you go.

LESSON 5

Jewelry

Some art is made to be worn. An example of this kind of art appears in Figure 13–17. We call this art, and the craft of making it, jewelry.

Some people wear jewelry made of colorful shells and feathers. Look once more at the necklace in Figure 13–17. From what animal feathers is this item made? Today people also wear jewelry made of precious stones and metals. Can you name any of these stones and metals?

WHAT YOU WILL LEARN

You will make a piece of paper jewelry with a particular wearer in mind. You will paint your jewelry with watercolors. You will choose either geometric or free-form shapes for your design. You will make a pendant, a pin, or a pair of earrings (Figures 13–18 and 13–19). The item must harmonize with the size and clothing style of the person for whom it is intended.

WHAT YOU WILL NEED

- Pencil and sheets of sketch paper
- Sheet of heavy watercolor paper, 9 x 12 inch (23 x 30 cm)
- Sheets of scrap paper
- Scissors
- Watercolor paints and brushes
- White glue
- Pin or earring backs
- Straight pin
- Polyurethane spray

WHAT YOU WILL DO

1. Identify the person for whom the piece is intended. Decide whether you will make a pin, a pendant, or a pair of earrings. Make pencil sketches experimenting with different shapes for your jewelry.

▲ **Figure 13–17   Feathers from tropical birds give color to this beautifully balanced necklace.**

Maranhão, Brazil, Kaapor tribe. *Tukanivar* (woman's feathered necklace). 20th Century. Toucan and cotinga feathers. 23 x 16 cm (9 x 6¼"). National Museum of the American Indian, Smithsonian Institution, Washington, D.C.

You may use either geometric or free-form shapes. Transfer your best sketches to the sheet of heavy watercolor paper. Set the paper aside.

2. On scrap paper, experiment with different colors and techniques for applying watercolor paints. (To review the different techniques, see Technique Tip **14**, *Handbook* page **275**.) If you are making the jewelry for yourself, think of your favorite colors. If the jewelry is to be a gift, think about the tastes of the person you have in mind.
3. Tear or cut out the paper shapes.
4. Paint your finished shapes. Make sure the colors you choose work together to create a feeling of harmony.

5. When the paint is dry, attach the pieces to a pin or earring backs with glue. If you are making a pendant, poke a hole near the top with the straight pin.

6. If you want to waterproof the jewelry, use polyurethane (pahl-ee-**your**-uh-thane) spray. *Make sure your teacher is present during this step.*

7. Display your finished jewelry. Note ways in which it is like and different from jewelry made by your classmates.

SAFETY TIP

Polyurethane sprays can be harmful if inhaled. Use these sprays outside or in rooms that are well ventilated. Use them only when an adult is present.

▲ Figure 13–18　Compare the free form of this paper jewelry to the balanced symmetry of the feathered necklace in Figure 13–17.

Ann Renée Weaver. *Paper Jewelry Pin.* 1989. Paper towels, white glue, opalescent acrylic, and textile paint. 7.6 cm (3") diameter. Private collection.

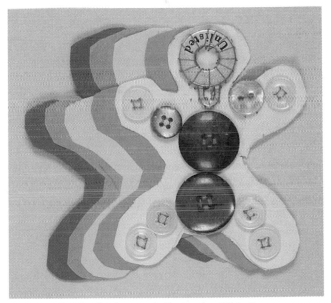

▲ Figure 13–19　Student work. Paper pin with buttons.

Try This!

STUDIO OPTIONS

■ Add other materials to your paper jewelry. Try fabric, buttons, string, or feathers.

■ Make a pin out of clay using the clay working techniques in Lesson 3.

How Can Textiles Tell a Story?

Faith Ringgold. *Bitter Nest Part II: Harlem Renaissance Party.* 1988. Acrylic on canvas, printed, tie-dyed, and pieced fabric. 238.8 x 208.3 cm (94 x 82"). National Gallery of Art, Washington, D.C.

Study the quilt on this page. Can you imagine the conversation around this table? What kinds of stories might the people be telling each other? People have enjoyed telling stories since the beginning of time. The earliest people told stories through gestures, similar to the game of charades. They also painted their stories on cave walls. Later, people told and preserved stories through spoken and written words.

There are many other ways to tell stories, however. For centuries, craftspeople have told stories through a variety of textile crafts. The word *textile* refers to cloth or fabric. Embroidery, tapestry, and quilting are all crafts related to textiles. Ancient embroidery and tapestry works often related stories from the Bible. They also showed scenes of historical events.

In the United States, quilting has been a popular textile craft since colonial times. Because fabric was difficult to find, pioneer women pieced together small scraps of fabric to make quilts. They told stories through album quilts. These quilts recorded important events such as births and marriages.

Today's craftspeople continue to tell stories through textiles. These artists are no longer limited to using only needlework on fabric, however. In *Bitter Nest Part II: Harlem Renaissance Party,* Faith Ringgold uses a combination of several media to tell her story. How does her choice of media and presentation help tell that story?

MAKING THE CONNECTION

- Who might the people in Ringgold's work be?
- Why do you think Ringgold chose to include words as well as pictures in this quilt?
- How would this work be different if the artist had used only the traditional needlework on fabric?

INTERNET ACTIVITY

Visit Glencoe's Fine Arts Web Site for students at:

http://www.glencoe.com/sec/art/students

REVIEW

 BUILDING VOCABULARY

Number a sheet of paper from 1 to 14. After each number, write the term from the list that best matches each description below.

crafts	loom
craftsperson	pottery
fibers	slab
fired	slip
glassblowing	warp
glazed	weaving
kiln	weft

1. Someone who has become an expert in an area of applied art.
2. The areas of applied art in which crafts-people work.
3. A craft in which strands of fiber are interlocked to make cloth or objects.
4. A frame used for weaving threads.
5. The craft of shaping melted glass by blowing air into it through a tube.
6. The craft of making objects from clay.
7. Hardened by heating in a kiln.
8. Any thin, threadlike materials.
9. Clay that has so much added water that it is liquid and runny.
10. A slice or sheet of clay.
11. Coated with a mixture of powdered chemicals that melt during firing into a hard, glasslike finish.
12. A special oven used to fire ceramics.
13. Threads attached to a loom.
14. Threads pulled across those already on the loom.

 REVIEWING ART FACTS

Number a sheet of paper from 15 to 20. Answer each question in a complete sentence.

15. What kinds of things do weavers use as fibers?
16. What is glass made of?
17. What are ceramics?
18. What are the different conditions of clay called?
19. Describe how clay pieces are joined in making pottery.
20. What method of claymaking is best for designing objects with straight sides?

 THINKING ABOUT ART

On a sheet of paper, answer each question in a sentence or two.

1. **Interpret.** What information would you need to have before accepting a drink out of a homemade ceramic cup?
2. **Extend.** Name two ceramic objects that would be best made using the slab method. Name two that would be best made using the pinching method. Give reasons for your choices.

MAKING ART CONNECTIONS

1. **Science.** Clay is the result of a certain type of rock decomposition. Research where clay is found and find out what is added to make it easier for artists to use. Report your results to the class.

2. **Industrial Arts.** Choose one of the products discussed in this chapter and find out how a similar product might be manufactured. Explain how the industrial methods differ from those of an individual craftsperson.

▲ The Taj Mahal has long been admired for its beauty. Did you know that it was built in the 1600s by an emperor as a tomb for his wife?

Taj Mahal. Agra, India. 1632–43.

CHAPTER 14

Architecture

When you look around any city, you notice many kinds of buildings. Houses, schools, churches, and office buildings are just a few of the different types of buildings. Each of them serves a different purpose.

Does the building on the left look familiar to you? What do you think it was used for? Who do you think used it? In this chapter you will explore the different purposes of buildings. You will also discover that buildings of the past still influence structural designs of today.

OBJECTIVES

After completing this chapter, you will be able to:

- Define architecture and explain what architects do.
- Describe three main uses of architecture.
- Explain how architects use floor plans and elevation drawings.
- Design a clay model of a house, a floor plan for a shopping mall, and a clay relief of a mall entrance.

WORDS YOU WILL LEARN

amphitheaters
architect
architecture
basilicas
elevation
facade
floor plan
post and lintel

PORTFOLIO IDEAS

Constant review of the entries in your portfolio is an important process. If you have been using it to hold all of your notes, sketches, and finished art works, you may want to revise or remove some of the entries. Think about how your viewers will see you as an artist when they look at the portfolio. Do the entries demonstrate how well you use the elements and principles of art? Do they show your growth as an artist? Entries from this chapter will represent a special interest—your ability to plan and construct examples of architecture.

LESSON 1

The Art of Architecture

Have you ever made a house out of playing cards or designed a sand castle? Maybe you have built a fortress from craft sticks. All these activities borrow ideas from the field of art called architecture. **Architecture** is *the planning and creating of buildings*. An **architect** is *an artist who works in the field of architecture*.

Architecture is considered to be both a fine art and an applied art. Like painters and sculptors, architects use color, line, shape, form, space, and texture. Like craftspeople, architects make works that are functional.

In this lesson you will look at the many uses of architecture. In later lessons you will try out some of the methods architects use in their work.

THE BEGINNINGS OF ARCHITECTURE

The first architects were cave dwellers who left their caves to build shelters from tree branches. Sun-dried mud and clay were some other materials used by early architects.

None of these materials, of course, could stand up long to wind or rain. In time, the buildings crumbled. Architects were faced with the task of finding or making stronger building materials. The early Egyptians found the solution by using stone. The most famous of their buildings are the pyramids. These amazing structures were built as tombs for the most important person in

▲ Figure 14–1 **The design of this Greek temple to the goddess Athena is a Golden Rectangle, which means it has perfect mathematical proportions.**

Parthenon. Acropolis, Athens, Greece. Begun 447 B.C.

Egyptian society, the Pharaoh. The Pharaoh was not only a king but also, in the eyes of his subjects, a god.

USES OF ARCHITECTURE

Because people need shelter to protect them from the weather and to provide privacy, creating dwellings has been a main purpose of architecture since earliest times. Other purposes were to create structures for prayer, business, and recreation. These remain key concerns of architects today.

Structures for Prayer

Because religion was central in their culture, the single most important building made by early Greek architects was the temple. The building on page **238** is an example of a Greek temple.

The Greeks did not gather inside their temples to worship. The temples were built as houses for their gods. Only priests and a few helpers were allowed inside. Everyone else prayed in front of the temple. For this reason Greek temples did not have to be large, nor provide areas for seats. Instead, Greek architects concentrated on making the temples perfectly proportioned. Their success is evident in the most famous Greek temple, the Parthenon (Figure 14–1).

In Europe in the 1200s and 1300s, larger churches were built. Architects also began exploring new ways of using line and balance. Figures 14–2 and 14–3 show two views of the same church. Notice how the architect created a feeling of lightness and openness, whether one is viewing the church from the inside or the outside. Colored light pouring into the interior through the stained glass windows added to the drama of this church.

Think of the churches you've seen in your neighborhood. Can you tell by their architectural style when they were built? In what ways are they different from churches of old? How are they similar?

▲ Figure 14–2 The repeated vertical lines of this building were intended to lead the viewer's eyes upward toward heaven.

Cathedral of Leon—Outside. 13th–14th centuries. Leon, Spain.

▲ Figure 14–3 Stained glass windows in churches like these were used to color the light inside. Does looking at the church from the inside communicate the same feelings as those in Figure 14–2? Why or why not?

Cathedral of Leon-Inside. 13th-14th centuries. Leon, Spain.

Structures for Business

The ancient Romans, like the Greeks before them, built temples. But Roman architects were also called upon to create many other kinds of buildings. Figure 14–4 shows a public arena used for sports contests and entertainment. *Huge meeting halls* called **basilicas** (buh-**sil**-ih-kuhs) were also built.

After the time of the Romans, other kinds of business buildings began appearing in cities. Banks were designed. Schools and government buildings were built.

In our own time, buildings used for business have taken a new direction—up. Strong metals such as steel have allowed architects to use space efficiently. The modern skyscraper can be found in major cities throughout the world. Buildings today are built on skeletons, or frames, of steel. One of the first buildings to use this technique is shown in Figure 14–5. It was designed by Louis Sullivan, a pioneer of modern architecture. How is this "skyscraper" different from the ones of today? How is it similar?

▲ **Figure 14–5** Rows of brick were used to cover the steel skeleton in Sullivan's building. Can you think of some coverings used today?

Louis Sullivan. Wainwright Building. 1890–1891. St. Louis, Missouri.

▲ **Figure 14–4** Eighty arched openings at the ground level enabled 50,000 spectators to leave the Colosseum so efficiently that it could be emptied in minutes.

Colosseum. Rome. A.D. 72–80.

Structures for Recreation

In addition to temples and buildings for business, the Romans designed amphitheaters (**am**-fuh-thee-uht-uhrs) for sporting events. **Amphitheaters** are *circular or oval buildings with seats rising around an open space.* The famous open-air amphitheater shown in Figure 14–4 could seat 50,000 people. Structures like this were early models of our modern sports arenas.

Sports arenas, of course, are not the only kinds of buildings designed for recreation. Concert halls and theaters are two others. Museums are a third. Figure 14–6 shows a museum by twentieth-century architect Frank Lloyd Wright. The building has one large main windowless room. The art works are hung on walls along a ramp that spirals upward. Would you know at a glance that this building is a museum? Why, or why not?

THE CHALLENGE OF ARCHITECTURE

Like other applied artists, architects are faced with a double challenge. That challenge is creating works that are both useful and pleasing to the eye. Since architecture is so much a part of everyday life, the search for new solutions is never-ending. These solutions show up not only in new styles but also in new and exciting building materials.

Take a close look at buildings going up in your town or city. There you are likely to see how architects combine a knowledge of engineering with an understanding of design to create buildings that are *both* attractive and functional.

✔CHECK YOUR UNDERSTANDING

1. What is architecture?
2. What are three main purposes of architecture?
3. What is an amphitheater?
4. Describe the double challenge facing every architect.

STUDIO ACTIVITY

Appreciating Local Architecture

The buildings around us can become so familiar we don't even notice them. This activity will help you appreciate local architecture as an art form.

Choose a building in your community you believe is interesting. Sketch the building as accurately as you can. In class, draw your building in the center of a sheet of 12 x 18 inch (30 x 46 cm) paper. In the space around your building, draw a new, imaginary setting. This setting should be an *ideal* one that allows your building to look its best. Without telling the name of your building, see if your classmates recognize it. Can you identify theirs?

P o r t f o l i o

Write a brief summary of your sketch, explaining why the building and landscape are unified. Keep the summary together with the sketch in your portfolio.

▲ **Figure 14–6** Not everyone liked Wright's design. Some said it looked like a giant cupcake. What do you think of it? Do you think it is an appropriate design for a museum?

Frank Lloyd Wright. Solomon R. Guggenheim Museum, New York, New York. 1988. Guggenheim Museum, New York, New York.

Building a Clay Model

To make a house of cards, you stand two cards on end and lay another across them. A similar approach was used by the architect of the temple in Figure 14–7. **Post and lintel** (**lint**-uhl) is *a building method in which a crossbeam is placed above two uprights*. The posts in this temple are the ridged columns. The lintels are the connected slabs of stone held up by the pillars. How many posts can you count in the picture? How many lintels?

WHAT YOU WILL LEARN

You will design and build a three-dimensional clay model for a vacation house. You will use the clay slab method you learned in Chapter 13 to cut and assemble a variety of square and rectangular shapes. Your house will have a porch built using the post and lintel method.

WHAT YOU WILL NEED

- Pencil and sheets of sketch paper
- Sheet of cloth 14 inches (36 cm) square
- 2 wood strip guides, each about 1/2 inch (13 mm) thick
- Clay
- Rolling pin and ruler
- Clay modeling tools and fork
- Container of water
- Slip

WHAT YOU WILL DO

1. Make pencil drawings to plan your house. Begin by drawing a floor plan. A **floor plan** is *a scale drawing of how a room or building would appear without a roof as if seen from above*. Floor plans show how the space inside a building is to be used. Don't forget to show the porch in your floor plan. Clearly label each room.

▲ **Figure 14–7** Posts and lintels were used to form the doorways and hallways of this ancient temple.

Parthenon. Acropolis, Athens, Greece. Begun 447 B.C.

2. Make a second drawing. This time, draw the front of the house as it would appear from outside. Such *a drawing of an outside view of a building* is called an **elevation**. An elevation can show any outside view. This one is of the **facade** (fuh-**sahd**), *the front of a building*. Your elevation should show a second view of your porch using posts and lintels.

3. To achieve a slab of clay of uniform thickness, place the wood strip guides on the cloth 8 inches (20 cm) apart. Place

the clay between the wood strips. Flatten it with the heel of your hand. Resting the rolling pin on the wood strips, roll out the clay.

4. Using the ruler and a needle tool, lightly mark off a large rectangle. This is to be the floor. Using the measurements from the length and width of your large rectangle, mark off two pairs of rectangles. One pair is to be the front and back walls. The second pair is to be the side walls. If you wish to have a house with a sloping or gabled roof, cut the front and back slabs so they come to a point. You will also need slabs for the roof. Carefully mark off windows and doors. Cut along the marks you have made and remove the clay rectangles. Keep each slab damp until you are ready to use it.

5. Using the fork to score the ends of the walls and some slip, attach the back wall and a side wall. Make sure they form an L. Carefully attach the joined walls to the floor. Then add the second side wall and the front wall.

6. Attach the floor, or deck, of the porch to the front wall. Attach the posts to the deck. Carefully add crossbeams, between posts and to the front wall.

7. Measure and cut additional clay slabs to be used for the roof and the porch. Attach these securely with slip after scoring.

8. Add decorations and details to your house by cutting into slabs or adding other details.

9. Fire your house in a kiln. Consider color schemes and glaze to add color and texture.

EXAMINING YOUR WORK

- **Describe**   Display the floor plan with your model house and the elevation drawing you used in planning your house. Identify the different rooms on your floor plan. Tell how each is to be used. Point out the posts and lintels you used in designing the porch. Tell how the slabs were tightly joined before your model was fired.

- **Analyze**   Show how your model is made from a variety of square and rectangular shapes. What forms have you created?

- **Interpret**   Tell how a viewer would know that your model represents a vacation house. What word would you use to describe the feeling your house gives — comfortable, peaceful, unusual? List ways in which the family living in your house could use the porch.

- **Judge**   Tell whether your work succeeds as architecture. Explain your answer. If you were to do another, what would you do differently?

10. *Optional*: Your house may be glazed and fired again, or you may wish to paint your model with acrylic paint. One or two coats of polymer resin coating will give acrylic colors a great luster.

Try This! COMPUTER OPTION

■ Use your computer art program to design a house to build from clay. Choose a variety of Shape and Straight Line tools to draw both a floor plan and a view of the facade. Use the Grids and Rulers menu, if available, and work in scale (¼" = 1 foot). Indicate doors, windows, and stairs. Label the floor plan with the Text tool and indicate the scale. Title and Save. Next, draw the front view with the Shape and Straight Line tools. Include surface textures—brick, wood, stone—on the facade. Title, Save, and Print both drawings.

Drawing Floor Plans

Architects work with and design space. In every instance, their designs must take into account the needs and desires of the people making use of the spaces they create. Typically, they develop these designs in an orderly fashion. First, they consider the purpose of the proposed structure. Then they make preliminary sketches showing the possible divisions of space within the building. They also sketch its outward appearance. Next they prepare more elevations and detailed floor plans (Figures 14–8 and 14–9). Elevations may provide views of the building from different vantage points. Their floor plans might show the location, size, and shape of rooms, corridors, windows, entrances, stairs, and elevators.

Imagine that your community is planning to build a new shopping mall. You are the architect selected by community leaders to design this new mall. They have asked you to design a unique structure that will provide enough space inside for businesses and shoppers to move about freely. They also want a large parking area for mall visitors. Most important, they want the mall to be an inviting, convenient, and pleasant place for people to shop.

WHAT YOU WILL LEARN

You will design a floor plan for a one-story shopping mall. Your mall will have one department store, 10 smaller shops, and two restaurants. The department store should be emphasized as the most prominent place of business in the mall. Divide the space in your mall so that large and small shops are cre-

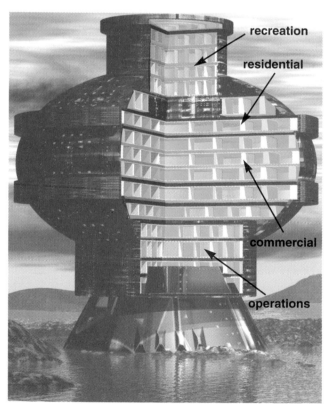

▲ **Figure 14–8** Have you ever imagined an enclosed city shaped like this one?

Computer-drawn elevation drawing of an imaginary city.

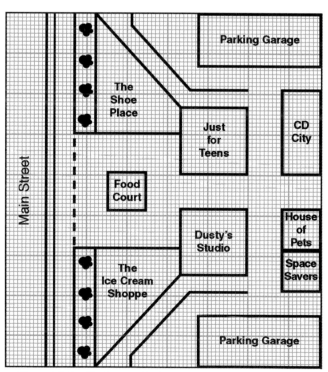

▲ **Figure 14–9** Student work. A computer-drawn section of a shopping mall floor plan.

ated. Your mall will also have a wide, roomy public walkway linking the different stores. Finally, it will have a large parking lot for mall visitors.

WHAT YOU WILL NEED

- Pencil, ruler, and eraser
- Sheets of sketch paper
- Sheets of white graph paper, 18 x 24 inch (46 x 61 cm)
- Transparent tape

WHAT YOU WILL DO

1. Using pencil, ruler, and sketch paper, create different possibilities for floor plans. (You may use malls you have visited for ideas. The final design, however, should be your own.) A large department store will be the focal point of the mall. Decide what kinds of businesses you will have among the 10 shops. Decide which businesses will be next to each other along the walkway. Decide whether either or both of the restaurants will serve fast food. Decide how much floor space each business will need. Provide a large parking lot. Use the foot as a unit of measurement. Develop a scale for your design, such as 1/4 inch equals 1 foot.

2. Carefully line up two sheets of the white graph paper so their long sides touch. Fasten them where they meet with transparent tape. Turn the paper over. Neatly transfer the final design of your floor plan to the large sheet. Use your ruler. Neatly label each store. Label the walkway and parking area.

EXAMINING YOUR WORK

- **Describe**   Tell which store in your mall received the most floor space. Explain why. Tell what other kinds of shops you placed in your mall.
- **Analyze**   Explain how you divided the space in your mall. Point out why some shops received more space than others. Explain how the department store is emphasized in your plan. Tell whether the walkways in your mall are wide and roomy. Tell whether there is enough parking space for times when the mall is busy.
- **Interpret**   Show what features you added to make your mall inviting to visitors. Tell whether the stores and restaurants will appeal to many different tastes. Tell whether visitors would find your mall pleasant to visit. Explain why.
- **Judge**   Tell whether you think your work succeeds as applied art. Explain your answer.

3. Show where the entrance to the mall will be. Add any details that will be used as decoration.
4. Display your floor plan alongside those of your classmates. How are the plans different?
5. *Optional*: Select one plan from the class and construct it out of cardboard as a group project.

Try This! STUDIO OPTIONS

■ Design a detailed floor plan for one of the stores in your mall. Decide whether the store will have wide or narrow aisles. Decide whether it will have counters or shelves. Draw your plan.

■ Draw two elevations for your mall—one from the front and the second from any angle you choose. Add details such as arched windows, floor tiles, skylights, and landscaping. Use colored pencils, watercolors, pen and ink, or crayons.

LESSON 4

Clay Entrance Relief

Has it ever occurred to you that buildings can have personalities? As with people, the faces, or facades, of buildings often suggest different personalities. Look at Figures 14–10 and 14–11. Both are entrances to churches. Would you describe either one as quiet and humble? Which seems to be bold and proud? How are these personalities suggested?

Imagine that your mall design in the previous lesson was so successful that you have been asked to plan another. This time, community leaders want you to begin by creating a model of the new mall entrance. They want this entrance to give the mall a definite personality.

WHAT YOU WILL LEARN

You will create a three-dimensional elevation of a mall entrance out of clay. Using the slab method, you will carve and model details to create a variety of light and dark values. A variety of different actual textures will be used. Your relief will give the mall a personality.

WHAT YOU WILL NEED

- Pencil and sheets of sketch paper
- Rolling pin and ruler
- Sheet of cloth, 14 inches (36 cm) square

▲ **Figure 14–10** How would you describe the mood of this church? Why?

Entryway at Kilpeck Church. Wales.

▲ **Figure 14–11** Compare this church entrance with the one in Figure 14–10. How are they different? How are they the same?

Mission San Jose. 18th century. San Antonio, Texas.

- 2 wood strip guides, each about 1/2 inch (13 mm) thick
- Clay and modeling tools

WHAT YOU WILL DO

1. Make pencil sketches of different mall entrance designs. As you work, think about the personality you would like the mall to have. Is the mall going to have a fun-filled look or a classic, expensive look? Think about what features would help capture the mood you prefer. Select your best drawing.

2. Place the wood strip guides on the cloth about 6 inches (15 cm) apart. Flatten the clay between the guide sticks, and roll out the clay. Measure and cut out a 6 x 8 inch (15 x 20 cm) rectangle.

3. Arrange the rectangle so a long side is facing you. Working from your elevation drawing, carve and model details of your mall entrance. These details should stick out or be cut into the clay to create a variety of dark and light values. As you work, consider the effects of gradual and abrupt value changes created by carving or adding rounded and angular details. (See Figure 4–12.) Use a needle tool to show the brick or other surface textures. Carve out doors and any details above or to the sides. If you like, include the name of the mall.

4. Using the pencil, poke a small, shallow hole in the back of your relief. The hole should be at the center and about an inch from the top, made at an upward angle.

5. When your relief is dry, fire it. Hang your finished relief from the hole you made in the back on a nail or hook.

- **Describe**   Point out the doors and other details of your mall entrance. Show the places in your relief where you carved. Show the places where you modeled. Point out the different actual textures you added to your relief. Show where light and dark values are created.
- **Analyze**   Explain how a variety of textures makes your mall more interesting. Explain why a variety of values was needed.
- **Interpret**   Identify the personality of your mall. Explain what you did to express this personality in your design of the mall entrance.
- **Judge**   Tell whether your work succeeds as applied art. Explain your answer.

▲ **Figure 14–12   Student work. Clay entrance relief work in progress.**

Try This! COMPUTER OPTION

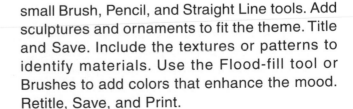

■ Design the entrance to an amusement park. Consider openings for different kinds of traffic—pedestrians, wheelchairs, and vehicles. Use the Symmetry tool or menu, if available, or Copy and Paste sections to create formal balance. Draw with the small Brush, Pencil, and Straight Line tools. Add sculptures and ornaments to fit the theme. Title and Save. Include the textures or patterns to identify materials. Use the Flood-fill tool or Brushes to add colors that enhance the mood. Retitle, Save, and Print.

Pyramids of Cheops, Chefren, and Mycerinus. Giza, Egypt. c. 2680–2565 B.C.

The Mystery of the Pyramids

Imagine that you are an architect hired by a king to design and build a skyscraper. The structure must be both functional, attractive, and last a very long time. There is a catch, however. You will not have any modern tools, electrical equipment, or heavy machinery with which to build it.

Your task would be similar to one facing the ancient Egyptians who built the pyramids at Giza. In the twenty-sixth century B.C., three Egyptian kings ordered the building of three enormous pyramids. The pyramids would serve as tombs for the rulers. One expert estimated that 100,000 men worked for 20 years to complete the enormous pyramids at Giza. The workers used more than two million stone blocks. Each stone weighed more than two tons.

How the Egyptians were able to build this structure without modern equipment and technology remains a mystery. The stone most likely came from limestone quarries found near Giza. To move the stones, many experts think that the Egyptians built a circular ramp around each pyramid. Then they moved the blocks up the ramp as the pyramid was constructed. Thousands of years later, the pyramids at Giza are the only one of the Seven Wonders of the Ancient World that still exists.

MAKING THE CONNECTION

- ✔ Why did the Egyptians choose limestone as the material for the pyramids?
- ✔ Why did the construction of the pyramids require so many workers and so many years to complete?
- ✔ Look for more information about pyramids. Why did ancient rulers use pyramids for their tombs?

INTERNET ACTIVITY

Visit Glencoe's Fine Arts Web Site for students at:

http://www.glencoe.com/sec/art/students

CHAPTER 14
REVIEW

BUILDING VOCABULARY

Number a sheet of paper from 1 to 8. After each number, write the term from the list that best matches each description below.

amphitheaters   elevation
architect   facade
architecture   floor plan
basilicas   post and lintel

1. The field of art dealing with the planning and creating of buildings.
2. An artist who works at planning and creating buildings.
3. Huge meeting halls.
4. Circular or oval buildings with seats rising around an open space.
5. A building method in which a crossbeam is placed above the two uprights.
6. A scale drawing of how a building would appear as if seen from above and there were no roof.
7. A drawing of an outside view of a building.
8. The front of a building.

REVIEWING ART FACTS

Number a sheet of paper from 9 to 18. Answer each question in a complete sentence.

9. Who were the first architects? What did they build? What media did they use?
10. What building material was used by the early Egyptians? What was an advantage of this material over ones used before it?
11. What are four main uses for architecture?
12. Why was it not important that Greek temples be large?
13. In what ways were churches of the 1200s and 1300s different from earlier temples?
14. What made it possible for architects to start building upward?
15. For what modern structures did early amphitheaters pave the way?
16. Name three kinds of buildings used for recreation.
17. What challenge faces every architect?
18. What kind of drawing reveals how the space inside a building is to be used?

THINKING ABOUT ART

On a sheet of paper, answer each question in a sentence or two.

1. **Compare and contrast.** What does architecture have in common with the other visual arts, such as painting and sculpture? In what ways is it unlike those arts?
2. **Analyze.** Why are both floor plans and elevations important in planning works of architecture?
3. **Extend.** From what you learned in this chapter, what other subjects besides art do you suppose architects study? Explain your answer.

MAKING ART CONNECTIONS

1. **Community Affairs.** A zoning law specifies what type of building may be built in a certain part of a city. In pairs or small groups, research whether there are laws that keep certain types of buildings away from schools. When research is complete, share your results with the class.

2. **Social Studies.** Research famous walls around the world, such as the Great Wall of China, the Berlin Wall, the Vietnam Veterans Memorial in Washington D.C., or Hadrian's Wall in Great Britain. Explain how these walls affected the people who lived near them, and explore the structure of these walls.

▲ **Advances in technology help artists create art in new ways. In this case, technology** *becomes* **the art work itself!**

Nam June Paik. *Technology.* 1991. 25 video monitors, 3 laser discs with unique 3 discs in a steel and plywood cabinet with aluminum sheeting and details of copper, bronze, plastic, and other materials. Approx. 332.6 x 192.1 x 131.7 cm (127 x 75⅝ x 51⅞"). National Museum of American Art, Smithsonian Institution, Washington, D.C. Museum purchase through the Luisita L. and Franz H. Denghausen Endowment.

CHAPTER 15

Photography, Film, Video, and Computers

Throughout this book you have learned about the many different ways that artists express themselves. Painters do this with brushes. Sculptors use clay, wood, or metal. Illustrators use pen or pencils.

Look at the photograph at the left. How is it like other works of art you have studied? How is it different? In this chapter you will learn about artists who use the camera, film, video, and the computer to produce their art works.

OBJECTIVES

After completing this chapter, you will be able to:
- Describe the history of photography.
- Tell how movies are made.
- Describe the characteristics of computer art programs.
- Make a photo essay, a silent movie, and a multi-media presentation.

WORDS YOU WILL LEARN

analog system
camera
cinematographer
daguerreotypes
digital system
director
microprocessors
motion picture
multi-media programs
negatives
photography
producer
wet plate

PORTFOLIO IDEAS

Select three art works created in this chapter that represent your ability to communicate a feeling, a mood, or an idea with photography, film, video, and computers. For each piece, write a self-reflection that identifies what you have learned, how the form of technology affected the finished art work, and why the piece is a good example of your growth as an artist. Mention any comments and feedback that you received from other artists and viewers about the works. Include the self-reflections and, whenever possible, the final art work in your portfolio.

The Art of Photography

What do all works of art have in common? All try to present an image in a way that makes it special. In recent times, artists have discovered new ways of creating special images. In this lesson you will learn about one of those ways—photography. In later lessons you will learn about three others—the arts of film, video, and computers.

PHOTOGRAPHY

Today we take photographs for granted. They are all around us. Newspapers, magazines, and books are full of them. It is strange to think that photography was an expensive and difficult process just over 150 years ago. **Photography** is *the art of making images by exposing a chemically treated surface to light*. Photographs are made using *a dark box with a hole controlling how much light enters*, better known as a **camera**.

THE HISTORY OF PHOTOGRAPHY

The idea of capturing an image using light is a very old one. Attempts to do this date back to the time of Leonardo da Vinci (Figure 15–1). It was not until the 1800s, however, that the first true photographs were made. L.J.M. Daguerre (duh-gehr) was the French inventor of an early method of photography. These were called **daguerreotypes** (duh-**gehr**-uh-types), *silvery, mirrorlike images on a copper plate*. Figure 15–2 shows a hand–colored version, taken by an unknown photographer. Notice how worn and scratched the image is. Can you identify the subject of this photograph without reading the credit line?

Daguerreotypes took a long time to make. They were also very costly. The wet plate method, introduced in the 1850s, brought improvements in both these areas. **Wet plate** is

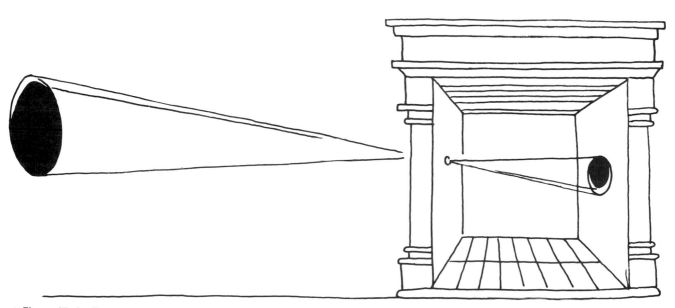

▲ **Figure 15–1** The camera obscura was an early attempt at photography. The word *camera* means "chamber" and *obscura* means "dark" in Italian. The first images were upside down until mirrors were combined with the lenses.

◀ Figure 15–2 Early photographs were hand-colored and viewed together in a stereopticon.

Unknown/French. *Street Flutists.* c. 1852. Stereograph daguerreotype. 8.7 x 16.8 cm (3⅜ x 6⅝"). International Museum of Photography, George Eastman House, New York.

a method of photography in which an image is created on glass that is coated with chemicals, then transferred to paper or cardboard, as in photography today. Also like photographs today, wet plate photographs used **negatives**, *reverse images of the object photographed*. The wet plate method was used to photograph important news events through the 1870s. Figure 15–3 was taken by Mathew Brady, a famous Civil War photographer. Figure 15–4 was taken by Dorothea Lange. She was a photojournalist in the 1930s. What could pictures like these add to a news account that words could not?

▲ Figure 15–3   In what ways are photographs like these more telling than a drawing would be?

Mathew Brady. *Civil War.* c. 1865. Photograph. National Archives, Washington, D.C.

▲ **Figure 15–4   If this were a painting, would its impact be different from this photograph? Why or why not?**

Dorothea Lange. *White Angel Breadline*. Photograph. Oakland Museum, San Francisco, California.

▲ **Figure 15–5** Photography and painting are combined in this art work. What mood does the finished work convey to you?

Jessica Hines. *Dream Series*. Hand-colored black-and-white photograph. 40.6 x 50.8 cm (16 x 20″). Private collection.

PHOTOGRAPHY AS ART

As picture taking methods improved, some photographers turned from recording images of the world around them, taking pictures of whatever captured their interest, to exploring photography's potential as art. Works by Dorothea Lange (Figure 15–4) and Alfred Stieglitz did more than just record interesting images—they were also carefully composed, in much the same way a painter composes a picture. In this way, photography became visually appealing art.

In recent years some artists have combined painting and photography to create a new kind of visual expression. Look closely at Figure 15–5. Notice how the artist has added painted areas to a black-and-white photograph of an automobile in front of a house. The finished work combines familiar images from the real world with ideas and feelings originating in the mind of the artist.

✔ CHECK YOUR UNDERSTANDING

1. Define *photography*. Define *camera*.
2. When were the first real photographs made?
3. What were two methods of making photographs in the 1800s?
4. Name two similarities between the photographs taken in the 1800s and the photographs taken today.

LESSON 2
Photo Essay

In the 1950s, Andy Warhol was such a successful commercial artist that even his show advertisements won an award. However, in 1962 he shocked the art world by exhibiting stenciled pictures of soup cans and sculptures of soap pad boxes. He was soon recognized as a leader in a new art movement known as Pop Art.

Robert and Ethel Scull were enthusiastic collectors of Pop Art. Robert Scull asked Warhol to make a photo essay, a collection of photographs that together make a statement about a subject. In this case, the subject was Mrs. Scull. The artist took Mrs. Scull to an ordinary photo booth where she posed for more than 100 photos. From these, Warhol selected the images used for the photo essay shown in Figure 15–6.

Look closely at these photos. How many different expressions and moods can you identify? What effect is achieved by the addition of the sunglasses? Do you think Mrs. Scull was pleased with Warhol's photo essay? Why or why not?

WHAT YOU WILL LEARN

You will create a black-and-white photo essay entitled "Feelings." To do this, you will select and mount no less than ten photographs of a single person exhibiting different expressions and emotions. You will give your essay variety and visual interest by combining full-size and cropped photographs showing the entire figure or parts of the figure.

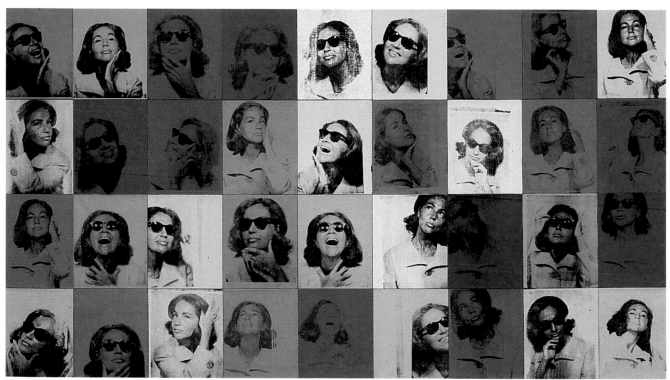

▲ **Figure 15–6** The artist took Mrs. Scull to a photo booth for these candid shots. Then he made them into photo silk screens to complete his painting.

Andy Warhol. *Ethel Scull 36 Times.* 1963. Synthetic polymer paint silk-screened on canvas. 202.6 x 363.9 cm (79¾ x 143¼") overall. Whitney Museum of American Art, New York, New York.

WHAT YOU WILL NEED

- Instant camera and a roll of 36 exposures of black-and-white film
- A sheet of mat boards (black or white) cut to a size to accommodate the photographs selected for the essay
- White glue

WHAT YOU WILL DO

1. Ask a friend to serve as the subject for your photo essay. Explain that he or she must model facial expressions, gestures, and postures suggesting a variety of different emotions. Discuss the different emotions that might be included in the essay and how these emotions might be exhibited.

2. Have your model demonstrate the different poses as you choose an angle from which you will take each photograph. Decide if photographing from above or below eye level will add interest to the photo. Also determine where close-up or long shots will be most effective.

3. Photograph your subject using all 36 exposures on the roll of film. Compose each photograph to make certain that you are capturing the exact expression, gesture, and pose needed to suggest a particular emotion or feeling.

4. Lay out all your developed photographs and select the best ones to include in your essay. Make certain to choose no less than ten that exhibit different emotions or moods.

EXAMINING YOUR WORK

- **Describe** Did you include at least ten photographs in your essay? Are there a number of different expressions, gestures, and poses exhibited?
- **Analyze** Do the photographs in your essay exhibit variety or harmony in any way? How? What kind of balance, formal or informal, is demonstrated by your essay?
- **Interpret** Does your photo essay clearly show different feelings or emotions? How many different emotions are provided? Could other students in your class identify these different emotions?
- **Judge** Do you feel that your photo essay is successful? What is its best feature—the photographs, their arrangement on the mat board, or both the photos and the arrangement? If you were to do another photo essay, what would you do differently?

5. Arrange your photographs on a sheet of white or black mat board cut to accommodate them. Experiment with different placements until you are satisfied with the overall effect. You may use either formal or informal balance. Carefully glue the photographs in place.

6. Exhibit your photo essay along with those created by other students.

Try This! STUDIO OPTIONS

■ Create another photo essay using color film. In this essay select a single emotion such as happy, sad, angry, impatient, jealous, or lonely as your theme.

■ Create a slide presentation showing one or several figures engaged in a humorous or serious activity. Select a musical recording that compliments your slide show. Give your slide presentation in class.

The Art of Film

"Lights. Camera. Action." These may not be words you would expect to hear spoken in an artist's studio. In some artists' studios, however, the words are spoken nearly every day. These are the kinds of studios where movies are made. The artist who speaks the words is known as the director.

In this lesson you will learn about the art of filmmaking.

THE BEGINNINGS OF FILM

After photographers learned to capture still images using light, they began looking ahead to the next form of creative expression. By the end of the 1800s inventors had found a way to capture moving images using light. The **motion picture,** *photographs of the same subject taken a very short time apart and flashed onto a screen,* made the image appear to be moving (Figures 15–7 and 15–8).

▲ Figure 15–7 Motion pictures can bring books to life, as in this version of *The Jungle Book.*

© Walt Disney, 1994/MPTV.

MAKING FILMS

Every motion picture, or movie, is the combined effort of hundreds of people. The three most important of those people are the director, the producer, and the cinematographer.

The Director

The director is the single most important person in the making of a movie. The **director** is *the person in charge of shooting the film and guiding the actors.* He or she also helps with the script.

The director's main job is deciding how every scene should be photographed. To get just the right look, a director may shoot the same scene dozens of times.

▲ Figure 15–8 Talented actors are an important part of successful movies. What mood is created by the actors in this scene from *Star Trek: Generations?*

© Paramount, 1994/MPTV.

The Producer

The **producer** is *the person in charge of the business end of making a movie.* The producer is the person who finds the story and hires the director. He or she also figures out how much money it will cost to make the movie. Some producers take part in selecting actors and in writing the script.

The Cinematographer

The **cinematographer** (sin-uh-muh-**tahg**-ruh-fuhr) is *the person in charge of running the camera or cameras.* Like other artists, cinematographers are trained in using light and color.

Before filming, or shooting, the director and cinematographer will go over the script together. They will discuss the different camera angles and techniques for shooting each scene.

THE ART OF FILM

The very first films made were silent. Since these films used no words, strong dramatic acting was required. They could be shown to audiences around the world. These films required strong and exaggerated acting.

The arrival of sound in the late 1920s opened up new doors to filmmakers. It also closed doors to actors whose voices did not sound right.

▲ Figure 15–10   Movies that feature computer animation are growing in popularity. What skills would you need to be part of the artist team for a movie such as *Toy Story*?

© Walt Disney, 1995/MPTV.

The next advance in film, color, made possible the first colored film classics. These were movies such as *The Adventures of Robin Hood* and *The Wizard of Oz.*

The films of today, of course, use dazzling effects the earliest filmmakers probably never dreamed of. Computers and other high-tech equipment have allowed directors to shoot "the impossible." (See Figures 15–9 and 15–10.) One can only guess what astonishing screen images tomorrow's breakthroughs will bring.

✔ CHECK YOUR UNDERSTANDING

1. What are motion pictures? When was filmmaking invented?
2. What is a director? What are some of the director's tasks?
3. What is a producer? What are some of the producer's tasks?
4. What are two advances that have been made in filmmaking since the days of silent films?

▲ Figure 15–9   The special effects in *Jurassic Park* captured the imagination of viewers everywhere. What challenges do you think the director of this movie faced?

© Universal, photo by Murray Close, 1993/MPTV.

Making a Silent Movie

Before the days of sound in movies, the filmmakers had their work cut out for them. They had to rely totally on action to tell the story (Figure 15–11). For those pioneering filmmakers, actions truly speak louder than words.

WHAT YOU WILL LEARN

You will be part of a group that makes a silent movie. The group will be headed up by a producer and director. A cinematographer for the group will shoot the film using a home video camera. Music will be used to help the audience feel the mood and action. Captions will be used to help the audience understand the action. (See Figure 15–12.)

WHAT YOU WILL NEED

- Pencil
- Large notepad divided in half by a vertical pencil line
- Hand-held video camera with tripod
- Sheets of white poster board
- Black broad-line marker
- Audio tape recorder

WHAT YOU WILL DO

1. The class is to be divided into two groups. Each group is to choose from among its members a producer, a director, a cinematographer, and a three-member writing team. Every other group member is to be an actor.
2. The producer for each group is to meet with the writers. Together, the producer and writers are to agree on a story idea. The story, which is to be original, may be funny, serious, or suspenseful. The story should have parts for as many actors as there are actors in the group. As the writers create, they should tell what each character is doing at any given moment. The final version of the story should be written on the left half of the notepad.
3. While the writers work, the director and cinematographer should test the equipment. At the director's instructions, the cinematographer should take long shots and close-ups. The two should test out indoor shots using the camera's lighting attachment. They should test different uses for the tripod.

▶ **Figure 15–11 Comedians were especially popular during the silent film era. Do you find this scene funny? Explain your answer. How is movement shown in this picture?**

Directed by Harold Lloyd. Still from *Safety Last.* 1923. The Museum of Modern Art, Film Stills Archive, New York, New York.

4. When the script is finished, the producer and director should read it. Together, they should decide which scenes need captions to help viewers understand the action. The producer should ask the writers to create these captions with poster board and marker. The producer and director should decide which actors are to play which parts. They should decide what kind of music best fits the mood of the story. The producer should search for and make tape recordings of particular pieces of music.

5. The director should read the script again, this time along with the cinematographer. The two should decide from which angle to shoot each scene or action. They should decide whether a scene calls for a close-up or a long shot. The director should make notes on the right side of the notepad. He or she should also note the points in the shooting where captions are needed.

6. The actors should rehearse the story. They will take their cues on where to stand and what to do from the director. The actors should try to show through their actions and expressions what is happening.

7. When the director feels the group is well prepared, shooting should begin. The finished film should be shown, with music, to the rest of the class.

EXAMINING YOUR WORK

- **Describe**   Describe what things the director did before and during shooting. Tell what decisions the director and producer made together. Tell what points the director and cinematographer discussed. Tell what decisions they reached. Tell whether the actors followed the director's instructions. Tell whether they showed what was happening through their actions and expressions.
- **Analyze**   Identify different ways the camera was used. Explain the results.
- **Interpret**   Tell what the story was about. Describe its mood. Explain how the captions helped tell the story and express the mood. Explain how the music added to the mood and emphasized the action.
- **Judge**   Tell whether you feel your work succeeds. Explain your answer.

▶ Figure 15–12   Students shooting a silent film.

COMPUTER OPTION

Try This!

■ Use a camcorder to make a silent video. Import the video into the computer using a digitizing card. Choose a multi-media program to edit and to add an introduction, transitions, ending, and any captions that would help to explain the plot. Select and include music to match the action. To achieve the effect of early movies, turn off the color in the Control Panel, and view the movie on the computer monitor in black and white.

The Art of Video and Computers

Photography and film changed the way artists looked at the world, how they captured images, and how they created works of art. More recently, two other technologies have surpassed film in the possibilities they offer to the artist—videotape and computers.

Video Technology

Videotape records and stores images and sounds as magnetic impulses, the same way a tape recorder registers sounds. Patterns of light beams and wavelengths are translated into electric waves, which are then picked up by the recorder and imprinted magnetically on film. *A system that uses electromagnetic energy to imprint both sound and pictures* is called an **analog system.** Think of analog systems as waves of water. (See Figure 15–13.)

Television studios were the first to record programs on videotape because the method was more efficient than film. Gradually, videotape and video cameras made their way into homes, so that anyone could tape broadcasts, watch the movie of their choice, or make and view their own home movies.

▲ Figure 15–14   The computer is a digital system. It processes on and off pulses of electricity that you control through a keyboard or a mouse.

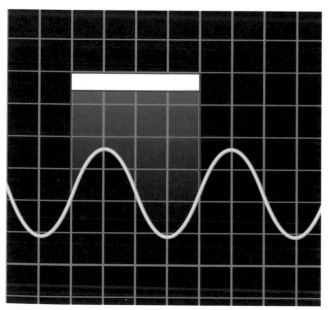

▲ Figure 15–13   The analog system uses electromagnetic waves to record sounds and images. One complete wave cycle is shown above.

The Art of Video

Why is videotape such a remarkable development? Videotape can imitate photography and film, and it can immediately record and play back. There is no film to be developed. Almost instantly, video artists record the sights, sounds, and scenes of nature or they create a totally new environment with moving and still images and sound. This technology paints a visual story or message, just like an artist who paints on canvas.

Perhaps more importantly, video can be combined with the tools available on the computer.

Computer Technology

The first computers were intended only for research and business, and they were slow and bulky. A computer uses a **digital system,** or *a system that processes words and images using a series of on and off switches.* Think of a digital system as a series of heart beats or bursts of energy. (See Figure 15–14.) The difference between the analog and the digital systems is the most important difference between video and computer technology. Thanks to the digital system, today's computers are becoming faster and smaller. *Tiny computers,* called **microprocessors,** can now operate computer programs that once required a computer the size of your classroom! (See Figure 15–15.)

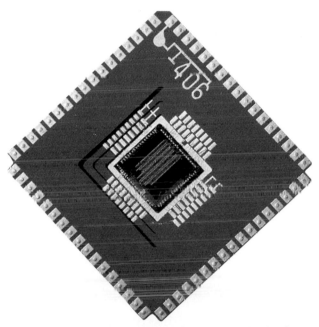

▲ **Figure 15–15** This tiny circuit is smaller than the tip of your finger, but powerful enough to run a computer.

The Art of Computers

Software programs are written for specific tasks on a computer and are tools for working, learning, and entertainment. With Paint or Draw programs, artists can draw, paint, manipulate, and design images. The art work in Figure 15–16 was created with a computer art program. More recent digital technologies, including scanning devices and virtual reality, provide even more exciting ways to stimulate an artist's imagination.

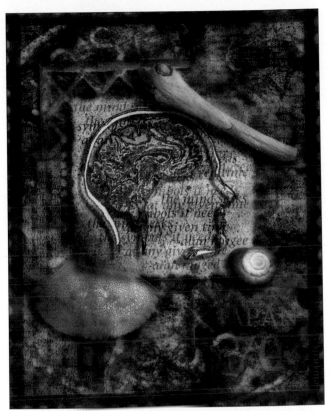

▲ **Figure 15–16** How is this computer-generated art work similar to an oil painting? How is it different?

Russell Sparkman. *The Mind Speaks.* 1995. Software: Collage by Adobe Photoshop.

Multi-media Art

Combining technologies on the computer is made easier by the development of **multi-media programs.** These are *computer software programs that help users design, organize, and combine text, graphics, video, and sound in one document.* With a little imagination, you can make reports, presentations, and art portfolios come alive. In the next lesson, you will create a multi-media presentation about an artist's life.

✔ CHECK YOUR UNDERSTANDING

1. What is an analog system?
2. What advantage does video have over film?
3. What is a digital system?
4. What is the advantage of a multi-media program?

LESSON 6

Multi-media Presentation

Imagine a classroom where students present their art work from a small disk or a videotape. The newest multi-media software programs make it possible to combine text, graphics, video, and sound in one document. Now you can select from a variety of electronic tools to create art works, depending upon your interests and available resources.

WHAT YOU WILL LEARN

With a group of three or four students, research, plan, and create a multi-media presentation about an artist's life. Consider the artist's country of birth, cultural influences, significant work and style, period of time, and place in art history. You will discover what people or events influenced his or her work, how this artist's work affected other artists, and why this artist's work is important today. Your presentation will include drawings, photographs or video, text, and sound to demonstrate what you have learned about the artist.

WHAT YOU WILL NEED

- Pencil and paper
- Resources such as books, magazines, newspapers, videos, CD-ROMs, laser discs, electronic encyclopedias, and on-line sources
- Art materials
- Technology tools, such as a computer, audio and videotape player and recorder, monitor, still camera, and camcorder

▲ Figure 15–17   Student work. A screen display of the introduction to a multi-media presentation.

WHAT YOU WILL DO

1. Select an artist that you and other group members would like to know more about. Research the artist using a variety of print and electronic resources. Use at least one resource that you have never previously explored. Include a bibliography of resources with the presentation.
2. Take notes on the information using paper and pencil or a word processing program. Discover information about the historic events as well as the work of other artists creating at the same time.
3. Make an outline of the information in chronological order. Be sure to notice how time and place influenced the artist.
4. Brainstorm and select a format for compiling and presenting facts and images about the artist and art works. Include music of the time or music to create a mood.
5. Choose such art materials as paint, oil pastels, pens, modeling clay, paper, and poster board to present examples of the artist's work.
6. You might present your report in the form of a drama or a play with costumes, props, and displays. Include at least one technology tool.

Try This! COMPUTER OPTION

- Make an electronic portfolio entry of your own art work. You might include all the art work created during this class or one example that you consider to be your best. Choose from a variety of hardware tools such as a still camera (either analog or digital), camcorder, tape recorder, and scanner. Select software for writing, drawing, and organizing the information. Include text, graphics drawn on an art program, photographs or video, and sound. Create a computer presentation using a multimedia software program.

Dorothea Lange. *Oregon or Bust.* c. 1936. Library of Congress, Washington, D.C.

Images of the Great Depression

The 1930s were some of the most difficult years in the history of the United States. After the stock market crash of 1929, the country entered into a period of economic depression. During the lowest point of the Great Depression, 25 percent of American workers were unemployed.

Many of those unemployed were farm workers. Agriculture was one of the industries hardest hit by the depression. In addition, over-use of the land and a severe drought had created serious problems in the midwestern farmlands. High winds had picked up the dry soil and created major dust storms. The area became known as the Dust Bowl, and more than half of the farmers lost their farms. Most of them packed their belongings and headed west, becoming migrant workers in search of jobs. Although they were sad to leave their homes, many were also hopeful that they would find a better life.

The images of these men and women were captured on film by photographers such as Dorothea Lange. In her photograph called *Oregon or Bust*, a single moment in time documents an entire era in United States history.

MAKING THE CONNECTION

- Which elements in this photograph tell you that the man is a migrant worker?
- What message, idea, or feeling does this photograph communicate to the viewer?
- Look for more information about the Dust Bowl. How was the farmland restored?

INTERNET ACTIVITY

Visit Glencoe's Fine Arts Web Site for students at:

http://www.glencoe.com/sec/art/students

REVIEW

 BUILDING VOCABULARY

Number a sheet of paper from 1 to 13. After each number, write the term from the list that best matches each description below.

analog system
camera
cinematographer
daguerreotypes
digital system
director
microprocessors
motion picture
multi-media
  programs
negatives
photography
producer
wet plate

1. The art of making images by exposing a chemically treated surface to light.
2. A dark box with a hole controlling how much light enters.
3. Silvery, mirrorlike images made on a copper plate.
4. A photography method in which an image is created on glass coated with chemicals.
5. Reverse images of an object photographed.
6. Photographs of the same subject taken a very short time apart and flashed onto a screen.
7. The person in charge of shooting a film and guiding the actors.
8. The person in charge of the business end of making a movie.
9. The person in charge of running the camera in the filming of a movie.
10. A system that uses electromagnetic energy to imprint both sound and pictures.
11. A system that processes words and images using a series of on and off switches.
12. Tiny computers.
13. Computer software programs that help users design, organize, and combine text, graphics, video, and sound in one document.

 REVIEWING ART FACTS

Number a sheet of paper from 14 to 19. Answer each question in a complete sentence.

14. Who is L.J.M. Daguerre? What contribution did he make to photography?
15. In what two ways was the wet plate an improvement over earlier methods?
16. What is a photo essay?
17. What is a cinematographer? What do they have in common with other artists?
18. Why were the first films made able to be shown to people around the world?
19. Why is the digital system faster than the analog system?

 THINKING ABOUT ART

On a sheet of paper, answer each question in a sentence or two.

1. **Compare and contrast.** In what ways are daguerreotypes and wet plate prints the same? In what ways are they different?
2. **Interpret.** Different shots of the same scene in a movie are called takes. In what way are takes similar to the studies done by painters and sculptors?

MAKING ART CONNECTIONS

1. **Social Studies.** Study the Brady photograph of the Civil War battlefield on page **253**. Notice the equipment and uniforms of the military personnel. Find news photos that document events from World War I or World War II. Report to the class how the dress and equipment have changed.
2. **Science.** Research the development of the materials used in photography and find out how the chemical process allows light to be captured on film.

▲ Working on group murals is an excellent way to practice
artistic skills, gain recognition, and at the same time, have fun.

HANDBOOK CONTENTS

1. Making Gesture Drawings

Gesture drawing is a way of showing movement in a sketch. Gesture drawings have no outlines or details. You are not expected to draw the figure. Instead, you are expected to draw the movement, or what the figure is doing. Follow these guidelines:

- Use the side of the drawing tool. Do not hold the medium as you would if you were writing.
- Find the lines of movement that show the direction in which the figure is bending. Draw the main line showing this movement.
- Use quickly drawn lines to build up the shape of the person.

2. Making Contour Drawings

Contour drawing is a way of capturing the feel of a subject. When doing a contour drawing, remember the following pointers:

- If you accidentally pick up your pen or pencil, don't stop working. Place your pen or pencil back where you stopped. Begin again from that point.
- If you have trouble keeping your eyes off the paper, ask a friend to hold a piece of paper between your eyes and your drawing paper. Another trick is to place your drawing paper inside a large paper bag as you work.
- Tape your paper to the table so it will not slide around. With a finger of your free hand, trace the outline of the object. Record the movement with your drawing hand.

- Contour lines show ridges and wrinkles in addition to outlines. Adding these lines gives roundness to the object.

3. Drawing with Oil Pastels

Oil pastels are sticks of pigment held together with an oily binder. The colors are brighter than wax crayon colors. If you press heavily you will make a brilliant-colored line. If you press lightly you will create a fuzzy line. You can fill in shapes with the brilliant colors. You can blend a variety of color combinations. For example, you can fill a shape with a soft layer of a hue and then color over the hue with a heavy layer of white to create a unique tint of that hue.

If you use oil pastels on colored paper, you can put a layer of white under the layer of hue to block the color of the paper.

4. Drawing Thin Lines with a Brush

Drawing thin lines with a brush can be learned with a little practice. Just follow these steps:

1. Dip your brush in the ink or paint. Wipe the brush slowly against the side, twirling it between your fingers until the bristles form a point.
2. Hold the brush at the beginning of the metal band near the tip. Hold the brush straight up and down.
3. Imagine that the brush is a pencil with a very sharp point. Pretend that pressing too hard will break the point. Now touch the paper lightly with the tip of the brush and draw a line. The line should be quite thin.

To make a thinner line still, lift up on the brush as you draw. After a while, you will be able to make lines in a variety of thicknesses.

5. Making a Grid for Enlarging

Sometimes the need arises to make a bigger version of a small drawing. An example is when you create a mural based on a small sketch. Follow these steps:

1. Using a ruler, draw evenly spaced lines across and up and down your original drawing (Figure T–1). Count

8″								
1	2	3	4	5	6	7	8
9	10	11	12	13	14	15	16
17	18	19	20	21	22	23	24
25	26	27	28	29	30	31	32
33	34	35	36	37	38	39	40
41	42	43	44	45	46	47	48

6″

▲ **Figure T–1**

the number of squares you made from side to side. Count the number of squares running up and down.

2. Measure the width of the surface to which the drawing is to be transferred. Divide that figure by the number of side-to-side squares. The resulting number will be the horizontal measure of each square. You may work in inches or centimeters. Using a ruler or yardstick, mark off the squares. Draw in light rules.

3. Measure the height of the surface to which the drawing is to be transferred. Divide that figure by the number of up-and-down squares. The resulting number will be the vertical measure of each square. Mark off the squares. Draw in pencil lines.

4. Starting at the upper left, number each square on the original drawing. Give the same number to each square on the large grid. Working a square at a time, transfer your image. (See Figure T–2.)

6. Using Shading Techniques

When using shading techniques, keep in mind the following:

- Lines or dots placed close together create dark values.
- Lines or dots placed far apart, on the other hand, create light values. To show a change from light to dark, start with lines or dots far apart and little by little bring them close together.
- Use care also to follow the shape of the object when adding lines. Straight lines are used to shade an object with a flat surface. Rounded lines are used to shade an object with a curved surface.

7. Using Sighting Techniques

Sighting is a technique that will help you draw objects in proportion.

1. Face the object you plan to draw. Hold a pencil straight up and down at arm's length. Your thumb should rest against the side of the pencil and be even with the tip.

2. Close one eye. With your other eye, focus on the object.

3. Slide your thumb down the pencil until the exposed part of the pencil matches the object's height. (See Figure T–3.)

▲ Figure T–3

4. Now, without moving your thumb or bending your arm, turn the pencil sideways.

5. Focus on the width of the object. If the height is greater, figure out how many "widths" will fit in one "height." If the width is greater, figure out how many "heights" will fit in one "width."

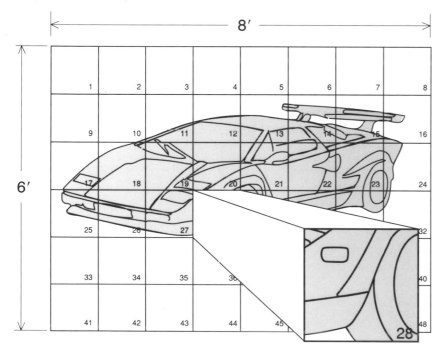

▲ Figure T–2

8. Using a Viewing Frame

Much in the way a camera is used to focus on one area of a scene, you can better zero in on an object you plan to draw by using a viewing frame (Figure T–4). To make a viewing frame do the following:

1. Cut a rectangular hole in a piece of paper about 2 inches (3 to 5 cm) in from the paper's edges.
2. Hold the paper at arm's length and look through the hole at your subject. Imagine that the hole represents your drawing paper.
3. Decide how much of the subject you want to have in your drawing.
4. By moving the frame up, down, sideways, nearer, or farther, you can change the focus of your drawing.

9. Using a Ruler

There are times when you need to draw a crisp, straight line. By using the following techniques, you will be able to do so.

1. Hold the ruler with one hand and the pencil with the other.
2. Place the ruler where you wish to draw a straight line.
3. Hold the ruler with your thumb and first two fingers. Be careful that your fingers do not stick out beyond the edge of the ruler.
4. Press heavily on the ruler so it will not slide while you're drawing.
5. Hold the pencil lightly against the ruler.
6. Pull the pencil quickly and lightly along the edge of the ruler. The object is to keep the ruler from moving while the pencil moves along its edge.

▲ Figure T–4

PAINTING TIPS

10. Cleaning a Paint Brush

Cleaning a paint brush properly helps it last a long time. *Always*:

1. Rinse the thick paint out of the brush under running water. Do not use hot water.
2. Gently paint the brush over a cake of mild soap, or dip it in a mild liquid detergent (Figure T–5).

▲ Figure T–5

3. Gently scrub the brush against the palm of your hand to work the soap into the brush. This removes paint you may not have realized was still in the brush.

4. Rinse the brush under running water while you continue to scrub your palm against it (Figure T–6).

▲ **Figure T–6**

5. Repeat steps 2, 3, and 4 as needed.

When it is thoroughly rinsed and excess water has been squeezed from the brush, shape your brush into a point with your fingers (Figure T–7). Place the brush in a container with the bristles up so that it will keep its shape as it dries.

▲ **Figure T–7**

11. Making Natural Earth Pigments

Anywhere there is dirt, clay, or sand, there is natural pigment. To create your own pigments, gather as many different kinds of earth colors as you can. Grind these as finely as possible. (If you can, borrow a mortar and pestle.) (See Figure T–8.) Do not worry if the pigment is slightly gritty.

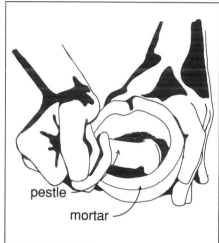

pestle

mortar

▲ **Figure T–8**

To make the binder, mix equal parts of white glue and water. Place a few spoonfuls of your powdered pigment into a small jar. Add a little of the binder. Experiment with different amounts of each.

When you work with natural pigments, remember always to wash the brushes before the paint in them has a chance to dry. The glue from the binder can ruin a brush. As you work, stir the paint every now and then. This will keep the grains of pigment from settling to the bottom of the jar.

Make a fresh batch each time you paint.

12. Mixing Paint to Change the Value of Color

You can better control the colors in your work when you mix your own paint. In mixing paints, treat opaque paints (for example, tempera) differently from transparent paints (for example, watercolors).

- *For light values of opaque paints.* Mix only a small amount of the hue to white. The color can always be made stronger by adding more of the hue.
- *For dark values of opaque paints.* Add a small amount of black to the hue. Never add the hue to black.
- *For light values of transparent paints.* Thin a shaded area with water (Figure T–9). This allows more of the white of the paper to show through.
- *For dark values of transparent paints.* Carefully add a small amount of black to the hue.

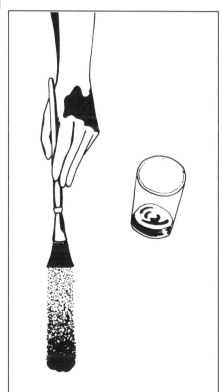

▲ **Figure T–9**

13. Working with Poster Paints (School Tempera)

When using poster paints (school tempera) remember the following:

- Poster paints run when wet. To keep this from happening, make sure one shape is dry before painting a wet color next to it.

14. Working with Watercolors

- If you apply wet paint to damp paper, you create lines and shapes with soft edges.
- If you apply wet paint to dry paper, you create lines and shapes with sharp, clear edges.
- If you dip a dry brush into damp paint and then brush across dry paper, you achieve a fuzzy effect.
- School watercolors come in semi-moist cakes. Before you use them, place a drop of water on each cake to let the paint soften. Watercolor paints are transparent. You can see the white paper through the paint. If you want a light value of a hue, dilute the paint with a large amount of water. If you want a bright hue, you must dissolve more pigment by swirling your brush around in the cake of paint until you have dissolved a great deal of paint. The paint you apply to the paper can be as bright as the paint in the cake.

15. Making a Stamp Printing

A stamp print is an easy way to make repetitive designs. The following are a few suggestions for making a stamp and printing with it. You may develop some other ideas after reading these hints. Remember, printing reverses your design, so if you use letters, be certain to cut or carve them backwards.

- Cut a simple design into the flat surface of an eraser with a knife that has a fine, precision blade.
- Cut a potato, carrot, or turnip in half. Use a paring knife to carve a design into the flat surface of the vegetable.
- Glue yarn to a bottle cap or a jar lid.
- Glue found objects to a piece of corrugated cardboard. Make a design with paperclips, washers, nuts, leaves, feathers, or anything else you can find. Whatever object you use should have a fairly flat surface. Make a handle for the block with masking tape.
- Cut shapes out of a piece of inner tube material. Glue the shapes to a piece of heavy cardboard.

There are several ways to apply ink or paint to a stamp:

- Roll water-based printing ink on the stamp with a soft brayer.
- Roll water-based printing ink on a plate and press the stamp into the ink.
- Apply tempera paint or school acrylic to the stamp with a bristle brush.

16. Working with Clay

To make your work with clay go smoothly, always do the following:

1. Dip one or two fingers in water.
2. Spread the moisture from your fingers over your palms.

Never dip your hands in water. Too much moisture turns clay into mud.

17. Joining Clay

If you are creating a piece of sculpture that requires joining pieces, do the following:

1. Gather the materials you will need. These include clay, slip, (a creamy mixture of clay and water), a paint brush, a scoring tool, (perhaps a kitchen fork) and clay tools.
2. Rough up or scratch the two surfaces to be joined (Figure T–10).

▲ Figure T–10

3. Apply slip to one of the two surfaces using a paint brush or your fingers (Figure T–11).

▲ Figure T–11

4. Gently press the two surfaces together so the slip oozes out of the joining seam (Figure T–12).

▲ Figure T–12

5. Using clay tools and/or your fingers, smooth away the slip that has oozed out of the seam (Figure T–13). You may wish to smooth out the seam as well, or you may wish to leave it for decorative purposes.

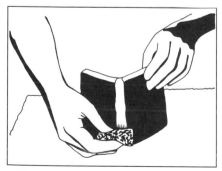

▲ Figure T–13

18. Making a Clay Mold for a Plaster Relief

One of the easiest ways to make a plaster relief is with a clay mold. When making a clay mold, remember the following:

- Plaster poured into the mold will come out with the opposite image. Design details cut into the mold will appear raised on the relief. Details built up within the mold will appear indented in the relief.
- Do not make impressions in your mold that have *undercuts* (Figure T–14). Undercuts trap plaster, which will break off when the relief is removed. When cutting impressions, keep the deepest parts the narrowest.
- In carving a raised area in the mold, take care not to create a reverse undercut (Figure T–15).

If you want to change the mold simply smooth the area with your fingers.

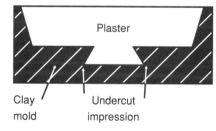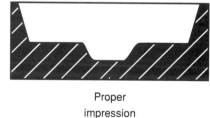

▲ Figure T–14

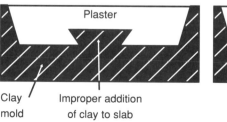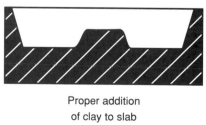

▲ Figure T–15

19. Mixing Plaster

Mixing plaster requires some technique and a certain amount of caution. It can also be a very simple matter when you are prepared. Always do the following:

- Use caution when working with dry plaster. Wear a dust mask or work in a well-ventilated room.
- Cover your work space to keep the dust from spreading.
- Always use a plastic bowl and a stick for mixing. Never use silverware you will later eat from.
- Always use plaster that is fine, like sifted flour. Plaster should never be grainy when dry.
- Always add the water to the bowl first. Sift in the plaster. Stir slowly.
- Never pour unused plaster down a drain. Allow it to dry in the bowl. To remove the dried plaster, twist the bowl. Crack the loose plaster into a lined trash can.

20. Working with Papier-Mâché

Papier-mâché (**pay**-puhr muh-**shay**) is a French term meaning "chewed paper." It is also the name of several sculpting methods using newspaper and liquid paste. These methods can be used to model tiny pieces of jewelry. They can also be used to create life-size creatures.

In creating papier-mâché sculptures, the paper-and-paste mixture is molded over a support. You will learn more about supports shortly. The molded newspaper dries to a hard finish. The following are three methods for working with papier-mâché:

- **Pulp Method**. Shred newspaper, paper towels, or tissue paper into tiny pieces. (Do not use glossy magazine paper; it will not soften.) Soak your paper in water overnight. Press the paper in a kitchen strainer to remove as much moisture as possible. Mix the mashed paper with commercially prepared papier-mâché paste or white glue. The mixture should have the consistency of soft clay. Add a few drops of oil of cloves to keep the mixture from spoiling. A spoonful of linseed oil makes the mixture smoother. (If needed, the mixture can be stored at this point in a plastic bag in the refrigerator.) Use the mixture to model small shapes. When your creations dry, they can be sanded. You will also be able to drill holes in them.
- **Strip Method**. Tear newspaper into strips. Either dip the strips in papier-mâché paste or rub paste on them. Apply the strips to your support (Figure T–16). If you do not want the strips to stick to your

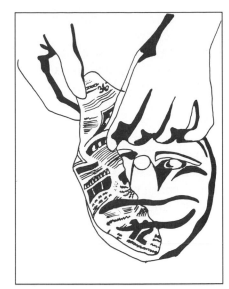

▲ Figure T–16

support, first cover it with plastic wrap. Use wide strips for large shapes. Use thin strips for smaller shapes. If you plan to remove your finished creation from the support, apply five or six layers. (Change directions with each layer so you can keep track of the number.) Otherwise, two or three layers should be enough. After applying the strips to your support, rub your fingers over the surface.

As a last layer, use torn paper towels. The brown paper towels that are found in schools produce an uncomplicated surface on which to paint. Make sure no rough edges are sticking up. Store any unused paste mixture in the refrigerator to keep it from spoiling.

- **Draping Method**. Spread papier-mâché paste on newspaper. Lay a second sheet on top of the first. Smooth the layers. Add another layer of paste and another sheet of paper. Repeat until you have four or five layers of paper. Use this method for making drapery on a figure. (See Figure T–17.) If you allow the lay-

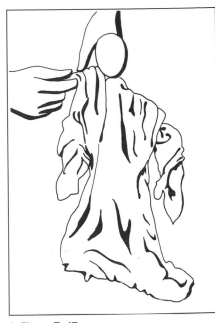

▲ Figure T–17

ers to dry for a day or two, they will become leathery. They can then be cut and molded as you like. Newspaper strips dipped in paste can be used to seal cracks.

Like papier-mâché, supports for papier-mâché creations can be made in several different ways. Dry newspaper may be wadded up and wrapped with string or tape (Figure T–18). Wire coat hangers may be padded with rags. For large figures, a wooden frame covered with chicken wire makes a good support.

▲ Figure T–18

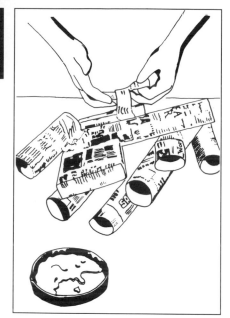

▲ Figure T–19

To create a base for your papier-mâché creations, tape together arrangements of found materials. Some materials you might combine are boxes, tubes, and bowls. (See Figure T–19.) Clay can also be modeled as a base. If clay is used, be sure there are no undercuts that would keep the papier-mâché from lifting off easily when dry. (For an explanation of undercuts, see Technique Tip **18**, *Handbook* page **276**.)

Always allow time for your papier-mâché creations to dry. The material needs extra drying time when thick layers are used or when the weather is damp. An electric fan blowing air on the material can shorten the drying time.

21. Making a Paper Sculpture

Another name for paper sculpture is origami. The process originated in Japan and means "folding paper." Paper sculpture begins with a flat piece of paper. The paper is then curved or bent to produce more than a flat

surface. Here are some ways to experiment with paper.

- **Scoring.** Place a square sheet of heavy construction paper, 12 x 12 inch (30 x 30 cm), on a flat surface. Position the ruler on the paper so that it is close to the center and parallel to the sides. Holding the ruler in place, run the point of a knife or a pair of scissors along one of the ruler's edges. Press down firmly but take care not to cut through the paper. Gently crease the paper along the line you made. Hold your paper with the crease facing upward.
- **Pleating.** Take a piece of paper and fold it one inch from the edge. Then fold the paper in the other direction. Continue folding back and forth.
- **Curling.** Hold one end of a long strip of paper with the thumb and forefinger of one hand. At a point right below where you are holding the strip, grip it lightly between the side of a pencil and the thumb of your other hand. In a quick motion, run the pencil along the strip. This will cause the strip to curl back on itself. Don't apply too much pressure, or the strip will tear. (See Figure T–20.)

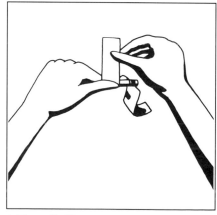

▲ Figure T–20

22. Measuring Rectangles

Do you find it hard to create perfectly formed rectangles? Here is a way of getting the job done:

1. Make a light pencil dot near the long edge of a sheet of paper. With a ruler, measure the exact distance between the dot and the edge. Make three more dots the same distance in from the edge. (See Figure T–21.)

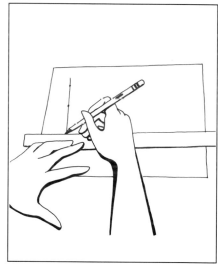

▲ Figure T–21

2. Line a ruler up along the dots. Make a light pencil line running the length of the paper.
3. Turn the paper so that a short side is facing you. Make four pencil dots equally distant from the short edge. Connect these with a light pencil rule. Stop when you reach the first line you drew. (See Figure T–22.)
4. Do the same for the remaining two sides. Erase any lines that may extend beyond the box you have made.
5. Trace over the lines with your ruler and pencil.

The box you have created will be a perfectly formed rectangle.

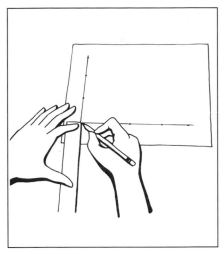

▲ Figure T–22

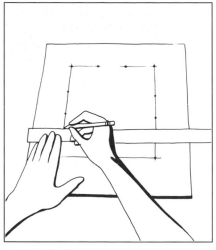

▲ Figure T–23

23. Making a Mat

You can add appeal to an art work by making a mat, using the following steps.

1. Gather the materials you will need. These include a metal rule, a pencil, mat board, cardboard backing, a sheet of heavy cardboard to protect your work surface, a mat knife with a sharp blade, and wide masking tape.

2. Wash your hands. Mat board should be kept very clean.

3. Measure the height and width of the work to be matted. Decide how large a border you want for your work. (A border of approximately 2½ inches on three sides with 3 inches on the bottom is aesthetically pleasing.) Your work will be behind the window you will cut.

4. Plan for the opening, or window, to be ¼ inch smaller on all sides than the size of your work. For example, if your work measures 9 by 12 inches, the mat window should measure 8½ inches (9 inches minus ¼ inch times two) by 11½ inches (12 inches minus ¼ inch times two). Using your metal rule and pencil, lightly draw your window rectangle on the back of the board 2½ inches from the top and left edge of the mat. (See Figure T–23.) Add a 2½ inch border to the right of the window and a 3 inch border to the bottom, lightly drawing cutting guidelines.

Note: If you are working with metric measurements, the window should overlap your work by 0.5 cm (centimeters) on all sides. Therefore, if your work measures 24 by 30 cm, the mat window measures 23 cm (24 − [2 x 0.5]) by 29 cm (30 − [2 x 0.5]).

▲ Figure T–24

5. Place the sheet of heavy, protective cardboard on your work surface. Place the mat board, pencil marks up, over the cardboard. Holding the metal rule firmly in place, score the first line with your knife. Always place the metal rule so that your blade is away from the frame. (See Figure T–24.) In case you make an error you will cut into the window hole or the extra mat that is not used for the frame. Do not try to cut through the board with one stroke. By the third or fourth stroke, you should be able to cut through the board easily.

6. Working in the same fashion, score and cut through the board along all the window lines. Be careful not to go beyond the lines. Remove the window.

7. Cut a cardboard backing for your art work that is slightly smaller than the overall size of your mat. Using a piece of broad masking tape, hinge the back of the mat to the backing. (See Figure T–25.)

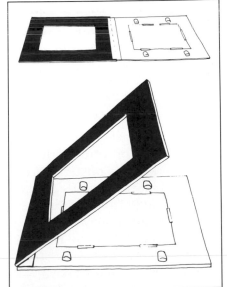

▲ Figure T–25

Position your art work between the backing and the mat and attach it with tape. Anchor the frame to the cardboard with a few pieces of rolled tape.

24. Mounting a Two-Dimensional Work

Mounting pictures that you make gives them a professional look. To mount a work, do the following:

1. Gather the materials you will need. These include a yardstick, a pencil, poster board, a sheet of heavy cardboard, a knife with a very sharp blade, a sheet of newspaper, and rubber cement.

2. Measure the height and width of the work to be mounted. Decide how large a border you want around the work. Plan your mount size using the work's measurements. To end up with a 3-inch (8 cm) border, for example, make your mount 6 inches (15 cm) wider and higher than your work. Record the measurements for your mount.

3. Using your yardstick and pencil, lightly draw your mount rectangle on the back of the poster board. Measure from the edges of the poster board. If you have a large paper cutter available, you may use it to cut your mount.

4. Place the sheet of heavy cardboard on your work surface. Place the poster board, pencil marks up, over the cardboard. Holding the yardstick firmly in place along one line, score the line with your knife. Do not try to cut through the board with one stroke. By the third try, you should be able to cut through the board.

▲ Figure T–26

5. Place the art work on the mount. Using the yardstick, center the work. Mark each corner with a dot. (See Figure T–26.)

6. Place the art work, face down, on a sheet of newspaper. Coat the back of the work with rubber cement. (*Safety Note:* Always use rubber cement in a room with plenty of ventilation.) *If your mount is to be permanent, skip to Step 8.*

7. Line up the corners of your work with the dots on the mounting board. Smooth the work into place. *Skip to Step 9.*

8. After coating the back of your art work, coat the poster board with rubber cement. Be careful not to add cement to the border area. Have a partner hold your art work in the air by the two top corners. Once the two glued surfaces meet, you will not be able to change the position of the work. Grasp the lower two corners. Carefully lower the work to the mounting board. Line up the two corners with the bottom dots. Little by little, lower the work into place (Figure T–27). Press it smooth.

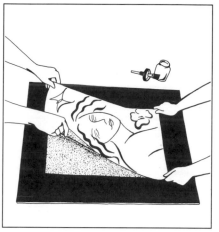

▲ Figure T–27

9. To remove any excess cement, create a small ball of nearly dry rubber cement. Use the ball of rubber cement to pick up excess cement.

25. Making Rubbings

Rubbings make interesting textures and designs. They may also be used with other media to create mixed media art. To make a rubbing, place a sheet of thin paper on top of the surface to be rubbed. Hold the paper in place with one hand. With the other hand, rub the paper with the flat side of an unwrapped crayon. Always rub away from the hand holding the paper. Never rub back and forth, since this may cause the paper to slip.

26. Scoring Paper

The secret to creating neat, sharp folds in cardboard or paper is a technique called scoring. Here is how it is done:

1. Line up a ruler along the line you want to fold.

2. Lightly run a sharp knife or scissors along the fold line. Press down firmly enough to leave a light crease. Take care not to cut all the way through the paper (Figure T–28).

▲ Figure T–28

3. Gently crease the paper along the line you made. To score curved lines, use the same technique. Make sure your curves are wide enough to ensure a clean fold. Too tight a curve will cause the paper to wrinkle (Figure T–29).

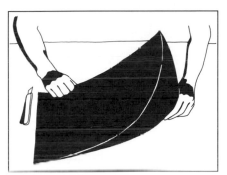

▲ Figure T–29

27. Making a Tissue Paper Collage

For your first experience with tissue, make a free design with the tissue colors. Start with the lightest colors of tissue first and save the darkest for last. It is difficult to change the color of dark tissue by overlapping it with other colors. If one area becomes too dark, you might cut out a piece of white paper, glue it over the dark area carefully, and apply new colors over the white area.

1. Apply a coat of adhesive to the area where you wish to place the tissue.
2. Place the tissue down carefully over the wet area (Figure T–30). Don't let your fingers get wet.
3. Then add another coat of adhesive over the tissue. If your brush picks up any color from the wet tissue, rinse your brush in water and let it dry before using it again.
4. Experiment by overlapping colors. Allow the tissue to wrinkle to create textures as you apply it. Be sure that all the loose edges of tissue are glued down.

28. Working with Glue

When applying glue, always start at the center of the surface you are coating and work outward.

- When gluing papers together don't use a lot of glue, just a dot will do. Use dots in the corners and along the edges. Press the two surfaces together. Keep dots at least ½ inch (1.3 cm) in from the edge of your paper.
- Handle a glued surface carefully with only your fingertips. Make sure your hands are clean before pressing the glued surface into place.
- *Note:* The glue should be as thin as possible. Thick or beaded glue will create ridges on your work.

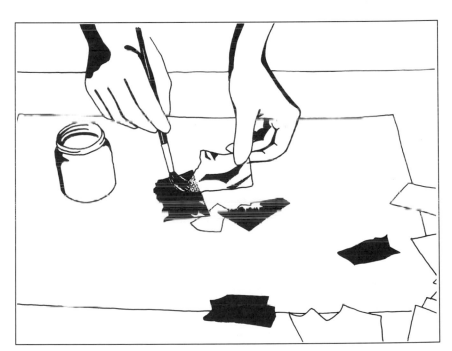

▲ Figure T–30

▲ Artists, down through the ages, have helped us visualize what we learn about history. Art historians are responsible for much of what we know about the artists who have lived in the past.

Mary Cassatt

1845–1926
American Painter

At the Opera
page **16**

Maternal Caress
page **35**

The Bath
page **161**

The second half of the 1800s was an unparalleled age of discovery. People had learned to harness the power of steam to run locomotives. Streetcars powered by electricity rumbled down cobblestone streets.

For American-in-Paris Mary Cassatt (kuh-**sat**) the age was also one of discovery — bitter discovery. Cassatt had come to Paris to continue the study of painting she had begun in Philadelphia. What she soon discovered was that women had to work twice as hard as men to get noticed in the Paris art world.

Cassatt, however, refused to be beaten. Back home in Pittsburgh, she had overcome her parents' resistance, who were against her becoming an artist. She would not give in now.

One day a painting in a shop window caught her eye. It was by the great artist Edgar Degas (day-**gah**). She was unable to take her eyes off the work. "I used to go and flatten my nose against the window," she later said. "It changed my life."

It also gave direction to Cassatt's career. The soft lines and gentle colors of Degas's Impressionist paintings set the tone for her own works. Works by Cassatt, such as *Maternal Caress*, (page **35**), combine great skill and sensitivity. Much of her work includes women and children as subjects. Today she is widely held to be one of America's finest painters.

The early 1500s were a time of conquest. The Spanish conquistadors had already conquered major parts of North and South America.

The spirit of conquest was being felt in other parts of the world as well. In the world of German art, a bold new conqueror had emerged. His name was Albrecht Dürer (**ahl**-brekt **dure**-uhr).

Dürer was born in Nuremberg, Germany. He was the second oldest in a family of 18 children. When Albrecht was young, his parents assumed he would become a goldsmith, like his father. But the young Dürer showed unusual skill at drawing. At 15, he was sent to study with a local painter.

Like most young German artists of the day, Dürer learned Gothic style. But a trip he made to Italy while in his early twenties changed everything. There the period of artistic awakening known as the Renaissance was in full progress.

Dürer returned to Nuremberg with a fresh view of the world and the artist's place in it. He turned away from his Gothic style and went about the task of becoming a Renaissance artist. Working hard, he learned how to capture the beauty and balance he found in Italian painting. The ideals he taught himself show up in such works as his engraving on page **158**.

Albrecht Dürer

1471–1528
German Painter, Printmaker

The Four Horsemen of the Apocalypse
page **158**

Winslow Homer

1836–1910
American Painter

Bermuda Sloop
   page xi, 180 (detail)

Right and Left
   page 2

The Fog Warning
   page 316

It is hard to think of any good coming out of a war. But for Winslow Homer, the American Civil War—or at least the scenes of the front lines he painted—were his passport to public recognition.

Homer was born in Boston. When he was six, his family moved to Cambridge, Massachusetts. At that time, Cambridge was mostly wilderness, and Homer learned to love the outdoors.

Like his love of nature, Homer's interest in art began early. By the time he was about 10, his talent for drawing was obvious to those around him. At 19, Homer went to work for a large Boston printing firm. There he designed covers for song sheets, a job he soon grew tired of.

For the next 17 years, Homer did magazine illustrations, mainly for *Harper's Weekly* in New York. It was for *Harper's* that he did his Civil War drawings and paintings.

After the war, Winslow traveled abroad. His work had become so much in demand that he paid for his trips with money earned by selling his paintings.

After 1883 he devoted his efforts almost totally to nature paintings. His home on the coast of Maine gave him a chance to study, and paint, the sea. Some of his best works, such as *The Fog Warning*, (page **316**), have the sea as their subject.

If you were going to fill a time capsule with symbols of life in mid-twentieth-century America, what would you include? One possibility might be a baseball. Another might be a photograph of a rock group.

Still another might be a painting by Edward Hopper. His works show the emptiness and loneliness that are as much a part of urban living as skyscrapers and traffic.

Hopper was born in Nyack, New York. He trained to be a graphic artist and worked for a time as an illustrator. Hopper did not turn to painting until he was close to 40.

From 1901 to 1906 he studied with Robert Henri, who headed the Ashcan School. Critics provided this label to describe some artists of this period. They used a stark, realistic treatment in their city scenes, painting ashcans and all. Like other members of the group, Hopper used the city as a setting for his pictures. Unlike other members, he did not focus on the glitter and excitement. Rather, Hopper's works capture the impersonal, unfriendly feeling of the big city. People rarely are seen in his pictures. When they are, they are often seen as alone and lonely.

A notable feature of Hopper's work is his use of color to capture a quiet mood. Such a mood can be seen in the bleak but soothing landscape of his *Cottages at North Truro, Massachusetts* (page **42**).

Edward Hopper

1882–1967
American Painter

Cottages at North Truro, Massachusetts
   page 42

Drugstore
   page 304

Wassily Kandinsky

1866–1944
Russian Painter

Improvisation #27
  page **39**

Several Circles
  page **85**

In the early 1900s two brothers named Wright proved that humans could harness the capability of flight. Their pioneering efforts at Kitty Hawk changed aviation history for all time.

Around the same time and a continent away, another person was changing history of a different sort. His name was Wassily Kandinsky (**vahs**-uh-lee kan-**din**-skee). The history he was changing for all time was art history.

Kandinsky was born in Russia in 1866. He studied law and worked as a lawyer through his twenties. In 1885 he visited an exhibit of French Impressionist paintings in Moscow. He was so impressed by the works that he found it hard to leave. In the months that followed, his thoughts drifted back to the paintings he had seen. Finally, he left his legal career and went to study painting in Munich, Germany.

In his early years as an artist, Kandinsky moved from one style to another. Then he spent some time experimenting with more original ideas. Around 1910 he completed an interesting watercolor. The work was bright and may have been based on some earlier landscape studies. What was most important about the work was that it had no recognizable subject. Non-objective art had been born! Today works such as *Improvisation #27* (page **39**) hang in the world's top art museums.

In 1889 the Eiffel Tower was built to celebrate the Paris Industrial Exposition. Around that same time, one of France's great artists began his career.

Henri Matisse (ahnj-**ree** mah-**tees**) had been born some 20 years earlier. Growing up in a small town in northern France, Matisse showed little interest in art. When he graduated from high school, his father sent him to Paris to study law.

When he was twenty-one years old, Matisse suffered an attack of appendicitis. He was forced to stay in bed for a long time. To ease his boredom, his mother bought him some paints. Suddenly Matisse felt as if a weight had been lifted. He had discovered an interest and a talent that changed his direction. He decided to become an artist.

While studying painting, Matisse began to experiment with different styles. By 1905, he had developed a style all his own. It made use of flat shapes and simple bold colors. An example of a work using this style is his painting *The Red Room* or *Dessert: Harmony in Red*, on page **128**.

While Matisse's paintings were revolutionary in his day, today they are hailed as masterpieces. They are seen as fulfillments of the goal Matisse had set for himself. That goal was to create "an art of purity and serenity without depressing subject matter."

Henri Matisse

1869–1954
French Painter

Femme au Chapeau (Woman with a Hat)
  page **4**

The Red Room or *Dessert: Harmony in Red*
  page **128**

Woman in a Purple Coat
  page **84**

Georgia O'Keeffe

1887–1986
American Painter

Sunrise
page 41

The 1920s marked the beginning of a new way of living in our country. The easygoing spirit of earlier times had been crushed by the arrival of the automobile. Americans suddenly found themselves rushing from one place to the next. Few had time to stop and think—to notice the beauty in the world around them.

One painter who took time to see beauty in her world was Georgia O'Keeffe. O'Keeffe had been raised on a small dairy farm in Wisconsin. Her strong interest in both nature and art had begun early. By the time she was 10, she knew she wanted to become a painter.

O'Keeffe's earliest training was in the styles of the great masters of Europe. Their subjects, however, held little interest for her. She wanted, instead, to paint the rocks, mountains, and wide open spaces around her. When she decided at age 29 to focus totally on nature, she burned her earlier work.

Among O'Keeffe's greatest achievements are the close-ups of flowers she began creating in the 1920s. To catch the attention of people too busy to notice, she made the close-ups huge. Each fills its canvas with graceful curved surfaces and flowing lines. The beauty of every petal is seen again and again in the greater beauty of the whole flower.

The 1880s brought the world many wonderful inventions, such as the adding machine, the bicycle, and the car. It also brought the world a painter who would produce some of the greatest art in the history of the Western world. His name was Pablo Picasso.

Picasso was born in Malaga, Spain, in 1881. As a boy, he never stopped drawing. In fact, his mother claimed he could draw before he could talk. Everywhere young Picasso went, his pad and pencil went. He liked betting his friends he could draw anything—in one unbroken line—and he always won.

One day his father, a painter and teacher, came home to a surprise. His young son had finished a portrait. After examining the work, Pablo's father gave the boy all his art materials. So great was the boy's work that the father vowed never to paint again.

In his long and full life, Pablo Picasso passed through many different styles. For some time he created the fractured images that were the hallmark of the Cubist movement. He later returned to paintings of the human figure. The painting of *Seated Woman (after Cranach)* on page 170 shows his mastery of media and technique.

Pablo Picasso

1881–1973
Spanish Painter, Sculptor

Seated Woman (after Cranach)
page 170

Raphael (Sanzio)

1483–1520
Italian Painter

St. George and the Dragon
page 104

The Small Cowper Madonna
page 132

It was the eve of Columbus's voyage of discovery to the New World. It was also the eve of a discovery within the art world. A young boy in Columbus's native Italy showed a gift for art that was rare. The boy's name was Rafaello — or, in English, Raphael.

Raphael was born in a small town in central Italy. His first teacher was probably his father, who was a painter for a noble family. While still a child, Raphael studied with an artist named Perugino (pehr-uh-**jee**-noh). Perugino taught the youth how to use soft colors and simple circular forms. He taught him how to create gentle landscapes. Soon the student's work began to be mistaken for the teacher's. Young Raphael knew it was time to move on.

He went to Florence to study the works of the leading artists of the day. Among his teachers there were the two giants of art, Leonardo da Vinci and Michelangelo. From Leonardo, he learned how to use shading to create a sense of depth. From Michelangelo, he learned how to breathe life into his figures. Both these ideas are present in his masterpiece *St. George and the Dragon* (page **104**).

Raphael died when he was only 37. Yet the works he left behind rank him as one of the great artists of the Renaissance.

After the Brooklyn Bridge opened in 1883, bridge building would never be the same. After an exhibition of paintings in Paris a year later, art would never be the same. The exhibition contained works by a group who came to be known — at first, jokingly — as Impressionists. One of the group's leaders was a man named Renoir.

Pierre Auguste Renoir (pee-**air** oh-**goost** ren-**wahr**) was born in 1841. His artistic talents became apparent early. By 13, he was already making a living as an artist in a porcelain factory. His job was painting scenes on pieces of china. His earnings helped pay for his education at a famous Paris art school, the Ecole des Beaux-Arts.

It was at school that Renoir met two other young artists, Claude Monet (moh-**nay**) and Alfred Sisley. The three soon became friends. They also began experimenting together by making paintings outdoors in natural sunlight. Their goal was to give objects a shimmering, sunlit quality. At first, their works were scorned by critics. Today they are among the most admired in the history of art.

Unlike most of his fellow Impressionists, Renoir was interested in painting the human figure. His painting, *Girl with a Watering Can* (page **121**) highlights the best features of his own Impressionist style.

Pierre Auguste Renoir

1841–1919
French Painter

Girl with a Watering Can
page 121

Regatta at Argenteuil
page 126

Henri de Toulouse-Lautrec

1864–1901
French Printmaker, Painter

La Gitane
page **36**

Jane Avril
page **190**

The year 1864 was one of promising beginnings and promising endings. Union troops marched into Georgia, signaling a swift end to the Civil War. The birth of a baby boy in the town of Albi, France, promised new happiness for the Toulouse-Lautrec (tuh-**loose** low-**trek**) family.

Although no one knew it, baby Henri's arrival also held great promise for the art world. The Toulouse-Lautrecs were an old and wealthy French family. Henri's parents taught their child from an early age to appreciate art. By the age of 10, young Henri was making sketches. This was no surprise since his grandfather, father, and uncle were all draftsmen.

When he was 14, Henri broke both legs in two separate accidents. Although the limbs healed, they never grew properly. All his life he was self-conscious about his deformed legs and dwarf-like appearance.

This did not prevent Toulouse-Lautrec from becoming interested in the dazzling night life of Paris. He loved to sit in cafes and watch the colorful scene. He always carried a sketchpad and often would record what he saw.

Today the remarkable prints he created, many based on his sketches, are thought to be art treasures.

By the late 1880s trains had become a popular form of transportation. A spirit of restlessness had gripped the Western world. Certainly one of the period's most important artists felt that restlessness. His name was Vincent van Gogh (van **goh**).

You may already know some of the facts of van Gogh's brief life. You have probably heard how he went mad and cut off his earlobe. You may know that he ended his own life at age 37. What you may not know is that this genius left the world 1600 remarkable art works.

Vincent van Gogh was born and raised in a small Dutch village. He spent much of his life contemplating his existence. He tried—and failed at—many different careers, including teaching and the ministry. At last he turned to art, which long had been a passion.

Van Gogh's first paintings were drab and dull. In 1886 he moved to Paris. There he was moved by several artistic forces. One was the color used in Impressionist paintings. Another was the style of Japanese woodcuts.

Van Gogh was not content simply to capture a scene. Instead, he needed to express his deep feelings about it. These feelings come through in short brush strokes of bright, intense color. An example of his unique style may be found in *Cypresses* (page **64**).

Vincent van Gogh

1853–1890
Dutch Painter

Cypresses
page **64**

Marie-Louise-Élisabeth Vigée-Lebrun

1755–1842
French Painter

Theresa, Countess Kinsky
page 131

La Princesse Barbe Gallitzin
page 149

When the French Revolution began in 1789, members of the ruling class fled. So did the woman who had painted many of them, Marie-Louise-Élisabeth Vigée-Lebrun (ay-**lee**-zah-bet vee-**zhay**-luh-**bruhn**).

Élisabeth Vigée-Lebrun's life story reads almost like a novel. She studied art in a convent. Before she was 20, she had painted many important French nobles. By age 25, she was working for Queen Marie-Antoinette. She did some 20 portraits of the queen.

The night the king and queen were arrested, Vigée-Lebrun escaped from Paris. The revolution had temporarily interrupted her career as a portrait painter. Luckily, she was able to continue her work in other capitals of Europe. Everywhere she went, there were requests for portraits. By the time she turned 35, she had earned over a million francs. This was a huge sum of money for an artist to have earned.

Vigée-Lebrun's portraits were very flattering to her subjects. She overlooked any flaws she saw. As in her portrait of *Theresa, Countess Kinsky* (page **131**), she gave all her subjects large eyes.

When Vigée-Lebrun died, a palette and brush were carved on her gravestone as she had asked. It was a fitting tribute to an artist who had completed over 800 paintings in her lifetime.

In the year 1917 the world was politically unsettled. Many of the major powers were at war. Russia was in the midst of a revolution. It was an odd time for an artist devoted to simple, quiet subjects to emerge. Such an artist is Andrew Wyeth.

Andrew Wyeth was the son of N. C. Wyeth, a successful illustrator of adventure stories. As a child, Andrew was sick much of the time. Since his father had little use for public schools anyway, Andrew was educated at home. As a boy, he was constantly drawing and painting with watercolors.

When Wyeth was 20, he had his first exhibit in New York. Every painting in the show was sold.

Several of Wyeth's paintings are based on Christina Olson, a family friend crippled by polio. One of these, *Christina's World* (page **115**), was made after Wyeth watched Christina bravely pull herself home using her arms. As Wyeth himself has explained, the work is more than a portrait. It is a glimpse of Christina's whole life and the things she experienced in it.

Wyeth creates his works by making many, many studies of a subject. For these, he uses both pencil and watercolor. He does his finished works using egg tempera.

Andrew Wyeth

1917–
American Painter

Christina's World
page 115
(detail) page 179

▲ There are many careers available in the field of commercial art. This group is discussing a display.

Advertising Artist

Every time you watch a TV commercial, you are experiencing the work of an advertising artist. The same goes for hearing radio commercials as well as reading magazine and newspaper ads. Advertising artists are people whose job is to help sell a product using art.

The field of advertising art dates back at least to ancient Egypt. A papyrus found in an ancient Egyptian tomb offers a reward for a runaway slave. In the Middle Ages, town criers often peppered their news announcements with advertisements for local businesses.

Nowadays advertising artists usually work as members of teams under the leadership of art directors. Some tasks of the ad artist might include designing illustrations and photographs for ads. Advertising artists are also often called upon to pick typefaces.

The success of advertising art is measured by how many people notice the advertisement and how well the product sells.

Animator

When the art of the motion picture was born, a number of fields were born with it. One of these was the field of animation. Animators are artists who create cartoons and cartoonlike figures for film and television.

Animators begin their work by picking a story to tell. They also choose the style of architecture and clothing that will fit the story. They then create the story in the form of storyboards. These are still drawings that show the action in the story. Storyboards are a series of panels that look similar to comic books but are larger. The animator will create about 60 sketches for each board. A short film will need three storyboards. A full-length film will require over 25 storyboards.

Once the storyboards have been created, the animators will create the major poses for each character. Other artists assist by filling in the many drawings that complete each movement.

Architect

Do you live in an apartment house or a private home? Whichever you live in, you are in a building designed by an architect. Architects are artists who design buildings of all kinds, including residences, office buildings, and museums.

The architect works with two major goals in mind. One is to make sure the building does what it was planned to do. The second goal is to make sure the building is pleasing to the eye. How a structure fits in with its surroundings is also a concern of the architect.

Architects must know a great deal about building materials. They must also understand how weather and other natural elements act on such materials. Architects are also trained in such matters as ventilation, heating and cooling, and plumbing.

Architects must have a strong background in mathematics and drafting. Most architects nowadays specialize in a particular type of building.

Art Adviser to Corporations

Up until a few years ago, the only art found in a company setting was purely decorative. A painting might be used to dress up a waiting area or conference room. Recently, there has been a growing interest among corporations in starting private art collections. With this interest, a new profession has been born — the corporate art adviser.

Art advisers to corporations have a number of duties and responsibilities. One duty is buying new art for the corporation collection. Another is advising the corporation head about tax laws having to do with art. A third duty is arranging traveling exhibitions and speaking to different groups about the collection.

Corporate art advisers often are hired as employees of the company. Sometimes they work on a free-lance basis and advise several companies at once.

Art Director for the Performing Arts

In order for a performance to run smoothly, a number of people must do their jobs well. In order for these people to do their jobs well, the show must have a strong director.

The art director oversees all the visual elements of the show and makes sure they fit together. Among the many people with whom the director works closely are scenery, costume, and lighting designers.

Art directors must have a background in art history as well as a knowledge of stagecraft. If a play is set in the past, the setting, furniture, and costumes all need to reflect that period.

Art Teacher

Many people with an interest in art and a desire to share their knowledge become art teachers.

A career in art teaching requires a college education. Part of that education is devoted to methods of teaching. Part is devoted to developing a broad background in art history, aesthetics, art criticism, and the use of art materials and techniques.

Good art teachers guide their students through a wide variety of art experiences. They give students the chance to create their own art and to react to the art of others. They also make sure their students learn about such important art subjects as aesthetics, art criticism, and art history.

Art Therapist

In recent years researchers have learned new ways of helping people with emotional problems. One of these ways is through art.

In the field called art therapy people trained as art therapists use art to open lines of communication with patients. Patients are invited to create images using different media. They are then encouraged to discuss the meanings of their creations. This process often serves to release feelings, allowing the therapists to better help the patients.

Art therapists find work in a number of different settings. Some work as members of teams in large hospitals. Others are employed by community health centers or clinics. Still others work in prisons. Some work in special schools for students with learning disabilities.

A career in art therapy requires professional training in psychology and art education.

City Planner

Have you ever wondered how big cities come to look the way they do? The two-word answer to this question is city planners.

City planners are people whose job is to supervise the care and improvement of a city. Every large American city has a planner.

A main task of city planners is to enforce zoning laws. These are laws controlling what part of a city may be used for what purposes. Thanks to city planners, garbage dumps are not located in residential communities.

A second task of the city planner is to look after the growth and development of the city. The planner works with the mayor and other city officials to create parks, harbors, and shopping malls.

City planners are trained as architects. Their knowledge of design helps them to plan a pleasing cityscape.

Exhibit and Display Designer

The next time you pass a display of clothing or other goods in a department store, look carefully. Somewhere within that display will be a hidden message: "Artist at Work."

Exhibit and display designers work in a number of retail and non-profit settings. Some are trade shows, department stores, showrooms, art galleries, and museums. Such designers plan presentations of collections, exhibits, and traveling shows of all kinds. They are responsible for such matters as deciding what items should be grouped together. They also take into account how displays should be lighted.

The display designer is an important part of the sales team. Displays attract customers. They can affect a customer's decision to buy. The way the display designer does his or her job can make all the difference between "sale" and "no-sale."

Fashion Designer

Some art is made to be worn. Creating art of this type is the work of the fashion designer. Fashion designers draw and plan clothing, hats, handbags, gloves, and jewelry.

Fashion designers must learn about different fabrics, colors, and their uses. Matters such as weight and texture are also important in the designing of clothing. A jacket designed for winter wear, for example, must not only be attractive, it must also be warm and comfortable.

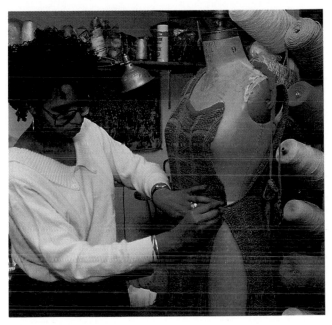

Some fashion designers become involved in high-fashion design. These are the trend-setting fashions that are usually very expensive.

Fashion designers may work either as freelance artists or for clothing manufacturers.

Industrial Designer

What do toys, vacuum cleaners, and cars have in common? All are designed to work easily and have a pleasing look. These and countless other items you see and use each day are the work of industrial designers.

Industrial designers work for makers of products. These artists work closely with engineers who develop the products. Sometimes industrial designers are asked to work on things as simple as tamper-proof caps for medicines. At other times they are asked to work on projects as complicated as space vehicles. Before they begin work, industrial designers need to know how the product is to be used.

Because different brands of the same product are sold, industrial design sometimes crosses over into advertising. The appearance of a design becomes especially important in the case of very competitive products such as cars and entertainment systems, for example.

Interior Designer

Architects give us attractive, functional spaces in which to live, work, and play. Interior designers fill those spaces with attractive and useful furnishings and accessories.

The job of the interior designer is to plan the interior space. This includes choosing furniture, fabrics, floor coverings, lighting fixtures, and decorations. To do this job well, the designer must take into account the wants and needs of the users of the space. In planning a home, for example, the interior designer will learn as much as possible about the lifestyle of the family that lives there.

Interior designers help their clients envision their ideas through the use of floor plans, elevations, and sketches. Once a client has agreed to a plan, the designer makes arrangements for buying materials. He or she also oversees the work for builders, carpenters, painters, and other craftspeople.

Landscape Architect

In recent years the role of the landscape architect increasingly has been recognized as very important in making the business and industrial areas of our cities environmentally healthy and aesthetic. Landscape architects are people whose job is to design outdoor areas around buildings. They also create arrangements of shrubs and flowers for playgrounds, parks, and highways.

Landscape architects work closely with architects and city planners to improve the natural setting. Their goal is to make the setting both easy to maintain and beautiful to look at. Landscape architects work with a number of different materials and landforms. These include flowers, plants, trees, rivers, ponds, walks, benches, and signs.

Some landscape architects work independently. Others work for architectural firms, government agencies, or private companies.

Museum Curator

Like universities and libraries, museums have the job of preserving and passing on culture. The person in charge of seeing that the museum does its job is the museum curator (**kyoor**-ayt-uhr).

Curators are part guardian, part restorer, and part historian. The tasks of the curator are many. They include acquiring, caring for, displaying, and studying works of art. The curator makes sure works of art in the museum collection are arranged so the viewer can enjoy as well as learn from museum exhibits.

As holders of advanced college degrees, curators carry on research in their special areas of interest. They report their findings in books, lectures, and journals.

LESSON 1

Print Motifs

Artists have always found nature to be a rich source for inspiration. Patterns created by repeated designs can be found in nature all around us. Something as common as interesting patterns left in the sand by an insect's tracks can inspire an artist's imagination.

Creating a pattern by repeating a motif can be easily accomplished by using a printing technique. Patterns on fabric, wallpaper, or wrapping paper are often printed. (See Figure S–1.)

WHAT YOU WILL LEARN

You will create a printed pattern to decorate wrapping paper for a special holiday. You will glue bits of plastic foam to a piece of wood to create a relief block for printing. Your wrapping paper will be decorated by a rhythmic pattern created by repeated printing.

WHAT YOU WILL NEED

- Scratch paper, pencil, and eraser
- Small piece of wood
- Foam packing trays, or any pieces of reusable plastic foam
- Scissors or cutting knife, glue
- Butcher paper, 12 x 24 inch (30 x 61 cm)
- Printer's ink or tempera paint, brushes
- Newspaper

WHAT YOU WILL DO

1. Consider some of the holidays that are less advertised. You might research a special holiday celebrated in another country, or you might decide to create wrapping paper that has a personal design for someone special. This person could be someone you know, someone famous, or even an imagined character.

▲ Figure S–1 **Wrapping paper decorated with a nature motif.**

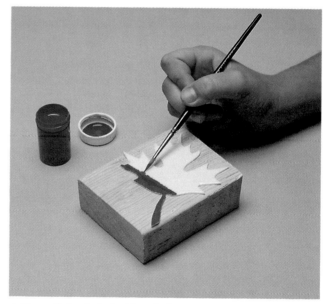

▲ Figure S–2 **A student is painting tempera on a foam stamp.**

2. Using pencil and scratch paper, sketch some designs that you might use. Remember you will be cutting out a piece of plastic foam to glue on a wood block. Use your pencil to draw the outline of a shape that can be cut out. Keep your design simple. Consider whether your design will have formal or informal balance. Remember even a small motif must have unity or a sense of wholeness to it.

3. Select your best sketch. Draw the shape on the plastic and cut it out. If you use more than one shape, carefully determine how they are to be arranged on the wood block. Remember the space between the shapes will be left white. Again think about the unity of your motif. When you are satisfied, glue the shape down.

4. Place a pad of newspaper under the butcher paper for better defined prints. Carefully paint the plastic foam shape on your wood block with ink or tempera paint, as shown in Figure S–2, and begin printing. Be sure to add more paint each time you make a print.

5. You may decide to make prints using different colors. Let the paint dry on your block before adding a new color. Be sure to plan ahead of time when a new color will be added to your pattern.

EXAMINING YOUR WORK

- **Describe**   Point out the shapes in your print. Point out which motifs in your pattern came out most clear. Tell what you did to achieve this clear print. Describe the theme of your wrapping paper.
- **Analyze**   Tell whether you used formal or informal balance to create unity in your motif. Tell how you created rhythm with your motif.
- **Interpret**   Tell what mood the theme of your motif suggests. Explain how adding different colors to your pattern enhanced the mood.
- **Judge**   Tell whether you feel your work succeeds. Explain your answer.

▲ Figure S–3   Cloth can also be printed and used for table cloths, napkins, pillow covers, and curtains.

Try This!

COMPUTER OPTION

■ Design a motif from nature or one that reflects a personal hobby or interest. Create the motif using only line and the Pencil, Straight Line, or Shape tools. Title and Save the line drawing. Select the Bucket tool to flood-fill areas, choosing from a variety of colors, patterns, textures, and gradients. Retitle and Save. Use the Lasso selection tool to select the motif. Go to the Edit menu and choose first the Copy, then the Paste command. While each copy is active, move it into a position and then glue it there by clicking anywhere on the screen. Fill the page, Retitle, Save, and Print.

Consider combining two motifs, or select the Transformation menu to rotate, flip, or turn alternating images to make an alternating rhythm.

LESSON 2
Action Painting

Look at the painting in Figure S–4. It was created by Jackson Pollock, who created his own technique to accomplish a style of painting, known as *action painting*. The colors in his paintings related to his feelings when he began the work. Notice how the lines appear to move or follow his feelings by being very quickly applied. Sometimes they are slowly dripped and drawn into his canvas. He did not use drawings or color sketches for his works but worked directly on the canvas.

▲ **Figure S–4** Jackson Pollock was known as an action painter. Can you see from this painting why he was called that?

Jackson Pollock. *Cathedral.* 1947. Enamel and aluminum paint on canvas. 181.6 x 89.1 cm (71½ x 35¹⁄₁₆"). Dallas Museum of Art, Dallas, Texas. Gift of Mr. and Mrs. Bernard J. Reis.

WHAT YOU WILL LEARN

You will create an action painting using tempera on a large sheet of white paper. Choose colors that reflect how you are feeling before you begin to work. Warm colors can be used for feelings of happiness, excitement, or anger. Cool colors can be used to reflect calm, peacefulness, sadness, or serenity.

WHAT YOU WILL NEED

- Sheet of white paper, 12 x 18 inch (30 x 46 cm)
- Tempera paints
- Brushes, varied sizes

WHAT YOU WILL DO

1. Select a color scheme that represents how you feel before you begin to paint. Remember the discussion in Chapter 4, Lesson 2, on the use of monochromatic, analogous, and complementary color schemes. You can create striking art work by combining colors in ways that use tints or shades of the same hue, (monochromatic). You may want to combine colors that share a hue, such as green, blue-green, and yellow-green, (analogous). Or you might choose a third way to combine colors using a complementary color scheme to achieve contrast colors that are opposite each other on the color wheel, for example, yellow and purple.

2. Put a layer or two of newspaper down on the floor and on your work area for protection. Tape the corners of your white paper to the newspaper. Tape the newspaper to the work surface to keep it from moving.

3. Load your brush with the paint. Hold the brush over your paper and let the paint drip from your brush. Let the paint drip to relate to your mood — fast or slow drips. Whether you have fast or slow drips depends on how full your brush is and on the consistency of the paint. A brush full of thin paint will result in fast drips. A brush that is not as full will have slower drips. Also, if the paint you use is thick the drips will be slower.

4. Observe that lines of color will probably dominate your work, but try to create shapes by accident. Be sure to create balance and harmony in your composition.

5. As you examine your art, also check to see if you are achieving balance and harmony. To check for balance look at your entire composition and see if any one area is too overpowering. However, keep in mind that balance need not be symmetrical. Next check for harmony. Make sure the various elements in your work (drip patterns, dark versus light, size of spatters) are blended in a pleasing way to create a harmonious whole.

6. Stop occasionally while you work to look at the parts from every side of the paper.

EXAMINING YOUR WORK

- **Describe**   Identify areas in the composition that were a result of fast and slow drips. Point to the way the colors were combined to form a color scheme.
- **Analyze**   Tell why you chose the colors you did. Are they warm or cool colors? Do you have fast or slow drips? Does a pattern show in your work? Is there any suggestion of subject in your painting?
- **Interpret**   Give your work a title. How do the colors make you feel? Do the drip patterns remind you of anything? Explain why you chose to use fast or slow drips.
- **Judge**   Tell whether you feel your work is successful. Explain your answer.

7. When you feel your art work is finished, make sure to give the painting enough time to dry in a flat position. If you must move the work to a drying area, carefully carry your painting (still attached to the newspaper) to a flat surface. Let the painting dry and then remove the tape and trim the edges to give a clean professional look to your painting.

8. Show your work to classmates and ask them to interpret your feelings.

Try This! STUDIO OPTIONS

■ To achieve another effect, you may want to dip strings into different hues of paint. Then holding the string at either end, keeping it taut, lay it down across the paper. Make several lines by redipping the string. Do one hue at a time, giving each a chance to dry before using the next color. By laying the strings across the paper in perpendicular patterns, you can make geometric designs.

■ Marble art is another technique. Choose three hues of paint and put each one in a different tin, filling the dish so there is a layer of paint covering the bottom. Put a marble in each tin.

■ Now fold some paper towels to use as you work. Place your art paper inside a shallow box lid. Take one of the marbles and put it in the lid on top of the paper. Tilt the lid so the marble rolls, causing paint tracks across the paper. Vary the track's shape and direction as you wish. When you are finished with that color, put the marble in the extra dish, wipe your hands and start on your next color. Don't make too many tracks the first time because you still have two more marbles to go. Let your art work dry in the lid or on a flat surface.

Group Mural

Have you ever seen large pictures painted on walls of buildings? These pictures are called murals. Look at the mural in Figure S–5. What are the dimensions of the mural? Do you wonder how the artist was able to draw the mural on the wall and keep everything in proportion to one another?

To make murals, artists begin by making a small drawing on paper. They add details and color. Next they create an enlarging grid that is in proportion to the finished product. Using the grid as a guide, the picture is drawn on the wall. (See Technique Tip 5, *Handbook* page **271**.)

WHAT YOU WILL LEARN

You will work with your classmates to create a wall mural. The mural will be planned for a specific wall in your school or community. Before you begin, get permission from your art teacher and school administrators and determine how the project will be financed. If that is not possible you can paint on butcher paper or plywood and display your art work temporarily in an appropriate area.

WHAT YOU WILL NEED

- Sketch paper, pencil, and eraser
- Ruler, tape measure, yardstick, or meter-stick
- Chalk
- Acrylic paints and brushes
- Specific wall to be painted
- Drop cloth
- Safe ladder
- Cleaning materials, such as sponges, soaps, and buckets of water

WHAT YOU WILL DO

1. As a group brainstorm ideas that could be used for a mural. The subject for your mural could be based on native traditions, school or community events, or social statements. Discuss possibilities and as a group decide on a theme for the mural.
2. Develop thumbnail sketches based on the theme. Show these sketches to community officials, school administrators, teachers, and other students. Make adjustments to the plan as needed.

▶ **Figure S–5** **This is an example of a wall mural. Wall murals are popular all over the world. Why do you think this is so?**

Daniel Alonzo. *A Whale of a Mural.* 1983. Two city blocks long.

3. Identify the specific wall where the mural may be painted. Measure the length and width of the area that the final product will take. Determine the materials which make up the wall. Consult with your teacher to find out what pre-treatment is necessary and what medium should be used on the wall.

4. Assign one or two people to render the final composition, which includes ideas and sketches from the entire group. Render the final design in color. Show it to the entire group and make adjustments as needed.

5. Develop an enlargement grid, as shown in Figure S-6, for the drawing and identify a scale for the smaller drawing to the mural. For instance, 1 inch on the grid equals a wall measurement of 1 foot.

6. Place drop cloths on the floor and protect the surrounding area as needed. Divide the wall into squares and number the squares on the wall to match the squares on the paper. Begin to enlarge the plan one square at a time.

7. Continue working until mural is complete.

EXAMINING YOUR WORK

- **Describe** Explain what medium you used to produce the work.
- **Analyze** Identify how the work achieved unity.
- **Interpret** Describe how the mural is a good representation of your school or community.
- **Judge** Explain why this is a successful work of art.

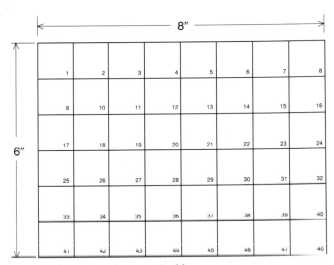

▲ Figure S–6 An enlargement grid.

Try This! COMPUTER OPTION

■ Make a group mural of a famous painting. First make a copy of the painting, then divide the picture into small rectangles or squares. Distribute one section among other group members to enlarge and redraw on the computer. Be sure to code the pieces so they can easily be reassembled.

Select the Grids and Rulers option on the computer so everyone will be using the same size. Redraw the piece using either the Pencil or small Brush tools. Title and Save. Use the Bucket and Brush tools to apply colors and textures to simulate the original art piece. Retitle, Save, and Print. Trim and assemble.

LESSON 4
Pop-up Cityscape

Art, as you have learned, may be judged using three different aesthetic views. One of these views holds that what matters most in a work is a realistic subject. A second view states that what is most important in art is form. A third view argues that content is what counts most. Look at the cityscapes in Figures S–7, S–8, and S–9. Which of these would be judged most successful by a critic of the first school, a critic of the second school, or a critic of the third school?

WHAT YOU WILL LEARN

You will create a three-dimensional pop-up cityscape. Your work will be guided by one of the three aesthetic views described previously. The cityscape will have three parts — a foreground, a middleground, and a background. You will use the principle of proportion to organize the element of space.

▲ **Figure S–7** **What aesthetic view do you think is best represented by this painting?**

Edward Hopper. *Drug Store*. 1927. Oil on canvas. 73.7 x 101.6 cm (29 x 40"). Museum of Fine Arts, Boston, Massachusetts. Bequest of John T. Spaulding.

WHAT YOU WILL NEED

- Pencil and sketch paper
- Four pieces of illustration board: one 3 x 12 inches (8 x 30 cm), one 6 x 12 inches (15 x 30 cm), one 9 x 12 inches (23 x 30 cm), one 10 x 12 inches (25 x 30 cm)
- School tempera paints and several brushes
- Ruler, scissors, masking tape and white glue
- Two scrap pieces of illustration board, 3 x 2 inches (8 x 5 cm)
- Two strips of heavy construction paper, 7 x 2 inches (18 x 5 cm)

◀ **Figure S–8   What kind of balance is represented in this painting?**

Stuart Davis. *Place Pasdeloup*. 1928. Oil. 92.1 x 73 cm (36¼ x 28¾"). Whitney Museum of American Art, New York, New York.

◀ **Figure S–9   What is the mood represented in this painting?**

El Greco. *View of Toledo*. Oil on canvas. 121.3 x 108.6 cm (47¾ x 42¾"). The Metropolitan Museum of Art, New York, New York. The H. O. Havemeyer Collection.

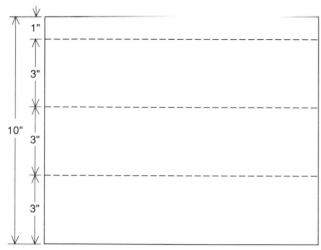

▲ Figure S–10   Light rules for lining up the foreground, middleground, and background of the cityscape.

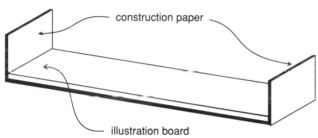

construction paper

illustration board

▲ Figure S–11   This is a connecting U-joint that supports the pop-up portions of the cityscape.

WHAT YOU WILL DO

1. Look once more at Figures S–7, S–8, and S–9. Decide which of the three paintings you want your cityscape to resemble most. Will it have a realistic subject, like Figure S–7? Will it focus on lines, textures, and shapes like Figure S–8? Will it capture a feeling, like the mood painting in Figure S–9?

2. Once you have chosen a style, make three sets of pencil sketches for your cityscape. One set should focus on the low buildings and shapes that will appear in the foreground. This set should have the most detail and color. A second should focus on the buildings and shapes of medium height that will appear in the middleground. A third should focus on the tall buildings and shapes that will appear in thc background. Include details of design. The three sections of illustration board should be cut at the top edge to show the roofline of the buildings on each.

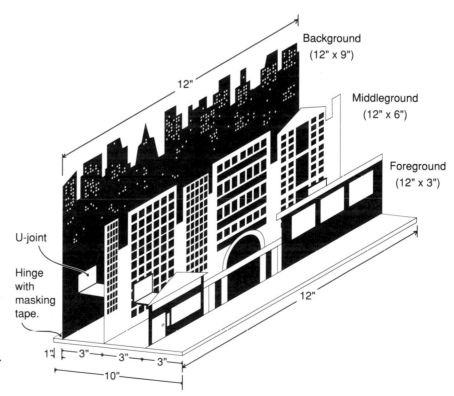

Background (12" x 9")

Middleground (12" x 6")

Foreground (12" x 3")

U-joint

Hinge with masking tape.

► Figure S–12   Attaching the U-joint to the middleground of the cityscape.

ADDITIONAL STUDIOS

3. Use the first three pieces of illustration board and transfer your best sketches to three of the sections of illustration board. Carefully paint the buildings and shapes in each section.

4. Turn the remaining piece of illustration board so the 12-inch (30-cm) side is facing you. Placing the ruler firmly against the near edge, make a pencil mark 3 inches (8 cm) from either end. Make two more pencil dots the same distance from the ends of the opposite side. Connect each pair of parallel dots with a light rule. (See Figure S–10.)

5. Line up the foreground panel (the smallest section) along one rule. Holding the foreground panel upright, attach it along its back to the base panel. Use strips of masking tape for this task. The tape should work as a hinge. Attach the middleground and background to the base in a similar fashion.

6. Center a scrap of illustration board on a strip of construction paper (Figure S–11). Join the two pieces with glue. When dry, bend the flaps up to form a letter U. Apply glue to one flap. Attach the flap to the back of the foreground panel. Be careful about keeping the U-joint as out of sight as possible. Apply glue to the other flap Attach it to the front of the middleground panel. Repeat this task to join the middleground and background panels. (See Figure S–12.)

7. Display your work. Compare it with that of other students.

EXAMINING YOUR WORK

- **Describe** Identify the aesthetic view that you chose. How did you express that aesthetic view in the design of your cityscape?
- **Analyze** Tell which art elements and principles you used. Tell how you used the principle of proportion. Explain how you organized the element of space.
- **Interpret** Does your work express a mood or feeling? Why did you choose to express this mood in your cityscape?
- **Judge** Tell whether you feel your work succeeds. Explain your answer.

▲ **Figure S–13   A finished pop-up cityscape.**

STUDIO OPTIONS

Try This!

■ Add to the three-dimensional feel of your cityscape. Create details out of illustration board, such as store awnings and window ledges. Paint these and glue them to your foreground panel.

■ Create a second pop-up cityscape, this time adding a fourth, near-foreground, panel. This fourth panel should contain cutouts of people, dogs, cars, and so on. The style of these objects should blend with that of the other three panels.

LESSON 5

Appliqué Banner

One type of craftsperson uses needle, thread, and fabric to create works of art. The craftsperson who created the tropical birds in Figure S-14 stitched them onto a satin robe using multicolored silk threads. The artist used many different stitches, but they are so fine that it is hard to see them in this reproduction.

WHAT YOU WILL LEARN

You will create a personal banner by sewing fibers and fabrics and small found objects onto a shaped piece of fabric. The banner must show objects or designs that are symbolic of you. Include your name or initials on the banner. To give the banner unity use harmony of color and rhythm through repetition

▶ **Figure S–14** This is one example of the art of stitchery. There are many different kinds of art that can be created this way.

of line and shape. Use variety in the size of the negative spaces between the shapes and in the textures of fabrics and stitches. See Figure S–15 for an example of a student banner.

WHAT YOU WILL NEED

- Sketch paper, pencil, and ruler
- Large sheet of newsprint
- Fabric scissors and straight pins
- Fabric for the banner
- Thick and thin sewing needles
- Small pieces of fabric
- A variety of fibers
- Small found objects
- *Optional:* A dowel rod or a wire coat hanger

▲ **Figure S–15** Student work. An appliqué banner.

WHAT YOU WILL DO

1. Plan the symbols you will include in your banner. List and draw them on your sketch paper. Remember to include your name or initials as one of the symbols. Collect a few small found objects that you might sew onto the banner such as a button from a special jacket, a ticket stub, an election button, a dried flower, a blue ribbon, or a stone from the river where you love to fish.
2. Practice some stitches on scrap fabric.
3. Plan the size and shape of your banner. Think about the space where you will hang it, and what you plan to include on it. If you plan to use a coat hanger, the banner can be no wider than the bottom rod of the coat hanger. Then design the way you will arrange the symbols on the shape of your banner. Remember to repeat lines and shapes to create a sense of rhythm. Vary the negative spaces. Make several rough sketches in your sketch book. Select your best design.
4. Make a pattern for the banner. Draw the shape on the newsprint paper. Use the ruler to measure and to make straight lines. Cut out the paper pattern. Pin it to your fabric, and cut the fabric to match the pattern.

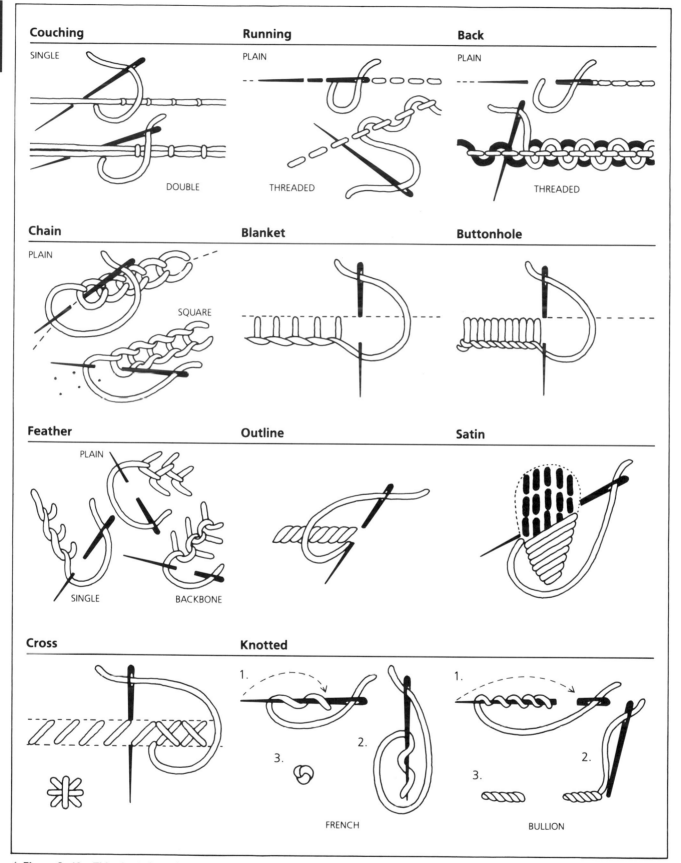

Couching

SINGLE

DOUBLE

Running

PLAIN

THREADED

Back

PLAIN

THREADED

Chain

PLAIN

SQUARE

Blanket

Buttonhole

Feather

PLAIN

SINGLE

BACKBONE

Outline

Satin

Cross

Knotted

1.

2.

3.

FRENCH

1.

2.

3.

BULLION

▲ **Figure S–16   This chart shows how to do some art stitches.**

5. Decide what harmonious color scheme you will use. Select fabrics and fibers to fit the color scheme.

6. Think about texture as you select fabrics and plan stitches. Decide which symbols will be made with fabric and sewn on to the banner, and which will be made with stitches. Draw on the scrap fabric with pencil and cut out the fabric pieces. Pin them in place, and sew them to the banner using the running stitch or the blanket stitch. Study the stitchery chart in Figure S–16. Draw the symbols to be made with stitches onto the banner and stitch them with a variety of fibers.

7. Turn the sides and bottom of your banner under ¼ inch and sew a hem. Sew the top over a thin dowel rod or the bottom rod of a wire coat hanger. Attach string to the rod so that you can hang it up or you may decorate the wire areas of the coat hanger.

8. Place your work on display with your classmates. Can you recognize any by the symbols alone? See Figure S-17 for ideas on different shapes for your banner.

- **Describe**   List the kinds of fabrics, fibers, and found objects you used in this project. List the symbols you included. List the stitches you used. Describe how you included your name or initials.
- **Analyze**   Describe the shape of your banner. What harmonizing color scheme did you use? Which lines and shapes did you repeat to create rhythm? Explain how you introduced variety into your design. Did you vary negative spaces? Did you vary textures?
- **Interpret**   Is your banner a symbol of you? Can your friends recognize the banner as your symbol?
- **Judge**   Are you satisfied with the quality of the banner? If not, what could you do to make it better?

▲ Figure S–17   Banners have many different uses. Can you name some of those uses?

Try This!

STUDIO OPTIONS

■ Working in groups of three or four, and using the above directions, make a large banner, (6 x 2 foot or 183 x 61 cm) to represent your school, community, or state.

■ Working on a square felt piece, make a stitchery design as a birthday present for a friend. Be sure to include symbols of that person in your design. Felt is easy to use because it doesn't require hemming. This allows you to make any style bottom edge you choose.

LESSON 6

Wire Sculpture

Look at the wire sculpture in Figure S–18. Do you recognize the subject? What is she doing? Notice how the artist has used the principles of movement and rhythm to make the figure seem alive.

WHAT YOU WILL LEARN

You will construct a freestanding wire sculpture. The finished sculpture will be a three-dimensional objective form. It will be created entirely of wire lines. You can bend, curve, and twist the wire to make a variety of large and small shapes. Your figure should show movement. It should also suggest a feeling, such as happiness, sadness, or fright.

WHAT YOU WILL NEED

- Sketch paper, pencil, and eraser
- 14-gauge steel wire, 35 inch (89 cm) piece
- Pair of needle nose pliers
- *Optional:* foam or wood block for base, 6 x 6 inch (15 x 15 cm)

WHAT YOU WILL DO

1. Study the wire sculpture in Figure S–19. Decide what subject you will use for your true-to-life form. Think of the features and feelings that will be associated with your figure. Identify other objects that may be part of your sculptural form, such as a bike, kite, or balloon.
2. Make a pencil sketch of the form you see in your imagination. Use one continuous line to create this true-to-life form. Keep your form simple and concentrate on the line used. Continue to reshape and re-draw until you are happy with your sketch.

▲ **Figure S–18** Art often displays a sense of humor. Do you think this piece shows humor?

Alexander Calder. *The Hostess*. 1928. Wire construction. Museum of Modern Art, New York, New York.

3. Grasp your wire at one end. Choose the part of the subject in your sketch where your sculpture will begin. (You will not be cutting the wire; your sculpture will be made of one continuous wire line.) Bend, curve, and twist the wire until it resembles the part you chose. Then move on to the next part. Continue working on one part at a time.

4. As you work, use a mixture of large, curved twists and small, tight twists. This will give interest and variety to your sculpture.
5. If your sculpture can stand on its own, you won't need to mount it on a base unless you want to. However, if your work needs mounting, attach it to a plastic foam or wood block, using wire bent into hooks, or small screws.
6. Display your finished sculpture with those of your classmates in a gallery in front of the class. Stroll through the gallery, comparing the different sculptures you and your classmates created. It is more important to catch the feeling of life, movement, and uniqueness than to be overly concerned with exact proportion and details.

=== SAFETY TIP ===

Before beginning to form your sculpture, cover both ends of the wire with masking tape or electrician's tape. While working, wear protective eye goggles. Both of these tips will help prevent you from scratching or poking your eyes and skin while you work.

EXAMINING YOUR WORK

- **Describe**   Point out the features in your work that identify the subject. Explain what features you added to create a true-to-life sculpture form.
- **Analyze**   Identify the variety of large and small shapes created in your wire line. Explain how your sculpture form shows movement.
- **Interpretation**   Explain how you made the sculpture express a mood.
- **Judge**   Explain why this is a successful work of art.

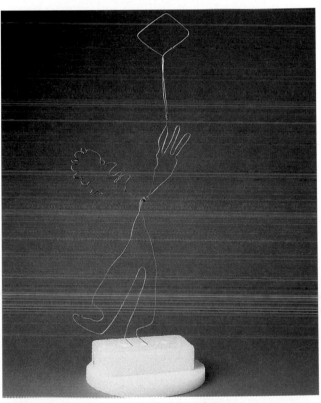

▲ Figure S–19   Student work. A wire sculpture.

Try This! COMPUTER OPTION

■ As a warm-up exercise before making the wire sculpture in this Studio Lesson, practice contour line drawing on the computer to capture the action and essence of the object or figure you will create from wire. Begin by completing one or two blind contour drawings of your hand or an object in the room.

Use the Pencil tool for the drawing and cover or darken the screen if you are tempted to peek. Then choose the subject of the wire sculpture and make some contour drawings with the Pencil while looking at the screen. Title, Save, and Print your best drawings.

LESSON 7
Freestanding Mobile

Artists have always been fascinated with representing motion and movement. Look at Figure S–20. Alexander Calder represents motion by making objects or mobiles that actually sway in the wind. A mobile is made up of objects that are delicately hung and balanced by other objects. Unlike other sculpture pieces, you do not have to walk around them to see them completely.

Figure S–20 is a suspended mobile. The moving objects are suspended from sturdy wire and metal crosspieces that are part of the sculpture.

WHAT YOU WILL LEARN

You will create a freestanding mobile based on natural forms—animals, birds, fish, or plants. The forms will be made from paper and may appear to be realistic or abstract. You will use the principle of balance when constructing your mobile.

▲ **Figure S–20** Do you think mobiles would be successful as art if they were not designed to move?

Alexander Calder. *Untitled*. 1976. Aluminum and steel. 9.1 x 23.2 m (29′10½″ x 76′). National Gallery of Art, Washington, D.C. Gift of the Collectors Committee.

WHAT YOU WILL NEED

- Cardboard from boxes, some pieces at least 16 inches (40 cm) long
- Pencil, ruler, and cutting knife
- Glue and string
- Construction paper
- 16-gauge wire, wire cutters, and round-nose pliers
- Paint and brushes

WHAT YOU WILL DO

1. Think of the natural forms—animals, birds, fish, or plants that can be used for your mobile. Decide if your forms will be realistic or abstract. Experiment with constructing the forms, using paper sculpture techniques. (See Technique Tip **21**, *Handbook* page **278**.)

2. Make the base for your freestanding sculpture. Study the diagram (Figure S–21) which shows how two pieces of cardboard can be joined together. Using a pencil and ruler draw the shape for the base. Measure one piece at least 16 inches (40 cm) tall. Make the other piece 3 or 4 inches (7.5 or 10 cm) tall and approximately 10 to 12 inches (25 to 30 cm) long to help make the base sturdy. Cut a slit about 2 inches (5 cm) long at the bottom of the large central piece. Cut a slit 2 inches (5 cm) long at the top of the bottom piece. Slip the cardboard slots together gently connecting the two pieces. Several smaller pieces of cardboard can be joined to the base to make it more interesting or to make it stand more solid. Continue joining them until the base stands alone and then glue the joint. Paint your base using colors that are appropriate to the theme of your mobile.

3. There are several ways that wire can be attached to the base. One way is to cut a small slot in the top of the cardboard and

then slide the wire down. This leaves both ends of the wire free for balancing objects on either side.

Another way is to poke about 3 or 4 inches (7.5 or 10 cm) of one end of the wire down between the cardboard layers. This leaves only one end free to hang objects.

4. Make your paper sculpture forms and decide how many you will suspend from your mobile. Consider proportion as you make the pieces and think of creative ways to balance the objects. Cut the pieces of wire to the desired lengths and use the round-nosed pliers to turn a small loop at the end. Use string to hang the paper sculptures from the wire loops.

5. Begin assembling your mobile with the lowest hanging pieces and continue working upward from there. After hanging two objects from either end of a piece of wire, locate its balance point by balancing the wire on your finger. Carefully form another loop in the wire to hang it from above.

6. When your work is complete display it in your classroom. (See Figure S–22.)

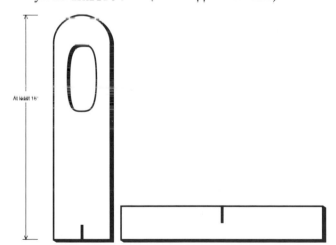

▲ Figure S–21   The base for the freestanding mobile.

- **Explain**   Identify the paper sculpture techniques that you used to create your paper forms. Describe how the base was constructed to give support to your mobile.
- **Analyze**   Tell how balance was achieved in the mobile. Explain whether your mobile creates visual movement.
- **Interpret**   Tell what natural form you had in mind while creating your mobile. Did you portray the form in an abstract or realistic view?
- **Judge**   Tell whether you feel your work succeeds. Explain your answer.

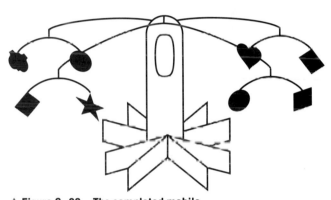

▲ Figure S–22   The completed mobile.

Try This!   STUDIO OPTIONS

- Make a mobile that is not free-standing, but is made to hang.
- Work with a partner. Each of you begin a cardboard base for a freestanding mobile. Find ways to connect your cardboard bases so that eventually you have one large base. Then, in cooperation with your partner, create one large mobile on the base.

 **LESSON 8**

A Picture That Tells a Story

Winslow Homer's painting in Figure S–23 shows a fisherman in a small boat surrounded by signs of danger. Can you identify these signs?

This work is a wonderful example of this artist's skill in arousing the viewer's curiosity. It suggests a great many questions and then allows the viewer to use his or her own imagination to answer these questions. For example, where is the fisherman looking? What does he see? What might he be thinking and feeling at this moment? Where must he go to reach safety?

In this lesson you will give your answer to one of the most important questions about this painting. You will decide the fate of the fisherman.

▲ **Figure S–23** Homer's paintings often tell stories. Can you see a story that might be told in this painting?

Winslow Homer. *The Fog Warning*. 1885. Oil on canvas. 76.2 x 121.9 cm (30 x 48"). The Museum of Fine Arts, Boston, Massachusetts. Otis Norcross Fund.

WHAT YOU WILL LEARN

You will complete a painting in which you show what happens to the fisherman in Homer's picture. As in Homer's painting you will use large and small shapes to suggest deep space. You will also use real and imaginary lines to guide the viewer's eyes to the most important objects in your work.

WHAT YOU WILL NEED

- Pencil and sketch paper
- White paper, 9 x 12 inch
- Tempera paint
- Brushes
- Mixing tray

WHAT YOU WILL DO

1. Imagine that Homer completed another painting entitled *Fog Warning II*. In this work he showed what happened to the fisherman. Discuss with other members of your class what this second picture might look like.
2. On your own complete several sketches showing your version of *Fog Warning II*. Include all the facts and details needed by viewers to determine the fisherman's fate. Suggest space by using large shapes in the foreground and smaller shapes in the distance. Use real and imaginary lines to direct attention to the most important features in your work.

EXAMINING YOUR WORK

- **Describe** Identify the objects in your picture. Explain how these were suggested by Homer's painting.
- **Analyze** Show how you used large and small shapes to create an illusion of deep space. Point to real and imaginary lines and explain how these are used to guide the viewer to the important parts of your picture.
- **Interpret** Determine if others are able to use your picture to learn the fate of the fisherman. Can they identify a happy or a sad ending to the story?
- **Judge** State whether you think your painting is successful or unsuccessful. What aesthetic view would you suggest to viewers trying to judge your work?

3. Transfer your best sketch to the paper or illustration board. Paint your picture with colors that suggest a happy or sad ending to the story of the fisherman.

COMPUTER OPTION

Try This!

■ Select another painting that you feel tells a story, but with a subject matter that is different from Homer's. Imagine the story it tells and then invent and draw the sequel on the computer. Use the Pencil or Brush tools to draw the images and the Bucket or Brush tools to apply color. Title, Save, and Print. On a word processing program, write your interpretation of the original painting and the sequel to the story. Save, Print, and post the writing with your art work.

 **LESSON 9**

Pinhole Camera Photography

Look at Figure S–24. This is a photograph by American photographer Ansel Adams. As with other works of art, learning to make photographs like this takes skill and practice. It does not, however, take an expensive camera. A simple homemade pinhole camera (Figure S–25) will allow you to test your skills as a photographer. Pinhole cameras work by letting the photographed image enter a darkened box through a tiny hole. The image is captured on a piece of film attached to the inside lid of the box.

WHAT YOU WILL LEARN

You will build a pinhole camera using simple materials found around the house. You will make a photograph using your camera.

WHAT YOU WILL NEED

- Scissors or cutting knife
- Empty round oatmeal box with a lid
- Flat black spray paint
- Square of heavy-duty aluminum foil, 2 inch (5 cm)
- Needle or sharp pin
- Masking tape
- Square of cardboard, 1 inch (3 cm)
- Sheets of Kodak Plus-X film, 4 x 5 inches (10 x 13 cm)
- Sheet of white paper, 12 x 18 inches (30 x 46 cm)

SAFETY TIP

Use spray paint outdoors or in a well ventilated area. Be careful not to inhale the fumes from the paint.

▶ **Figure S–24 Photography is an art form that can be used in many different ways. What are some ways photography is used?**

Photograph by Ansel Adams.

WHAT YOU WILL DO

1. Using the scissors or cutting knife, cut a ½-inch (13 mm) square hole in the bottom of the oatmeal box. The hole should be as close to the center as possible. Paint the inside of the box and the lid with spray paint. Set them aside to dry.
2. Hold the piece of aluminum foil against a hard, flat surface. Using the needle or pin, carefully poke a pin-size hole at the center. Make sure the hole is crisp and sharp. A ragged or too-large hole will produce a blurry image.
3. Place the foil inside the box. Line it up so the pinhole is centered over the hole at the bottom. Using masking tape, attach the foil to the bottom of the box. Place the cardboard square over the hole on the outside bottom of the box. Fasten the square along one side with tape, making a hinged flap. (See Figure S–25.)
4. In a darkroom, cut a piece of film to fit inside the lid of the box. Try to handle the film by the edges only because touching the film may cause blurs on the image. Tape the film in place. Place the lid on the box. Hold the cardboard flap closed until you are ready to shoot a picture.
5. Choose a subject that is outdoors in bright sunlight. Standing about 10 feet away from your subject, set the camera down on a flat unmoving surface. Prop the camera with cloth or crumpled paper towel, so it won't roll or move while you are taking your picture. Aim the bottom of the box at your subject. Lift the flap, and hold it open for about 15 seconds. Close the flap. Holding it in place, return to the darkroom to develop your photo.

EXAMINING YOUR WORK

- **Describe** Show that all inside surfaces of your camera are coated with paint. Tell whether you held the camera steady and kept the cardboard flap open for 15 seconds.
- **Analyze** Tell whether your photograph was blurry or clear. If blurry, explain why. If the photograph is too light or too dark, explain why.
- **Interpret** Explain how a viewer would recognize your work as a portrait. Give your photograph a title.
- **Judge** Tell whether you feel your work succeeds. Explain your answer.

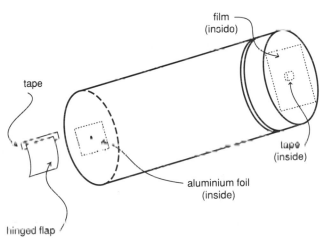

▲ Figure S–25   This shows how a pin-hole camera is constructed.

STUDIO OPTIONS

Try This!

■ Take a second photograph of a subject indoors. Experiment to find out how long the flap needs to be open for indoor light.

■ Set up an indoor group portrait. Have your subjects strike an interesting pose. Take your photograph.

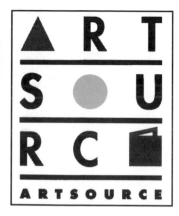

Performing Arts Handbook

T he following pages of content were excerpted from *Artsource®: The Music Center Study Guide to the Performing Arts,* developed by the Music Center Education Division, an award-winning arts education program of the Music Center of Los Angeles County.

The following artists and groups are featured in the Performing Arts Handbook.

Music   *Paul Tracey*

A R T
S ● U
R C ▮
ARTSOURCE

PERFORMING ARTS

Paul Tracey is an international minstrel (songwriter and entertainer). He draws upon his cultural heritage and broad personal experience to communicate ideas about life by writing and performing original songs. Born in South Africa and raised in England, he returned to his homeland at the age of 18 where he learned about farming and building. It was also during this time that he developed an appreciation for the music of other cultures, especially African folk songs. He now lives in the United States where he has performed on Broadway and written songs for the Muppets. Currently he performs his one-man shows to worldwide audiences.

Paul Tracey, international minstrel. Photo © 1995 by Craig Schwartz.

■ DISCUSSION QUESTIONS

1. Look carefully at the photograph of Paul Tracey. What do you see that identifies his cultural heritage?
2. The music of Paul Tracey is influenced by his British and South African cultures. What aspects of your heritage could be a source of inspiration for a poem, dance, song, or painting?
3. Think about your heritage. Identify colors, symbols, patterns, sounds, rhythms, movements, objects, or words that you could use in an art work that portrays your heritage.

■ CREATIVE EXPRESSION ACTIVITIES

Music   Based on your responses to Discussion Questions 2 and 3, create original lyrics for a song that you compose about your life. If you wish, you can use your lyrics with a melody that you already know. Perform the song to an audience of your classmates.

Geography   Use a world atlas, map, or globe to locate South Africa, England, and the United States. Share what you know about the land and people who live in these places. How might these cultures have influenced Paul Tracey's music?

John Adams, composer. Photo © 1994 by Deborah Feingold.

John Adams is an American composer, born in Worcester, Massachusetts. He is called a "minimalist" composer, which means his compositions use simple musical elements and a great deal of repetition. He also tries to make his music sound different by using harmony and melody in unique ways. With these techniques he creates new ways to express familiar ideas through music. When composing his piece "Short Ride in a Fast Machine," John Adams had a mental image of "moving through space at tremendous speeds, while in some kind of vehicle." Adams then wrote challenging music for various instruments in the orchestra to create this image.

■ **DISCUSSION QUESTIONS**

1. If you could compose a musical piece about traveling at tremendous speed, what rhythms and sounds do you think would convey your idea? What musical instruments would you select to create those sounds? How would these instruments be played so your audience will enjoy your composition?

2. What other titles can you think of for a musical composition about traveling?

■ **CREATIVE EXPRESSION ACTIVITIES**

Music Working with other students in small groups, compare the titles you created in Discussion Question 2. Then choose one and use simple musical instruments and vocal sounds to compose a short piece to match the title. Perform the piece for the class.

Language Arts In small groups, brainstorm a list of words that might describe the rhythms and sounds in "Short Ride in a Fast Machine." Then create a short story or poem using the words. Decorate your story or poem with designs or symbols.

Sandy Spieler is the director of In The Heart of the Beast Puppet and Mask Theatre. The theatre group presents original and imaginative performances with puppets made of recycled materials. Members of the group combine sculpture and painting with poetry, music, and dance to magically bring the puppets to life. Their May Day Parade is a glorious pageant and ceremony celebrated annually. It features giant rod puppets over twenty feet tall. Each large puppet has a name that symbolizes a different element of nature, such as Prairie, Sky, River, Woods, and the Tree of Life.

In the Heart of the Beast Puppet and Mask Theatre. Sandy Spieler, artistic director. May Day Parade and Festival. Photo courtesy of In the Heart of the Beast Puppet and Mask Theatre.

■ DISCUSSION QUESTIONS

1. Think about parades or pageants you have experienced, then study the photo on this page. How is it similar to, or different from, the parades or pageants you have seen?
2. Imagine you are in charge of planning a parade to celebrate the cycle of life. What ideas do you have for puppets to include in your parade? What recycled material could you use to create your puppets? How would you plan the parade?

■ CREATIVE EXPRESSION ACTIVITIES

Multi-Media   In a small group, use some of the ideas you had in Discussion Question 2 to plan a parade celebrating a specific theme or event. For example, you might honor a historical figure or celebrate an important event in your community.

Social Studies   Share what you know about parades or pageants of various cultures, such as Mardi Gras, Chinese New Year, Day of the Dead, and so on. Discuss each one's purpose, theme, and characteristics.

Dance

Lewitzky Dance Company

Lewitzky Dance Company. Bella Lewitzky, director. "Impressions #2." Featured dancers: Kimo Kimura, Kenneth Bowman, Kenneth B. Talley, John Pennington. Photo by Vic Luke.

Dancer and choreographer Bella Lewitzky grew up in the Mojave Desert in California. The vast open space, stillness, and beauty of her surroundings would later influence her dance. Her art has also been inspired by the work of visual artists. "Impressions #2" is part of a trilogy of dances, each one based on Ms. Lewitzky's responses to the art works of three different artists—Henry Moore, Vincent van Gogh, and Paul Klee. "Impressions #2" was inspired by the art of Vincent van Gogh.

■ DISCUSSION QUESTIONS

1. Study van Gogh's painting in Figure 4–15 on page 64. List action words that describe what you see. Now look at the photo of the dancers on this page and use action words to describe what you see. How are your lists similar? How are they different?

2. Again look at *Cypresses* and notice the intensity and value of the colors. Dancers would use terms such as *strong, weak, heavy,* or *light* to describe the same concepts. How would you use your body to "show" these colors in movement?

■ CREATIVE EXPRESSION ACTIVITIES

Language Arts   Describe an imaginary dance that shows how you would translate the elements of art used in Figure 4–15 into dance movements. You may wish to organize your dance into three parts—either a beginning, middle, and end or an entrance, middle, and exit.

Dance   Dancers use the movements of their bodies to express action as it relates to weight, flow, space, and time. Explore ways to show the following eight actions using dance movements: press, flick, punch, float, slash, glide, wring, and dab.

Choreographer Donald McKayle is a performing artist who has broken many barriers. He was the first African-American male dancer selected to join the famous Martha Graham Dance Company. He also went with the company on its historic tour of Asia in the late 1950s. Among his many dances is a piece called "Rainbow 'Round My Shoulder," based on prisoners' dreams of freedom. McKayle focuses on prisoners in the south who were chained together as they worked. In the dance he incorporates the strong, repetitive rhythm of work movements and prison songs. He believes that the more truthful artists are, the more their art will communicate to others. His dances, as well as his life, reflect this belief.

The Alvin Ailey American Dance Theater. Donald McKayle, choreographer. "Rainbow 'Round My Shoulder." Featured dancers: Elizabeth Roxas and Desmond Richardson. Photo by Jack Mitchell.

■ DISCUSSION QUESTIONS

1. Share what you know about the life of prisoners working on a chain gang. What kind of movements would a choreographer use to portray a prisoner's hard and repetitive life? Explain your choices.
2. Look at the photo of the dancers on this page. What principles of art can you identify in the photo?
3. Why do you think a choreographer would choose the title "Rainbow 'Round My Shoulder" as a title for a dance about prisoners? What does a rainbow symbolize? What symbols would you choose if you were creating a work of art expressing a wish for freedom?

■ CREATIVE EXPRESSION ACTIVITIES

Dance Working with a partner or in small groups, think of movements that suggest actions associated with physical work. You might use such repetitive movements as hauling, dragging, pushing, pulling, lifting, carrying, and breaking rocks. Create several variations for each. Perform the movements for the class.

Language Arts List words that describe the feelings of someone who is imprisoned and longs for freedom. Use your list to write a poem or short story about this person and his or her feelings.

Bali and Beyond. Cliff DeArment and Maria Bodmann. "Gamelan Music." Photo by Craig Schwartz.

Bali and Beyond is the name of a musical group that performs the Balinese gamelan, one of the world's ancient musical traditions. Maria Bodmann and Cliff DeArment, pictured on this page, believe that performing gamelan music is an important way to share cultures. In Indonesia, the gamelan instruments accompany ceremonies in the temple and during rice planting. They are also used at birthdays, anniversaries, births, and funerals. Although Bali and Beyond features metallophones (percussion instruments with metal bars that are struck with hammers or mallets), other instruments are frequently used in the Balinese gamelan. Larger ensembles include gongs and drums of various sizes, bamboo flutes, zithers, Indonesian violins, cymbals, harps, reed horns, and bells.

■ **DISCUSSION QUESTIONS**

1. Locate Bali on a map and name the chain of islands it belongs to. Identify countries which lie immediately to the north, east, south, and west. In what ways could the people of one country influence the people and culture of another country?
2. Percussion instruments are ones which are struck by beaters or sticks to produce sound. Identify percussion instruments that you know. Describe the shape, size, and design of the instruments and give their origin, if you know it.

■ **CREATIVE EXPRESSION ACTIVITIES**

Music   Using your body as a percussion instrument, create and practice two or more simple rhythm patterns. When each pattern has been learned thoroughly, join other students to combine your patterns into a rhythmic piece. Perform the piece for your class.

Science   Use science books to discover how different lengths of the bars on metallophones produce different sounds. Share what you learn with your class.

Although he was talented, Arthur Mitchell had no formal dance training when he auditioned for the New York City High School of the Performing Arts. Accepted into the dance program, four years of study followed. After his graduation, he was invited to study classical dance at the School of American Ballet. Eventually, Mr. Mitchell's mastery of technique, sense of style, and elegance earned him a position with the New York City Ballet. He was the first African-American male to become a permanent member of a major American dance company, and he proved that he could be judged by his dancing, not the color of his skin. When Dr. Martin Luther King, Jr. was assassinated, Mr. Mitchell decided to establish a school of classic ballet, which became the Dance Theatre of Harlem. His dance company has been known for its performance of *Firebird*, shown on this page. Based on an old Russian folktale, Mr. Mitchell reset the story in a tropical rain forest.

Dance Theatre of Harlem. Arthur Mitchell, founder and artistic director. *Firebird*. Photo by Martha Swope.

■ DISCUSSION QUESTIONS

1. Look at the photo on this page. What physical qualities do you think are needed for this dancer to accomplish this movement? Consider her balance, muscular strength, and flexibility.

2. Why do you think the choreographer might use a Russian folktale for a dance idea, but place it in a tropical rain forest setting? Does the dancer's costume reflect this setting?

3. Why do you think the death of Martin Luther King inspired Arthur Mitchell to start a classical ballet company for African Americans?

■ CREATIVE EXPRESSION ACTIVITIES

Language Arts   Use books, poems, and/or photos to study the characteristics of various birds. Choose two birds and list some of the characteristics of each. Select several characteristics and write a poem about one of the birds. You could also write a poem contrasting the two birds.

Dance   Interpret the poem you wrote in the Language Arts activity above or find another poem about birds. Using body gestures and movements, capture the images in the poem to express the qualities of each bird.

The Children's Theatre Company. *The Story of Babar, the Little Elephant.* 1996 Season. Courtesy of The Children's Theatre Company.

The Children's Theatre Company in Minneapolis, Minnesota, is known for its vivid recreation of the storybook page on stage. The play featured in the photograph on this page is *The Story of Babar, the Little Elephant,* based on the familiar children's story by Jean De Brunhoff. The biggest challenge when bringing a book's characters to life on the stage is expanding two-dimensional art work from a book into three dimensions on stage. It is critical that designers create an accurate scale drawing of the book's characters. Illustrations in the book served as blueprints to the costume designers. The Children's Theatre Company's creative team left nothing to chance. They invented action for the scenes in the story and carefully choreographed every movement.

■ **DISCUSSION QUESTIONS**

1. The costumes for Babar and his elephant friends had to look accurate and have the flexibility for the character to move and even dance! If you were a costume designer, how would you create a costume that transforms an actor into an elephant?
2. What type of fabrics could you use for this costume? Discuss texture, color, flexibility, and the material that you would use to shape the basic structure.
3. Think of yourself as the director of a play. Identify problems you might face in bringing a specific children's book to life on a stage. With a partner, brainstorm solutions to these problems.

■ **CREATIVE EXPRESSION ACTIVITIES**

Art Experiment with fabric remnants and artificial fur to make puppets of the Babar characters. You might instead use characters from another children's book. When finished, write a script based on the story and present a puppet play.

Theatre Select a favorite Babar book or another children's picture book. Create action and scenes that are based on the book's illustrations. You might first arrange and pose the actors as they appear in the scene. Then say "Action!" and give the characters one minute to make up movement and/or language to bring the scene to life.

The World Kulintang Institute Performance Ensemble, shown on this page, is the only organization of its kind. Group members are dedicated to making people aware of the kulintang music of the Southern Philippines. The term *kulintang* can refer to the group of gongs and drums or to a solo melody instrument. This instrument consists of eight bronze and brass gongs laid out in a single row. Kulintang music is preserved in the oral tradition. That means that one musician teaches the music to another without written music. Hundreds of rhythmic and melodic motifs must be memorized by a kulintang student before they are combined into compositions. The music is used for various ceremonial rituals.

World Kulintang Institute Performance Ensemble. Photo by Craig Schwartz.

■ DISCUSSION QUESTIONS

1. Kulintang is an oral tradition. Can you identify an art form from another culture that is preserved in the oral tradition?
2. Listening skills are important to kulintang music because it is not recorded in writing. How are listening skills important in your life? What can any artist learn by improving his or her listening skills?
3. Look at the photo of the kulintang musicians. Use the elements and principles of art to describe their instruments and also the clothing they wear.

■ CREATIVE EXPRESSION ACTIVITIES

Music/Art Listen to a popular song. Show the direction of the melody by drawing a continuous line illustrating its movement up or down. If the melody stays on the same pitch, keep the line straight to show that it is a repeated pitch. Share the "picture" of the music with your class.

Art The traditional clothing worn by people of the Southern Phillippines is called "Malongs." It is made from colorful, hand-woven material with geometric figures in various designs and carefully arranged colors on selected backgrounds. Using traditional color schemes of red, yellow, purple, gold, green, orange, and light blue, draw a design made of geometric figures using any combination of these colors to fill in the negative spaces.

Music

Xochimoki

Xochimoki. Jim Berenholtz and Mazatl Galindo. Photo by Sylvia Mautner.

Xochimoki (So-she-**mo**-key) is a musical group that features unique musicians. Jim Berenholtz and Mazatl Galindo combine original music of Pre-Colombian civilizations with contemporary acoustic and electronic instruments. The result is an interesting mix of the old with the new. One source of inspiration was found when they visited some of Mesoamerica's most exciting murals in the Lacandon rain forest near Yaxchilan. Here they studied art works that depicted dancers and musicians of that ancient world. Using the murals to guide their creativity, Xochimoki composed "Bonampak," an original work using the same instruments illustrated in the murals.

■ DISCUSSION QUESTIONS

1. In the mural described above, musicians are shown playing gourd trumpets, ocarinas, tall wooden drums with skin heads, log drums, turtle shell drums struck with deer antlers, and seed pod rattles worn on the ankles. What modern instruments do you think would be similar to these?

2. List types of music that are popular today and the instruments used to play this music. Explain how examples of these instruments or music would help future civilizations understand today's society.

■ CREATIVE EXPRESSION ACTIVITIES

Art   Using the list created in Discussion Question 2, work with a partner or in a small group to design a mural that preserves contemporary music trends. Share your design with the class.

Art/Language Arts   Sketch your vision of musical instruments of the future. Let your art work illustrate how the instruments are played, as well as how they look. Write detailed descriptions of each, describing the sounds they produce, the materials from which they are made, and how they produce sounds.

THE WOOLLOOMOOLOO CUDDLE   1991 © / Remy Charlip

Remy Charlip is a gentle, playful man who has developed unique and delightful approaches to creating dances. His Air Mail dances begin with a series of 20 to 40 drawings which serve as a dance score. The drawings show the positions the dancers are to take. Individual dancers make the decision of how to move from one position to the other. Drawings from "Woolloomooloo Cuddle," shown on this page, were created for the Sydney Dance Company in Australia. Remy came to Australia to create a dance for the company, but was unable to join the dancers. He solved the problem by creating drawings and sending them to the company dancers to interpret in their own way. He now sends drawings of dances to soloists and companies all over the world.

An Air Mail Dance by Remy Charlip. © 1991. "Woolloomooloo Cuddle." Art courtesy of Remy Charlip.

■ DISCUSSION QUESTIONS

1. Explain how Charlip's technique of creating Air Mail dances is different from that of most other choreographers.
2. Study the drawings from "Woolloomooloo Cuddle." What steps would you take to create a dance based on these drawings?
3. When faced with a problem, Remy Charlip solved it in a clever way. Think of a time when you found a creative solution to a problem. Share the experience with the class and discuss positive ways to deal with problems and conflicts.

■ CREATIVE EXPRESSION ACTIVITIES

Language Arts   Print the letters of your first name on a piece of paper. Study the lines of the letters, then explore ways to interpret each letter into a body design. Practice a way to move smoothly from one letter design to the next using only four counts. Make sure to use different levels when moving.

Dance   In pairs, pretend you are dancers and recreate the designs from "Woolloomooloo Cuddle" on this page. Choose a sequence for the positions and practice moving smoothly from one to the other. Change the sequence and try a new dance combination.

Lewitzky Dance Company. Bella Lewitzky, director. "Impressions #1." Featured dancers: Jennifer Handel, Nancy Lanier, Laurie McWilliams, Theodora Fredericks, Deborah Collodel, Claudia Schneiderman. Photo by Vic Luke.

Bella Lewitzky is a modern dance performer, choreographer, and dance educator who has performed for over sixty years. She frequently uses works of art as a source of inspiration for dance movements. In particular, she has focused on the work of Henry Moore. Since it was impossible to bring his sculptures into her studio, she and her dancers worked from photos. They observed that his sculptures have true, physical weight and mass and have two or three balance points, or places where the sculpture touches the ground. There are also holes, or negative spaces, that encourage the viewer to look through, altering their perspective. Eventually these observations and movement explorations evolved into a dance work called "Impressions #1."

■ DISCUSSION QUESTIONS

1. Review the characteristics of sculpture. How does the process differ from painting?
2. Look at the photo of the dancers on this page. Use the elements of line, shape, form, and texture to describe what you see.
3. Use art books to locate a sculpture by Henry Moore. Observe it in terms of weight, negative and positive space, form, and number of balance points. Discuss how these concepts might be communicated through movement.

■ CREATIVE EXPRESSION ACTIVITIES

Dance In partners, take turns sculpting each other into different three-dimensional forms. Join with other pairs of students and position yourselves in relationship to each other to make more complex forms. Present your forms to the class.

Science Select an object in your classroom and describe it in the following terms: Is it light or heavy? How does it move or balance? How many points are touching the ground? What is the object's shape? Observe it from different perspectives (i.e upside down, above your head, far away, tilted, and so on).

ART
S●U
RC
ARTSOURCE

PERFORMING ARTS

Geri Keams was born and raised on the Navajo Nation in the Painted Desert region of Arizona. Her grandmother, a well-known Navajo rug weaver, taught her the importance of passing on the stories of the "Old Ones." True to the wishes of her grandmother, Geri dramatically brings traditional Native American myths and legends to life on stage. One of these stories, "The Quillwork Girl," tells the tale of a young girl with an extraordinary talent for embroidering porcupine quills on buckskin. In her dreams she learns of seven brothers who she sets out to find. Their reunion leads to a confrontation with members of the Buffalo Nation, which ends in their creation of the Big Dipper.

Geri Keams, storyteller. Photo © 1990 by Craig Schwartz.

■ DISCUSSION QUESTIONS

1. Look carefully at the photo on this page of Geri Keams and describe her costume. How can you tell it is Navajo? What crafts were involved?
2. "The Quillwork Girl" tells about the creation of the Big Dipper. Do you know any other myths or legends about the constellations? What culture are they from?
3. What story from your childhood do you remember most vividly? Who told it or read it to you? What aspects of the story make it memorable?

■ CREATIVE EXPRESSION ACTIVITIES

Language Arts Animals are often the subject of folk tales. In small groups, share and discuss animal stories that you know. Were crafts included in the stories?

Language Arts Create a myth explaining a mystery of nature, such as "why the moon has phases" or "why peacocks have eyes on their tails." Write it and share it with your class.

Theatre Learn a myth or legend from a culture of your choice. Become a storyteller and relate it in your own words, dramatizing aspects with both gestures and changes in the quality of your voice.

Cast of We Tell Stories. Carl Weintraub, artistic director. Photo courtesy of We Tell Stories.

We Tell Stories is the name of a group of actors who bring stories to the stage. A trunk filled with colorful and sometimes wacky costumes and props help create the magic as the tales unfold. One of the stories they perform is called "The Two Skyscrapers Who Decided to Have a Child," by Carl Sandburg. It is a story of two skyscrapers who were stuck in one place. They wanted to have a child who could travel and be free. Carl Weintraub, the artistic director of We Tell Stories, hopes that children will be inspired to read the stories performed by the group.

■ DISCUSSION QUESTIONS

1. Think of such stories as "The Three Little Pigs" and the three architectural structures they built with different materials—straw, sticks, and bricks. What might these three types of homes represent about the personalities of the pigs?
2. Discuss the following types of structures, some of which are shown and described in Chapter 14: the Parthenon; a cathedral; temple; the Colosseum; basilicas; amphitheaters; sports arenas, pyramids, and skyscrapers. Select one and describe it as if it were a person talking about itself.

■ CREATIVE EXPRESSION ACTIVITIES

Theatre   In small groups use your bodies to construct three of the styles of architecture described in Discussion Question 2. Study their characteristics so you can be specific.

Language Arts   Choose a character from a favorite book. Tell the story from the point of view of the character or as the character narrating the story.

Theatre   Form a "magic story circle" in your class. Sit in a circle with other students and have one person start a story. Other students build onto the story by passing it from person to person around the circle. Think of who, what, when, where, and why when expanding the story.

John Ramirez, storyboard artist.

Animator John Ramirez likes to mix art with music. Working with professional musicians such as Paul Tracey, he draws storyboards that bring music and words to life. As a child he always loved to draw. Eventually, he began to create his own comic strips, which are similar to storyboards, and later his own animated films. When he was 12 years old, he met a professional animation teacher who gave him the skills, discipline, and opportunities to pursue animation as his career. At age 13, John was an exchange student in Japan where he expanded his artistic skills and his perspective on world cultures. John is now working as an animator and storyboard artist with many of the professionals who he once knew as a student.

■ DISCUSSION QUESTIONS

1. In the eighth grade, John Ramirez made a 60-second film called *Midnight in the Park,* in which a man takes a walk and statues come alive. If you could make your own 60-second film, what topic would you choose? Why?

2. If you were an animator combining music with a visual segment, would you compose the music first then design the visual segment, or design the visual segment before the music? Explain your response.

■ CREATIVE EXPRESSION ACTIVITIES

Language Arts/Art   Write a short scene that takes place in a specific place, such as under the water, in outer space, or on a busy city street. Sketch a storyboard, or a series of drawings, to show the scene. Arrange these sketches in a sequence and use them to show the action for the scene. You might select a piece of music and point to your sketches as you play the music to show how the music and art work together.

Visual Arts   Choose a favorite short story or humorous tale to use as the basis for a storyboard of 7 to 10 frames.

Artists and Their Works

Artists and Their Works

Glossary

A

Acrylic (uh-**kril**-ik)   A quick-drying water-based synthetic paint. (Ch. 10–1)

Additive   A sculpting method produced by adding to or combining materials. (Ch. 12–1)

Aesthetics (ess-**thet**-iks)   The philosophy or study of the nature and value of art. (Ch. 2–2)

Aesthetic views   Ideas, or schools of thought, on what to look for in works of art. (Ch. 2–2)

Amphitheaters (**am**-fuh-thee-uht-uhrs)   Circular or oval buildings with seats rising around an open space. (Ch. 14–1)

Analog system   A system that uses electromagnetic energy to imprint both sound and pictures. (Ch. 15–5)

Analogous colors (uh-**nal**-uh-gus)   Colors that are side by side on the color wheel. (Ch. 4–2)

Analyzing   Noting how the principles are used to organize the elements of color, line, texture, shape, form, and space. (Ch. 6–3). Noting the style of a work. (Ch 7–3)

Applied art   Art made to be functional, as well as visually pleasing. (Ch 1–2), (Ch. 6–6)

Architect   An artist who works in the field of architecture. (Ch. 14–1)

Architecture   The planning and creating of buildings. (Ch. 14–1)

Art critic   A person who practices art criticism. (Ch. 6–1)

Art criticism   The process of studying, understanding, and judging art works, consisting or four stages: describing, analyzing, interpreting, and judging. (Ch. 6–1)

Art history   The study of art from past to present, consisting of four stages: describing, analyzing, interpreting, and judging. (Ch. 7–1)

Art movement   A group of artists with similar styles who have banded together. (Ch. 7–3)

Artists   People who use imagination and skill to communicate ideas in visual form. (Ch. 1–2)

Assembling   A sculpting method in which different kinds of materials are gathered and joined together. (Ch. 12–1)

B

Balance   A principle of art concerned with arranging the elements of art so that no one part of a work overpowers, or seems heavier than, any other part. (Ch. 5–1)

Basilicas (buh-**sil**-ih-kuhs)   Huge meeting halls. (Ch. 14–1)

Binder   A liquid to which the dry pigment is added. (Ch. 3–3), (Ch. 10–1)

Blending   A shading technique that involves adding dark values little by little by pressing harder on the drawing medium. (Ch. 8–1)

Brayer   A roller with a handle. (Ch. 9–1)

C

Camera   A dark box with a hole controlling how much light enters. (Ch. 15–1)

Carving   A sculpting method in which material is cut or chipped away. (Ch. 12–1)

Casting   A sculpting method in which melted material is poured into a mold. (Ch. 12–1)

Cinematographer (sin-uh-muh-**tahg**-ruh-fuhr)   The person in charge of running the movie camera or cameras. (Ch. 15–3)

Collage (kuh-**lahzh**)   Art arranged from cut or torn materials pasted to a surface. (Ch. 1–4), (Ch. 7–6)

Color wheel   An arrangement of colors in a circular format. (Ch. 4–2)

Complementary colors   Colors opposite each other on the color wheel. (Ch. 4–2)

Composition   How the principles are used to organize the elements. (Ch. 2–1)

Content   Message, idea, or feeling. (Ch. 2–1)

Contour drawing   Drawing an object as though your drawing tool is moving along all the edges and the ridges of the form. (Ch. 8–3)

Crafts   The different areas of applied art in which craftspeople work. (Ch. 13–1)

Craftsperson   Someone who has become an expert in an area of applied art. (Ch. 13–1)

Credit line   A listing of important facts about an art work. (Ch. 2–1)

Crosshatching   A shading technique using two or more lines that crisscross each other. (Ch. 8–1)

Glossary

Daguerreotypes (duh-**gehr**-uh-types)   Silvery, mirrorlike images on a copper plate. (Ch. 15–1)

Describing   In art criticism, making a careful list of all the things you see in the work. (Ch. 6–1); In art history, telling who did a work, and when and where it was done. (Ch. 7–1)

Digital system   A system that processes words and images using a series of on and off switches. (Ch. 15–5)

Director   The person in charge of shooting the film and guiding the actors. (Ch. 15–3)

E

Edition   A group of identical prints all made from a single plate. (Ch. 3–2), (Ch. 9–1)

Editorial designers   Graphic artists who arrange words and illustrations and prepare the material for printing. (Ch. 11–1)

Elements of art   Basic visual symbols artists use to create works of visual art. The elements of art are line, shape, form, space, color, and texture. (Ch. 4–1)

Elevation   A drawing of an outside view of a building. (Ch. 14–2)

Emphasis   A principle of art that stresses one element of art or makes an area in a work of art stand out. (Ch. 5–3)

Encaustic (in-**kaw**-stik)   A painting medium in which pigment is mixed into melted wax. (Ch. 10–1)

Facade (fuh-**sahd**)   The front of a building. (Ch. 14–2)

Fauves (**fohvs**)   An art movement begun early in this century in France, in which the artists use wild, intense color combinations in their paintings. (Ch. 7–3)

Fibers   Any thin, threadlike materials. (Ch. 13–1)

Fine art   Art made purely to be experienced visually. (Ch. 1–2)

Fired   Hardened by heating in a kiln. (Ch. 13–1)

Floor plan   A scale drawing of how a room or building would appear without a roof as if seen from above. (Ch. 14–2)

Form   An object with three dimensions—height, width, and depth. (Ch. 4–5)

Freestanding   Surrounded on all sides by space. (Ch. 3–5), (Ch. 12–3)

Fresco (**fres**-koh)   A painting medium in which pigment is applied to a wall spread with wet plaster. (Ch. 10–1)

Gesture drawing   Drawing lines quickly and loosely to show movement in a subject. (Ch. 8–2)

Glassblowing   The craft of shaping melted glass by blowing air into it through a tube. (Ch. 13–1)

Glaze   A thin, transparent layer of paint. (Ch. 10–1)

Glazed   Coated with a mixture of powdered chemicals that melt during firing into a hard, glasslike finish. (Ch. 13–1)

Graphic artists   Artists that work in the field of art known as graphic design. (Ch. 11–1)

Graphic design   The field of art that uses pictures and words to instruct or to communicate a specific message. (Ch. 11–1)

H

Harmony   A principle of art concerned with blending the elements of art in a pleasing way. (Ch. 5–3)

Hatching   A shading technique that involves drawing a series of thin lines running parallel, or in the same direction. (Ch. 8–1)

High relief   Relief that stands out boldly from its background. (Ch. 12–2)

Hue   A color's name. (Ch. 4–2)

I

Illustrators   Graphic artists who create printed materials that explain or teach. (Ch. 11–1)

Impasto (im-**pahs**-toh)   Thick, buttery layers. (Ch. 10–1)

Intaglio (in-**tal**-yoh)   A printmaking method in which the image to be printed is cut or scratched into a surface. (Ch. 9–2)

Intensity   The brightness or dullness of a hue. (Ch. 4–2)

Interpreting   In art criticism, determining and explaining the meaning, mood, or idea of the work of art. (Ch. 6–4); In art history, noting how time and place affect an artist's style and subject matter. (Ch. 7–5)

Judging   In art criticism, making a decision about a work's success or lack of success and giving reasons to support that decision. (Ch. 6–6); In art history, deciding whether a work introduces a new style or if it is an outstanding example of a particular style. (Ch. 7–7)

K

Kiln   A special piece of equipment used to fire ceramics. (Ch. 13–1)

L

Layout   The arrangement of words and pictures on a page. (Ch. 11–1)

Line   The path of a dot through space. (Ch. 4–4)

Line quality   The unique character of any line. (Ch. 4–4)

Line variation   The thickness or thinness, lightness or darkness of a line. (Ch. 4–4)

Lithograph (**lith**-uh-graf)   A print made by lithography. (Ch. 9–2)

Lithography (lith-**ahg**-ruh-fee)   A printmaking method in which the image to be printed is drawn on limestone with a special greasy crayon. (Ch. 9–2)

Logo   A special image representing a business, group, or product. (Ch. 11–2)

Loom   A frame or machine that holds a set of threads that runs vertically. (Ch. 13–1)

Low relief   Relief that stands out in space only slightly. (Ch. 12–2)

M

Madonna   A work showing the mother of Christ. (Ch. 7–5)

Medium of art   A material such as paint, clay, or glass used to create a work of art. (Ch. 3–1)

Microprocessors (my-kroh-**prahs**-es-uhrs)   Tiny computers. (Ch. 15–5)

Mixed media   The use of more than one medium to create a work of art. (Ch. 3–1)

Modeling   A sculpting method in which a soft or workable material is built up and shaped. (Ch. 12–1)

Monochromatic colors (mahn-uh-kroh-**mat**-ik)   Different values of a single hue. (Ch. 4–2)

Monoprinting   A printmaking method in which the image to be printed is put on the plate with ink or paint and then transferred to paper or cloth by pressing or hand-rubbing. (Ch. 9–2)

Motif (moh-**teef**)   A unit that is repeated over and over in a pattern or visual rhythm. (Ch. 4–3)

Motion picture   Photographs of the same subject taken a very short time apart and flashed onto a screen. (Ch. 15–3)

Movement   A principle of art that leads the viewer to sense action in a work or a path that the viewer's eye follows throughout a work. (Ch. 5–5)

Multi-media programs   Computer software programs that help users design, organize, and combine text, graphics, video, and sound in one document. (Ch. 15–5)

N

Negatives   Reverse images of the object photographed. (Ch. 15–1)

Non-objective   Having no recognizable subject matter. (Ch. 2–1)

Non-objective art   A work with no objects or subjects that can be readily identified. (Ch. 6–1)

Oil paint   Paint with an oil base. (Ch. 10–1)

Opaque (oh-**pake**)   Does not let light through. (Ch. 10–1)

Glossary

Palette Any tray or plate where paints are mixed before use. (Ch. 10–1)

Patrons of the arts Sponsors, or supporters, of an artist or art-related places and events. (Ch. 1–3)

Perceive To become aware through the senses of the special nature of objects. (Ch. 1–1)

Perception Awareness of the elements of the environment by means of the senses. (Ch. 8–1)

Photography The art of making images by exposing a chemically treated surface to light. (Ch. 15–1)

Pigment A finely ground, colored powder that gives paint its color. (Ch. 3–3), (Ch. 10–1)

Point of view The angle from which the viewer sees the scene. (Ch. 1–1)

Portfolio A pad of drawing paper on which artists sketch, write notes, and refine ideas for their work.

Post and lintel (lint-uhl) A building method in which a crossbeam is placed above two uprights. (Ch. 14–2)

Pottery The craft of making objects from clay. (Ch. 13–1)

Principles of art Guidelines that govern the way elements go together. (Ch. 5–1)

Print An image that is transferred from a prepared surface to paper or fabric. (Ch. 3–2)

Printing plate A surface onto or into which the image is placed. (Ch. 9–1)

Printmaking Transferring an inked image from a prepared surface to another surface. (Ch. 9–1)

Producer The person in charge of the business end of making a movie. (Ch. 15–3)

Proportion A principle of art concerned with the size relationships of one part to the whole and of one part to another. (Ch. 5–3)

Registration Careful matching up of plates in prints with more than one color. (Ch. 9–2)

Relief A type of sculpture in which forms and figures are projected from the front only. (Ch. 3–5), (Ch. 12–2)

Relief printing A printmaking method in which the image to be printed is raised from a background. (Ch. 9–2)

Renaissance (ren-uh-sahns) A French word meaning "rebirth." (Ch. 7–5)

Reproduction A photograph of a print. (Ch. 3–2)

Rhythm A principle of art concerned with repeating an element of art to create the illusion of movement. (Ch. 5–5)

Scoring Roughing or scratching clay with a clay tool (or fork). (Technique Tip **17** *Handbook,* page **275**)

Screen printing A printmaking technique in which the artist transfers the design to the screen through various processes. (Ch. 9–2)

Serigraph (sir-uh-graf) A screen print that has been handmade by an artist. (Ch. 9–2)

Shading The use of light and shadow to give a feeling of depth. (Ch. 8–1)

Shape An area clearly set off by one or more of the other five visual elements of art. (Ch. 4–5)

Sketchbook A carefully selected collection of art work kept by students and professional artists.

Slab A slice or sheet of clay. (Ch. 13–3)

Slip Clay that has so much added water that it is liquid and runny. It is used to fasten pieces of clay together. (Ch. 13–1)

Solvent A liquid that controls the thickness or thinness of the paint. (Ch. 3–3), (Ch. 10–1)

Space The distance or area between, around, above, below, and within things. (Ch. 4–5)

Stippling A shading technique achieved by using dots. (Ch. 8–1)

Style An artist's personal way of expressing ideas in a work. (Ch. 3–3), (Ch. 7–3)

Subject The image viewers can easily identify. (Ch. 2–1)

Subtractive A sculpting method produced by removing or taking away from the original material. (Ch. 12–1)

Super-realism A style of art devoted to extraordinarily realistic works. (Ch. 2–2)

Synthetic paints Manufactured paints with plastic binders. (Ch. 10–1)

T

Tempera (**tem**-puh-rah)   A painting medium in which pigment mixed with egg yolk and water is applied with tiny brush strokes. (Ch. 10–1)

Texture   How things feel, or look as though they might feel, if touched. (Ch. 4–7)

Three-dimensional   Having height, width, and depth. (Ch. 3–5)

Transparent   Clear. (Ch. 10–1)

Two-dimensional   Having height and width but not depth. (Ch. 3–5)

Typefaces   Styles of lettering for the printed material. (Ch. 11–1)

U

Unity   The arrangement of elements and principles with media to create a feeling of completeness. (Ch. 5–7)

V

Value   The lightness or darkness of a hue. (Ch. 4–2)

Variety   A principle of art concerned with combining one or more elements of art to create interest. (Ch. 5–3)

W

Warp   The lengthwise threads attached to the loom. (Ch. 13–4)

Watercolor   A painting medium in which pigment is blended with gum arabic and water. (Ch. 10–1)

Weaving   A craft in which fiber strands are interlocked to make cloth or objects. (Ch. 13–1)

Weft   The crosswise threads pulled across the warp. (Ch. 13–4)

Wet plate   A method of photography in which an image is created on glass that is coated with chemicals, then transferred to paper or cardboard. (Ch. 15–1)

Work of art   Any object created or designed by an artist. (Ch. 2–1)

Glossary/Glosario

A

Acrylic/Acrílico   Una pintura sintética a base de agua que se seca rápidamente. (Capítulo 10–1)

Additive/Agregar   Un método de hacer esculturas en que se añaden o combinan materiales. (Capítulo 12–1)

Aesthetics/Estética   La filosofía que estudia la naturaleza del arte y su valor. (Capítulo 2–2)

Aesthetic views/Opiniones estéticas   Ideas o corrientes de opinión sobre lo que se debe buscar en una obra de arte. (Capítulo 2–2)

Amphitheaters/Anfiteatros   Edificios de forma redonda u ovalada con gradas alrededor de un espacio abierto. (Capítulo 14–1)

Analog system/Sistema analógico   Un sistema que utiliza energía electromagnética para grabar el sonido y las imágenes. (Capítulo 15–5)

Analogous colors/Colores análogos   Colores que están adyacentes en la rueda de colores. (Capítulo 4–2)

Analyzing/Analizar   Notar cómo los principios del arte han sido usados para organizar los elementos de color, línea, textura, contorno, forma y espacio. (Capítulo 6–3) Notar el estilo de una obra. (Capítulo 7–3)

Applied art/Arte aplicado   Obras que no sólo son agradables a la vista, sino útiles también. (Capítulo 1–2), (Capítulo 6–6)

Architect/Arquitecto   Un artista que diseña edificios. (Capítulo 14–1)

Architecture/Arquitectura   El planear y crear edificios. (Capítulo 14–1)

Art critic/Crítico de arte   Una persona que ejerce la crítica del arte. (Capítulo 6–1)

Art criticism/Crítica de arte   El proceso de estudiar, comprender y evaluar obras de arte que consiste de cuatro etapas: describir, analizar, interpretar y evaluar. (Capítulo 6–1)

Art history/Historia del arte   El estudio del arte del pasado al presente que consiste de cuatro etapas: describir, analizar, interpretar y evaluar. (Capítulo 7–1)

Art movement/Movimiento artístico   Un grupo de artistas con estilos similares que hacen causa común. (Capítulo 7–3)

Artists/Artistas   Personas que usan su imaginación y sus habilidades para comunicar sus ideas de manera visual. (Capítulo 1–2)

Assembling/Ensamblar   Un método de hacer esculturas en el que distintos tipos de materiales se reúnen y se juntan. (Capítulo 12–1)

B

Balance/Equilibrio   El principio artístico que trata de la disposición de los elementos artístico de tal manera que ninguna parte de una obra domine a otra. (Capítulo 5–1)

Basilicas/Basílicas   Un edificio grande que servía de sitio de reunión. (Capítulo 14–1)

Binder/Aglutinante   Un líquido al que se le añade el pigmento seco. (Capítulo 3–3), (Capítulo 10–1)

Blending/Matizar   Una técnica para sombrear un dibujo en la que poco a poco se va apretando el instrumento de dibujar. (Capítulo 8–1)

Brayer/Rodillo   Un rodillo con mango. (Capítulo 9–1)

C

Camera/Cámara   Una caja oscura con un agujero que controla la cantidad de luz que le entra. (Capítulo 15–1)

Carving/Tallar   Un método de hacer esculturas en que se corta o desprende el material. (Capítulo 12–1)

Casting/Vaciado   Un método de hacer esculturas en el que un material líquido se vierte en un molde. (Capítulo 12–1)

Cinematographer/Director de fotografía   La persona encargada de operar la cámara o cámaras de filmar películas. (Capítulo 15–3)

Collage/Collage   Una obra hecha de pedazos de materiales que han sido cortados o arrancados y pegados a una superficie. (Capítulo 1–4), (Capítulo 7–6)

Color wheel/Rueda de colores   Los colores, organizados alrededor de un círculo. (Capítulo 4–2)

Complementary colors/Colores complementarios   Colores que están opuestos en la rueda de colores. (Capítulo 4–2)

Composition/Composición   La manera en que los principios del arte se usan para organizar los elementos. (Capítulo 2–1)

Content/Contenido   El mensaje, idea o sentimiento. (Capítulo 2–1)

Contour drawing/Dibujo de contorno Dibujar un objeto como si el instrumento de dibujar se estuviera moviendo por los bordes y puntos salientes de una forma. (Capítulo 8–3)

Crafts/Artesanía Las artes aplicadas en que trabajan los artesanos. (Capítulo 13–1)

Craftsperson/Artesano Alguien que se ha hecho experto en una de las artes aplicadas. (Capítulo 13–1)

Credit line/Rótulos de crédito Una lista de los datos importantes acerca de una obra de arte. (Capítulo 2–1)

Crosshatching/Sombreado con líneas cruzadas Una técnica para sombrear una ilustración que usa dos o más líneas que se cruzan. (Capítulo 8–1)

Daguerrotypes/Daguerrotipos Imágenes plateadas, parecidas al reflejo que se ve en un espejo, en una placa de cobre. (Capítulo 15–1)

Describing/Describir En la crítica del arte, hacer una lista minuciosa de todo lo que ves en la obra. (Capítulo 6–1) En la historia del arte, decir quién creó una obra, y cuándo y dónde fue creada. (Capítulo 7–1)

Digital system/Sistema digital Un sistema que procesa palabras e imágenes por medio de una serie de interruptores. (Capítulo 15–5)

Director/Director La persona que está a cargo de filmar una película y de guiar a los actores. (Capítulo 15–3)

Edition/Edición Un grupo de grabados idénticos hechos de la misma plancha. (Capítulo 3–2), (Capítulo 9–1)

Editorial designers/Diseñadores editoriales Artistas gráficos que arreglan las palabras e ilustraciones y preparan el material que va a ser impreso. (Capítulo 11–1)

Elements of art/Elementos del arte Símbolos visuales básicos que usan los artistas para crear obras de arte visual. Los elementos del arte son línea, contorno, forma, espacio, color y textura. (Capítulo 4–1)

Elevation/Alzado Un dibujo de una de las vistas de afuera de un edificio. (Capítulo 14–2)

Emphasis/Énfasis El principio artístico que le da mayor importancia a uno de los elementos del arte o resalta una de las secciones de una obra. (Capítulo 5–3)

Encaustic/Encáustico Un tipo de pintura en la que el pigmento se mezcla con cera derretida. (Capítulo 10–1)

Facade/Fachada El frente de un edificio. (Capítulo 14–2)

Fauves/Fauvismo Un movimiento artístico, que comenzó a principios de este siglo en Francia, en el cual los artistas utilizan en sus pinturas combinaciones extrañas de colores intensos. (Capítulo 7–3)

Fibers/Fibras Hebras finas de cualquier material. (Capítulo 13–1)

Fine art/Bellas artes Las artes que se crean para ser percibidas visualmente. (Capítulo 1–2)

Fired/Cocido Endurecido en un horno caliente. (Capítulo 13–1)

Floor plan/Plano Un dibujo a escala de como luciría desde arriba una habitación o un edificio sin techo. (Capítulo 14–2)

Form/Figura Un objeto que tiene tres dimensiones—alto, ancho y hondo. (Capítulo 4–5)

Freestanding/De pie Totalmente rodeado por espacio vacío. (Capítulo 3–5), (Capítulo 12–3)

Fresco/Al fresco Un método de pintar en que se aplica el pigmento a una pared cubierta de yeso mojado. (Capítulo 10–1)

G

Gesture drawing/Dibujo de gestos Dibujar rápida y aproximadamente las líneas de un sujeto para mostrar su movimiento. (Capítulo 8–2)

Glassblowing/Soplado del vidrio El oficio de darle forma al vidrio derretido, soplando aire dentro de él por medio de un tubo. (Capítulo 13–1)

Glaze/Glasear Aplicar una capa de pintura fina y transparente. (Capítulo 10–1)

Glazed/Vidriado Recubierto con una mezcla de substancias químicas en polvo que se derriten al cocerse el objeto y forman una capa que parece de vidrio. (Capítulo 13–1)

Glossary/Glosario

Graphic artists/Artistas gráficos   Artistas que trabajan en el campo del diseño gráfico. (Capítulo 11–1)

Graphic design/Diseño gráfico   El campo del arte que utiliza ilustraciones y palabras para enseñar o comunicar un mensaje específico. (Capítulo 11–1)

Harmony/Armonía   El principio artístico que se refiere a la combinación de los elementos del arte de manera agradable. (Capítulo 5–3)

Hatching/Sombreado con trazos finos   Una técnica para sombrear una ilustración que utiliza una serie de líneas finas que son paralelas o que van en la misma dirección. (Capítulo 8–1)

High relief/Altorrelieve   El tipo de relieve en que las figuras resaltan mucho del fondo. (Capítulo 12–2)

Hue/Tono   El nombre de un color. (Capítulo 4–2)

Illustrators/Ilustradores   Artistas gráficos que crean materiales impresos que explican o enseñan. (Capítulo 11–1)

Impasto/Empastar   Aplicar la pintura en capas gruesas. (Capítulo 10–1)

Intaglio/Entallar   Un método de imprimir en el cual la imagen que se va a grabar se corta en una superficie. (Capítulo 9–2)

Intensity/Intensidad   Lo brillante o apagado que es un tono. (Capítulo 4–2)

Interpreting/Interpretar   En la crítica del arte, significa determinar y explicar el sentido, atmósfera o idea de una obra de arte. (Capítulo 6–4) En la historia del arte, significa notar cómo la época y sitio donde vivió un artista afectan su estilo y sus temas. (Capítulo 7–5)

Judging/Evaluar   En la crítica del arte, significa tomar una decisión acerca del éxito de una obra y dar razones que apoyen esa decisión. (Capítulo 6–6) En la historia del arte, significa determinar si una obra introduce un nuevo estilo o si es un ejemplo excepcional de un estilo en particular. (Capítulo 7–7)

Kiln/Horno   Un aparato que se usa para cocer los objetos de cerámica. (Capítulo 13–1)

Layout/Maquetación   La disposición de las palabras y las ilustraciones en una página. (Capítulo 11–1)

Line/Línea   El trayecto de un punto a través del espacio que crea una raya. (Capítulo 4–4)

Line quality/Cualidades de la línea   Las características particulares de una línea. (Capítulo 4–4)

Line variation/Variación en la línea   Lo gruesa o fina, clara u oscura que es una línea. (Capítulo 4–4)

Lithograph/Litografía   Un grabado hecho por medio de la litografía. (Capítulo 9–2)

Lithography/Litografía   Un método de imprimir en que la imagen que se va a grabar se dibuja en una piedra caliza con un lápiz grasoso especial. (Capítulo 9–2)

Logo/Logotipo   Una imagen especial que representa a un negocio, grupo o producto. (Capítulo 11–2)

Loom/Telar   Un bastidor o máquina que sujeta una serie de hilos verticales. (Capítulo 13–1)

Low relief/Bajorrelieve   El tipo de relieve en el que las figuras resaltan muy poco del fondo. (Capítulo 12–2)

Madonna/Madona   Una obra que representa a la madre de Cristo. (Capítulo 7–5)

Medium of art/Medio de expresión   El material del que está hecha una obra, tal como pintura, arcilla o vidrio. (Capítulo 3–1)

Microprocessors/Microprocesadores   Computadores muy pequeños. (Capítulo 15–5)

Mixed media/Técnica mixta   El uso de más de un medio de expresión para crear una obra arte. (Capítulo 3–1)

Modeling/Modelar   Un método de hacer esculturas en el cual se le da forma a un material suave y moldeable y se le añaden más pedazos si se desea. (Capítulo 12–1)

Monochromatic colors/Colores monocromáticos
Los distintos tonos de un color. (Capítulo 4–2)

Monoprinting/Grabado único Un método de imprimir en que se pinta una imagen en una placa con tinta o pintura, y después se traslada a papel o tela al frotar o apretar éste con la mano. (Capítulo 9–2)

Motif/Motivo Una imagen que se repite muchas veces de acuerdo a un patrón o siguiendo un ritmo visual. (Capítulo 4–3)

Motion picture/Película cinematográfica Fotografías de un mismo sujeto que se toman seguidamente y se proyectan en una pantalla. (15–3)

Movement/Movimiento El principio artístico que hace que el que mira una obra se sienta como si alguna acción estuviera ocurriendo o hace que su mirada siga un senderao a través de la obra. (Capítulo 5–5)

Multi-media programs/Programas multimedia Programas de software para computadores, que ayudan a los usuarios a diseñar, organizar y combinar texto, gráficos, video y sonido en el mismo documento. (Capítulo 15–5)

Negatives/Negativos Imágenes de un objeto fotografiado que están al revés. (Capítulo 15–1)

Non-objective/Sin objeto Que no tiene ningún su jeto que se pueda reconocer. (Capítulo 2–1)

Non-objective art/Arte sin objeto Una obra que no tiene objetos o sujetos que se puedan identificar con facilidad. (Capítulo 6–1)

Oil paint/Pintura al óleo Un tipo de pintura que se hace a base de aceite. (Capítulo 10–1)

Opaque/Opaco Que no permite que traspase la luz. (Capítulo 10–1)

Palette/Paleta Cualquier bandeja o plato donde se mezclan las pinturas antes de usarse. (Capítulo 10–1)

Patrons of the arts/Patrocinadores de las artes Los que ayudan o apoyan a un artista o a lugares o acontecimientos artísticos. (Capítulo 1–3)

Perceive/Percibir Darse cuenta de la naturaleza particular de los objetos por medio de los sentidos. (Capítulo 1–1)

Perceiving/Percibir Mirar con cuidado y pensar bien sobre lo que uno ve. (Capítulo 1–1)

Perception/Percepción La habilidad de observar detenidamente y profundizar sobre un objeto. (Capítulo 8–1)

Photogram/Fotograma Una imagen que se produce en papel de trazar planos por medio de luz y de gases. (Capítulo 15–2)

Photography/Fotografía El arte de utilizar luz para fijar imágenes en una superficie que ha sido tratada con substancias químicas. (Capítulo 15–1)

Pigment/Pigmento El polvo fino que le da color a la pintura. (Capítulo 3–3), (Capítulo 10–1)

Point of view/Punto de vista El ángulo desde el cual el observador ve la escena. (Capítulo 1–1)

Portfolio/Carpeta de trabajos Una colección de obras de arte que un estudiante o artista profesional selecciona con cuidado y conserva.

Post and lintel/Puntal y dintel Un método de construcción en el que un madero horizontal se coloca encima de dos postes. (Capítulo 14–2)

Pottery/Alfarería El oficio de hacer objetos de arcilla. (Capítulo 13–1)

Principles of art/Principios del arte Las pautas que gobiernan cómo los elementos del arte se combinan. (Capítulo 5–1)

Print/Grabado Una imagen que se traslada de una superficie preparada a un papel o tela. (Capítulo 3–2)

Printing plate/Placa de imprimir Una superficie en la cual se coloca o talla la imagen. (Capítulo 9–1)

Printmaking/Grabar Transferir una imagen cubierta de tinta de una superficie preparada a otra superficie. (Capítulo 9–1)

Producer/Productor El que está a cargo de los asuntos financieros de hacer una película. (Capítulo 15–3)

Proportion/Proporción El principio artístico que trata de la correspondencia en tamaño entre una parte del objeto y el objeto entero y de la correspondencia en tamaño entre las distantas partes. (Capítulo 5–3)

Glossary/Glosario

Registration/Registro La alineación cuidadosa de las placas cuando se hacen grabados de más de un color. (Capítulo 9–2)

Relief/Relieve Un tipo de escultura en la que sólo se representa el frente de las figuras. (Capítulo 3–5), (Capítulo 12–2)

Relief printing/Grabado en relieve Un método de imprimir en que la imagen se sale del fondo. (Capítulo 9–2)

Renaissance/Renacimiento Un movimiento artístico cuyo nombre en inglés viene del francés y significa "volver a nacer." (Capítulo 7–5)

Reproduction/Reproducción Una fotografía de un grabado. (Capítulo 3–2)

Rhythm/Ritmo El principio artístico que trata de la repetición de elementos para crear la impresión de movimiento. (Capítulo 5–5)

S

Scoring/Marcar Arañar o rayar la arcilla con un instrumento (o con un tenedor). (Technique Tip **17** *Handbook*, page **275**)

Screen printing/Serigrafiado Una técnica de hacer grabados en la que el artista usa varios procesos para trasladar el diseño a una pantalla. (Capítulo 9–2)

Serigraph/Serigrafía Un grabado impreso a través de una pantalla, y hecho a mano por el artista. (Capítulo 9–2)

Shading/Sombrear El uso de claridad y sombra para dar la impresión de profundidad. (Capítulo 8–1)

Shape/Contorno Una imagen de dos dimensiones, destacada por uno o más de los otros elementos visuales del arte. (Capítulo 4–5)

Sketchbook/Cuaderno de bocetos Un bloc en el que un artista dibuja, toma notas y perfecciona sus ideas para una obra.

Slab/Pedazo Una tajada o trozo de arcilla. (Capítulo 13–3)

Slip/Barbotina Arcilla a la que se le ha añadido tanta agua que está líquida. Se usa para sujetar pedazos de arcilla unos a otros. (Capítulo 13–3)

Solvent/Solvente Un líquido que controla lo espesa que es una pintura. (Capítulo 3–3), (Capítulo 10–1)

Space/Espacio El área entre, alrededor, arriba, debajo y dentro de las cosas. (Capítulo 4–5)

Stippling/Puntear Una técnica para sombrear en la que se dibujan pequeños puntos. (Capítulo 8–1)

Style/Estilo La manera particular que tiene un artista de expresar sus ideas en una obra. (Capítulo 3–3), (Capítulo 7–3)

Subject/Sujeto La imagen que el observador puede identificar con facilidad. (Capítulo 2–1)

Subtractive/Suprimir Un método de hacer esculturas en que se quita o separa parte del material original. (Capítulo 12–1)

Super-realism/Superrealismo Un estilo artístico tan realista que los objetos en las obras parecen verdaderos. (Capítulo 2–2)

Synthetic paints/Pinturas sintéticas Pinturas manufacturadas con aglutinantes plásticos. (Capítulo 10–1)

T

Tempera/Al temple Un medio de pintar en el que se mezcla el pigmento con yemas de huevo y agua, y se pinta con pinceladas muy pequeñas. (Capítulo 10–1)

Texture/Textura La manera en que las cosas se sienten o parcee que deben sentirse al tocarlas. (Capítulo 4–7)

Three-dimensional/Tridimensional Que tiene alto, ancho y hondo. (Capítulo 3–5)

Transparent/Transparente Claro. (Capítulo 10–1)

Two-dimensional/Bidimensional Que tiene alto y ancho, pero no hondo. (Capítulo 3–5)

Typefaces/Tipo de imprenta Distintos estilos de letras que se usan para imprimir. (Capítulo 11–1)

U

Unity/Unidad La manera en que los elementos están arreglados en el medio de expresión, según los principios artísticos, para dar la sensación de que la obra está completa. (Capítulo 5–7)

Value/Opacidad Lo claro u oscuro que es un tono. (Capítulo 4–2)

Variety/Variedad El principio artístico que trata de la combinación de elementos para crear interés. (Capítulo 5–3)

Warp/Urdimbre Los hilos largos que sujetan el telar. (Capítulo 13–4)

Watercolor/Acuarela Un tipo de pintura en que el pigmento se mezcla con goma arábiga y agua. (Capítulo 10–1)

Weaving/Tejeduría Un trabajo manual en el cual hilos de fibra son entrelazados para hacer tela u objetos. (Capítulo 13–1)

Weft/Trama Los hilos que se cruzan con la urdimbre para hacer una tela. (Capítulo 13–4)

Wet plate/Placa mojada Un método de tomar fotografías en el cual la imagen se crea en un cristal cubierto de substancias químicas especiales, y se traslada a un papel o cartulina. (Capítulo 15–1)

Work of art/Obra de arte Cualquier objeto creado o diseñado por un artista. (Capítulo 2–1)

Bibliography and Resource List

The following resources provide information in various areas of art and education. The entries are organized by subject and each title is followed by a brief description to help you choose the subjects you wish to read about.

Art History

Anderson, Bjork. *Linnea in Monet's Garden*. New York: R and S Books, 1985. When Linnea visits Claude Monet's garden in Giverny, she gets to stand on the bridge over his lily pond and walk through his house. Later, when she sees his paintings in Paris, she understands what it means for a painter to be called an Impressionist. This delightful book contains photographs of Monet's paintings as well as old family snapshots.

Avi-Yonah, Michael. *Piece by Piece! Mosaics of the Ancient World*. Minneapolis, MN: Lerner, 1993. This book describes ancient and modern techniques as well as early Greek, Roman, and Byzantine mosaics.

Barnicoat, John. *Posters: A Concise History*. New York: Thames and Hudson, 1985. Readers discover the importance of the poster, including its role in various artistic movements.

Capek, Michael. *Artistic Trickery: The Tradition of Trompe L'Oeil Art*. Minneapolis, MN: Lerner, 1995. From the ancient Greeks to contemporary designers, artists have long been inspired to play visual jokes. This book lets the reader in on some of the gags.

Davidson, Rosemary. *Take a Look: An Introduction to the Experience of Art*. New York: Penguin, 1993. This book introduces the history, techniques, and functions of art through discussion and reproductions of paintings, photographs, drawings, and design elements. It also includes valuable diagrams and information about seeing and looking at art.

"Introduction to the Renaissance," *Calliope: World History for Young People*. Peterborough, NH: Cobblestone Publishing, May/June 1994. This issue of *Calliope* deals with many aspects of the arts and sciences during the Italian Renaissance. It features articles on artists such as Michelangelo and Leonardo da Vinci, rulers such as Isabella d'Este, and composers such as Monteverdi.

Biography

Gilow, Louise. *Meet Jim Henson*. New York: Random House, 1993. The creator of the Muppets, puppet stars of television and the movies, is the subject of this biography.

Greene, Katherine, and Richard Greene. *The Man Behind the Magic: The Story of Walt Disney*. New York: Viking, 1991. This biography of Walt Disney discusses his boyhood on a Missouri farm, his struggles as a young animator, and his building of a motion picture and amusement park empire.

Heslewood, Juliet. *Introducing Picasso: Painter, Sculptor*. Boston: Little, Brown, 1993. By examining the life of the well-known modern painter and the historical and artistic influences on his work, this book gives young readers a sense of who Picasso was and how his art developed. Photographs illustrate his work and his life.

Kastner, Joseph. *John James Audubon*. New York: Harry N. Abrams, 1992. This biography chronicles the life of Audubon from his childhood in France to his adventures in the New World, and shows how he captured these adventures in his artwork.

Neimark, Ann E. *Diego Rivera: Artist of the People*. New York: HarperCollins, 1992. Diego Rivera is brought to life in this comprehensive biography. It is illustrated with reproductions of Rivera's artwork.

Newlands, Anne. *Meet Edgar Degas*. New York: Lippincott, 1988. Degas talks to the reader about 13 of his paintings, describing what it's like to be a young artist in Paris.

Careers

Gordon, Barbara. *Careers in Art: Graphic Design*. VGM Career Horizons, 1992. Provides descriptions of careers in the graphic design field including art directors, book and magazine publishers, industrial designers and production artists. Information on courses and training requirements, job opportunities, and portfolio preparation.

Kaplan, Andrew. *Careers for Artistic Types*. Brookfield, CT: Millbrook, 1991. The author interviews 14 people who work in careers that are of interest to young people who like art.

Media and Techniques

James, Jane H. *Perspective Drawing: A Point of View.* 2d ed. Englewood Cliffs, NJ: Prentice Hall, 1988. This book is written for students who want to learn more about perspective.

Kehoe, Michael. *A Book Takes Root: The Making of a Picture Book.* Minneapolis, MN: Carolrhoda, 1993. This book traces the process of making a picture book from idea to manuscript to final production. Color photographs accompany the text and make this a fun-to-read and informative book.

Lauer, David A. *Design Basics.* 2d ed. New York: Holt, Rinehart and Winston, 1985. A resource for design students.

Mayer, Ralph. *The Artist's Handbook of Materials and Techniques.* 5th ed., rev. and updated. New York: Viking-Penguin, 1991. An up-to-date reference on art materials and techniques.

Meilach, Dona Z., Jay Hinz, and Bill Hinz. *How to Create Your Own Designs: An Introduction to Color, Form and Composition.* New York: Doubleday and Co., 1975. An excellent introduction to the elements of design.

Patterson, Freeman. *Photography and the Art of Seeing.* Rev. ed. San Francisco: Sierra Club Books, 1990. This book offers good advice on creative photography and is of particular interest to the beginning photographer.

Porter, Albert W. *Expressive Watercolor Techniques.* Worcester, MA: Davis Publications, 1982. A useful resource with valuable information on techniques and processes.

Sheaks, Barclay. *Drawing Figures and Faces.* Worcester, MA: Davis Publications, 1987. A helpful resource for students who wish to expand their drawing techniques.

Weldon, Jude. *Drawing: A Young Artist's Guide.* London: Dorling Kindersley, 1994. This well-designed and beautifully illustrated book guides the young artist through a wide variety of artistic experiences. Each idea is illustrated with master drawings and paintings. Topics include light and shade, color, imagination, and storytelling.

Multimedia Resources
Laserdiscs

American Art from the National Gallery A collection of 2,600 paintings and sculpture by American artists spanning three centuries.

Louvre Compendium Includes more than 5,000 works of art and 35,000 detailed images in a three-volume series.

Videodisc Volume I: Painting and Drawings

Videodisc Volume II: Sculpture and Objets d'Art

Videodisc Volume III: Antiquities

The National Gallery of Art A guided tour of the National Gallery featuring more than 1,600 masterpieces. A printed catalog and on-screen captions identifying each work are included.

The National Gallery of Art Laserstack Use this laserstack to create your own notes or slide lists for presentations. Works may be arranged by artist, nationality, period, style, date, medium, or subject.

Regard for the Planet A resource for 50,000 photographs documenting world cultures, places, and events of the last 40 years.

CD-ROMs

Art and Music Series Focuses on art and music from medieval times to Surrealism, with text linked to a 24-volume student encyclopedia and glossary. Events, challenges, and achievements of each time period are highlighted. (lab packs available) WIN & MAC

National Museum of Women in the Arts Access to 200 artworks from the collection. Available on CD-ROM or videodisc.

With Open Eyes Access to images through time line, geographical location, and close-ups. View 200 multimedia and multicultural artworks from the collection of the Art Institute of Chicago. View any object in a virtual-reality gallery to get a sense of scale. Includes games, music, poetry, and sound effects. WIN & MAC

Index

Index

Index

Credits

The following students contributed exemplary art for the Studio Activities and Studio Lessons.

Figure 1–11 **Grace Turner,** Holston Middle School, Knoxville, TN; Figure 2–9 **Jason McDermott,** McGary Middle School, Evansville, IN; Figure 3–6 **J.T. Helms,** Sneed Middle School, Florence, SC; Figure 3–11 (bottom) **Kate Baltzell,** Sneed Middle School, Florence, SC; Figure 3–17 **Matthew C. Lewis,** Helfich Park Middle School, Evansville, IN; Figure 3–24 **Layla Tapia,** Whittle Springs Middle School, Knoxville, TN; Figure 4–10 **Marshall Coleman,** Sneed Middle School, Florence, SC; Figure 4–23 **Tristan Hilliard,** Sneed Middle School, Florence, SC; Figure 4–24 **Lindsay Huggins,** Sneed Middle School, Florence, SC; Figure 5–6 **Sorren Young,** Whittle Springs Middle School, Knoxville, TN; Figure 5–16 **Robert Kotz,** Chisholm Trail Middle School, Round Rock, TX; Figure 6–5 **Jessie McManaway,** Sneed Middle School, Florence, SC; Figure 6–12 **Kate Baltzell,** Sneed Middle School, Florence, SC; Figure 7–16 **Malcolm McCray,** Whittle Springs Middle School, Knoxville, TN; Figure 8–7 **Jon Clemons,** Holston Middle School, Knoxville, TN; Figure 8–9 **Kristen J. Alters,** Valleywood Middle School, Kentwood, MI; Figure 8–14 **Michele Cannon,** Junction Middle School, Palo Cedro, CA; Figure 8–15 **Niki Granger,** Junction Middle School, Palo Cedro, CA; Figure 9–10 **Bobbie Daulton,** Cammack Middle School, Huntington, WV; Figure 9–11 **Nini Jin,** Cammack Middle School, Huntington, WV; Figure 9–15 **Kayci Mackey,** Junction Middle School, Palo Cedro, CA; Figure 9–17 **Janet Spivey,** Baldwin Jr. High, Montgomery, AL; Figure 10–10 **Ellen Knight,** Sneed Middle School, Florence, SC; Figure 11–7 **Merryl Arazie,** Sneed Middle School, Florence, SC; Figure 11–9 **B.J. Canestaro,** Bearden Middle School, Knoxville, TN; Figure 11–11 **David J. Estevez,** Junction Middle School, Palo Cedro, CA; Figure 11–13 (left) **J.T. Helms,** Sneed Middle School, Florence, SC; Figure 11–13 (right) **Dustin Wade,** Sneed Middle School, Florence, SC; Figure 11–15 **Jennifer Brooks,** Junction Middle School, Palo Cedro, CA; Figure 12–7 **Lindsay Huggins,** Sneed Middle School, Florence, SC; Figure 12–9 (left) **Katherine Bailey,** Sneed Middle School, Florence, SC; Figure 12–9 (right) **Doug Snowden,** Sneed Middle School, Florence, SC; Figure 12–11 **Amber Greenlee,** David A. Brown Middle School, Wildomar, CA; Figure 13–11 **Kristen Rae Williams,** Sneed Middle School, Florence, SC; Figure 13–19 **Allison Hengemuhle,** Junction Middle School, Palo Cedro, CA; Figure 14–9 **Dustin Wade,** Sneed Middle School, Florence, SC; Figure 15–18 **Ashley Wyrick,** Holston Middle School, Knoxville, TN; Figure S–15 **Amanda Lehman,** McGary Middle School, Evansville, IN; Figure S–19 **Angela L. Baker,** Junction Middle School, Palo Cedro, CA.